Critical Approaches to the Films of Robert Rodriguez

EDITED BY FREDERICK LUIS ALDAMA
AFTERWORD BY ALVARO RODRIGUEZ

University of Texas Press ⟶ *Austin*

Requests for permission to reproduce material from this work should be sent to:
    Permissions
    University of Texas Press
    P.O. Box 7819
    Austin, TX 78713-7819
    http://utpress.utexas.edu/index.php/rp-form

♾ The paper used in this book meets the minimum requirements of
ANSI/NISO Z39.48-1992 (R1997) (Permanence of Paper).

Library of Congress Cataloging-in-Publication Data
Critical approaches to the films of Robert Rodriguez / edited by
Frederick Luis Aldama. — First edition.
       pages   cm
    Includes bibliographical references and index.
    ISBN 978-0-292-76355-5 (cloth : alk. paper)
    ISBN 978-1-4773-0240-8 (pbk : alk. paper)
1. Rodriguez, Robert, 1968–, Criticism and interpretation. I. Aldama, Frederick
Luis, 1969–, editor.
    PN1998.3.R633C86 2015
    791.4302′33092—dc23

                                                                2014017669

doi:10.7560/763555

Critical Approaches to the Films of Robert Rodriguez

Contents

Critical Approaches to the Films of Robert Rodriguez

Rodriguez's Cinema of Possibilities: An Introduction

FREDERICK LUIS ALDAMA

Robert Rodriguez is hands down the most productive U.S. Latino film-maker working today. With sixteen films (including two shorts) "shot, chopped, and scored" (his identifiers often appearing at the beginning of his films) since his first breakout success *El Mariachi* in 1992, he has single-handedly carried U.S. Latino filmmaking into twenty-first-century global cinema.

Rodriguez is a Latino filmmaker who is at once an insider and outsider to the mainstream entertainment machine. With the exception of only a couple of missed years, he has created a film every year—and in some years, more than one film. This flow continues today. Two years after the release of *Spy Kids 4D* in 2011, his *Machete Kills* came out in a 2013 release while *Sin City: A Dame to Kill For* was in postproduction; the first install-ment, *Machete*, came out in 2010.

Rodriguez has captured the attention of the media since the making of his first film, *El Mariachi*. The news of his shooting the film in 14 days and on a $7,000 budget created a blitz of buzz terms like "mariachi style" and "guerilla filmmaker." The media loved, too, that he came up with part of the money for the making of the film by checking into a local pharmaceu-tical company where he was a paid human lab rat for its drug trials.

While Rodriguez has been a near-constant fixture in the mainstream media, the systematic scholarly study of his films is only just beginning. There has been a sprinkle of academic essays on his work, and only two book-length studies. With only three of his films yet released (*El Mariachi*, *Desperado*, and *From Dusk till Dawn*), in 1998 Mary J. Marvis recognized that Rodriguez should be the subject of a very light biographical book series for children on significant Latino figures. With Europeans having taken an early interest in Rodriguez, it is not surprising that the first book-length scholarly study of his films should appear in Italy—a big producer of westerns (spaghetti) and horror (zombie) films; in several of Rodriguez's films one can see much inspiration coming from directors such as Sergio Leone and Dario Argento, among others. In 2009 Fabio Migneco published *Il cinema di Robert Rodriguez*. However, written in Italian and as of yet untranslated, Migneco's book remains limited to a European publishing market. The editing of this book with Zachary Ingle's edited collection of substantive interviews, *Robert Rodriguez: Interviews* (published by the University of Mississippi Press), along with my single-authored book, *The Cinema of Robert Rodriguez* with the University of Texas Press, marks a shift in the tide. Ingle expands his contribution in a chapter included in this volume. Yet another author in this volume, Christopher González, is special issue editor of *POST SCRIPT: Essays in Film and the Humanities*, which focuses on the films of Robert Rodriguez.

The aim of this volume is to attend to nearly all of Rodriguez's films in ways that enrich our understanding of how each is made (choice of lens, angle, sound design, and edit, for instance) and consumed (our perception, thought, and feeling). Individually and collectively, the volume aims to turn the spotlight onto Rodriguez's films as an area that necessitates serious scholarly study. It aims to fling open the doors and windows to more scholarship to come.

Filmmaker *in Time*

That Rodriguez was born in 1968 is significant. He would grow up during a sociohistorical epoch when he could realize his dream to become a filmmaker. I mean by this that Rodriguez was definitely born at the right time. Already in his early teens, technologies for recording and watching film were becoming more and more cost-accessible to the average middle-class family. As a young adult, he witnessed the advances in filmmaking technology moving decisively away from the expensive, cumbersome cameras and editing machines of yesteryear. Already in making *Desperado* (1995) he had learned to use the lightweight, infinitely maneuverable Steadicam. By the early 2000s he was able to get his hands on and master digital filmmaking technology along with postproduction computer graphic editing software.

Rodriguez came of age as a Latino filmmaker in the era of VHS, allowing him access to films for studying as well as the video camera recording and editing equipment to make the films. If he had been born during

Kubrick's day or even before during the time of Kazan or Eisenstein, the cumbersome cameras and other laborious technical machines involved in the shooting, editing, and screening processes would have likely been out of his reach—too costly even for a middle-income Latino family living in the Southwest.

Latino Auteur

Rodriguez is an auteur, of sorts. We think of Rodriguez's brand of auteurism, however, as more of the guerilla filmmaking variety. His auteurism is to have total control over the final product, but in a do-it-yourself way. As a former professor of Rodriguez's, Charles Ramírez Berg writes in "A Teaser before the Show" (the foreword to *The Cinema of Robert Rodriguez*),

> The "Mariachi Aesthetic," the movie-making method Robert devised to make *El Mariachi*, was revolutionary. Strip the list of things you think you must have to make your film down to zero—because that laundry list is only preventing you from getting to the business of actually making your movie. Instead, make a list of the resources you *do* have, then fashion a movie around them. (x–xi)

Indeed, as Rodriguez often mentions in his "Ten Minute Film School" episodes (often included as a feature in the DVDs of his films), he usually learns with great technical proficiency all the skills involved in the making of a film to maintain creative control over the final result as well as to save money. For instance, rather than send the film out postproduction for a composer to come up with a sound design that takes up much time and money, he learned how to compose on the spot. Rather than hire a Steadicam operator for *Desperado*, he learned how to do it on the spot. The same can be said of his learning all the other elements of the filmmaking process. The net result: his films are made inexpensively (relative to Hollywood budgets) and have a distinctive Rodriguez quality to them. As Ramírez Berg sums up of his career thus far, "He's spending way more than $7,000 per picture, yet the Mariachi Aesthetic remains intact: the innovation of ideas as well as vitality of creation realized in his cinema of possibilities continue to trump concerns over exorbitant blockbuster budgets" ("A Teaser before the Show" xi–xii).

With Rodriguez we have an auteur in the sense of a creative mind who has a *total vision* and a *total control* of the making of the whole *with a specific audience in mind*—an audience that seeks above all else to be entertained. He pushes the envelope on cinematic language, creating the seemingly unimaginable in films like *Sin City*, but in ways that still aim, as the sine qua non, to entertain.

Rodriguez's Browning of America

Rodriguez exists within a larger U.S. Latino filmmaking tradition that includes notables such as Miguel Arteta, Carlos Ávila, Jesse Borrego, Patricia Cardoso, Peter Bratt, Paul Espinosa, Hector Galán, Sandra Guardado, Aurora Guerrero, Cristina Ibarra, Cheech Marin, Ramón Menéndez, Sylvia Morales, Gregory Nava, Edward James Olmos, Lourdes Portillo, Alex Rivera, Nancy De Los Santos, Jesús Salvador Treviño, and Luis Valdez, among others. At the same time, he represents a new generation of Latino filmmaker—one that doesn't necessarily only include in its focus explicitly, say, Latino issues: generational divisions and assimilation (Luis Valdez's 1987 *La Bamba* or Gregory Nava's 1995 *Mi Familia*, for instance); disenfranchisement and sense of noncitizen status (Allison Anders's 1993 *Mi Vida Loca* and Edward James Olmos's 1992 *American Me*); urban- and rural-set exploitation and oppression (Gregory Nava's 1984 *El Norte* and Paul Espinosa's 1995 adaptation of . . . *and the earth did not swallow him*); the border and immigration policy (Cheech Marin's 1987 *Born in East L.A.* and Gregory Nava's 2006 *Bordertown*, for instance). Several film scholars have used broad brushstrokes to characterize these and other films that make up the corpus of Latino cinema. Such a cinematic tradition, Chon Noriega remarks, "seeks to define difference . . . against the backdrop of the 'non-Chicano,' and it does so in the name of an ethnic nation, community, or culture" (xxxi).

Rodriguez's cinema is this—and more. Indeed, several scholars in this collection comment on how Rodriguez's sense of Latino identity and experience is arguably more expansive, or the expression, in Christopher González's words, of a "post-post-Latinidad."

Elsewhere, Charles Ramírez Berg gives rich nuance to the different phases of Chicano/Latino cinema, positioning Rodriguez in ushering in the most recent phase: one that seeks to make visible the Latino condition, even to mainstream it. The first phase (1969–1976) was characterized by an "anti-stereotyping aesthetic" (*Latino Images* 5) whereby Latino directors sought to resist, overturn, and complicate Hollywood's stereotypical representations. Directors who make films with a "rebellious, not separatist" (186) spirit typify the second wave. This second wave of films is laced with anger, but it is ultimately "channeled into more accessible forms" (186). The third wave gains visible momentum in the 1990s and emphasizes oppression, exploitation, or resistance. Ramírez Berg gives Rodriguez's "Bedhead" and *El Mariachi* as examples of films that take for granted Latino-ness in the United States. Ethnicity simply *is*. In this third wave of Latino cinema, as Ramírez Berg states, "political content is embedded within the deeper structure of the genre formulas the filmmakers employ rather than being on the surface" (187).

In many ways Rodriguez's at once spotlighting and mainstreaming Latinos is a reflection of what is going on with Latinos in the United States generally. Latinos exert a huge demographic weight in the United States. At 50 million-plus and counting, our presence is huge (hence Rodriguez's naturalizing our presence). Yet, in the media we are still few and far between (hence Rodriguez's continuing to put a spotlight on Latinos). When we are present, the mainstream media like to depict us as preternaturally hot-tempered, violent, and ravenously sexual. Indeed, as Mary Beltrán discovers, while we see sprinkles of Latinas appearing in "interesting and compelling roles" (108), the general trend is that they continue to be held fast to the spitfire stereotype.

It is the case that Rodriguez represents a new model of Latino filmmaking today—one whereby the director can (1) choose to completely make natural the presence of a character's Latino ethnicity—it simply *is* as it *is* for Anglo characters in most films; (2) cast Latino actors in Latino roles—or any other role (he insisted on casting the then-unknown Salma Hayek in *Roadracers* and also insisted that the Hollywood-produced action/Western *Desperado* include a large Latino cast; indeed, Latino actors such as Hayek, Danny Trejo, Cheech Marin, and Antonio Banderas, among others, appear again and again in all his films; and, with the filmmaking under his total control, he would consider Latinos infinitely moveable, casting Jessica Alba as the Irish stripper in *Sin City* and then as the Latina stepmom in *Spy Kids 4D*); and (3) choose to highlight Latinidad, or Latino-ness, in ways that playfully foreground or overturn the stereotypes.

New Millennial Latino Filmmaker

Rodriguez's life very much reflects the growing of this generation of Latinos with an urban worldview: massively diversified in its cultural products and tastes. Born June 20, 1968, Rodriguez grew up in a large family (nine siblings) in the urban environment of San Antonio, Texas. His father, Cecilio, worked as a traveling salesperson, selling cookware, china, and crystal; his mother, Rebecca, worked as a nurse. The education of Rodriguez's varied film tastes started early. He learned to play the guitar and the saxophone. And, living in an urban environment offered the possibility of the mother's taking the children to the movies at the local barrio (or neighborhood) revival house, the Olmos Theatre. In an interview with Peter Travers he recalls how "we'd sit with food hidden under diapers and watch movies two or three times" (*Rolling Stone* 3/18/93, Issue 652). Rodriguez would watch double and sometimes triple features, from the films of the Marx Brothers to those of Alfred Hitchcock. In *Rebel Without a Crew*, he considers these outings to be some of the most significant of his early childhood memories. As a teenager, this home-school-styled film education would continue with the renting and watching of movies on VHS tapes. Some of his favorites included George Miller's *The Road Warrior* (the second film in the *Mad Max* series) and John Carpenter's *Escape from New York*. As Alvaro Rodriguez so gracefully puts it in the Afterword to this volume, he and Rodriguez escaped the "sweltering South Texas heat" not only to immerse themselves in the storyworld of Manhattan-Island-cum-maximum-security-prison but so that Rodriguez could catalogue for Alvaro's "eager ears a run-through of how Carpenter shot this sequence and that, already informing what would become his own style."

His fascination with understanding how films could tell stories and create certain responses in audiences began to realize itself materially in his own making of stop-motion stories with his father's Super 8 camera. When his father came home with a new four-head JVC videocassette recorder and camera, he was able to set aside the more technologically arduous Super 8. He began shooting videos of everything, including clay animations and short action comedies with his siblings. It had an audio dub feature that allowed him to erase then rerecord sound over the films; he learned to edit with the camera and how to lay the music over later. To make the visual and audio synching easier, he also learned to shoot as little footage with as few takes as possible. To become more and more efficient at this, he trained himself more and more to see, as he states, "the movie edited in my head beforehand" (*Rebel* x). He continued to hone his filmmaking (and cartooning) craft while attending St. Anthony's High School Seminary, a private high school in San Antonio. He was hired to cover the football games, creatively shooting audience expression and spiraling footballs. And it was here that he would meet another aspiring filmmaker, Carlos Gallardo. Both wanted to become better and better filmmakers. Gallardo wanted to cut his teeth making action features ("The Guy from the Land Down Under") and Rodriguez to sharpen his making shorts and trailers that would eventually allow him to make a feature action film—with a Latino protagonist.

In 1986, Rodriguez enrolled at the University of Texas, Austin, which would prove to be more than just a place for higher-minded learning and thinking. It became yet another training ground for Rodriguez as a comic strip author/artist (his popular "Los Hooligans" strip based on his siblings ran in the *Daily Texan* for three consecutive years) and as a filmmaker. UT Austin housed the very well regarded and extremely competitive Radio-Television-Film (RTF) program. Rodriguez knew that to take his craft to the next level, he had to be able to train on 16mm cameras. Working three jobs while carrying a full load, however, didn't serve his GPA well. With only thirty open spots and a hundred applicants, he knew he would have to use other means to open the door to the RTF program. On his own time and using borrowed Super-8 and video recording camera equipment and then a camcorder that he bought with money he earned from a cholesterol experiment and then antidepressant drug studies, he made a series of shorts titled *Austin Stories*. One of these was "Bedhead," which he circulated at small film fests, picking up several notable awards. He showed the film to Professor Charles Ramírez Berg and Steve Mims, who taught production in the RTF program. His homegrown low-tech video making and editing skills—and self-discipline and perseverance— paid off. He was in the RTF program—by other means. In the RTF program Rodriguez grew the support and admiration of Mims and also the seminal Latino film theorist Charles Ramírez Berg. Rodriguez also gained access to the 16mm camera equipment he longed to train on.

With the success of his $800-made short "Bedhead" Rodriguez figured out that even if he used a 16mm camera with its more expensive film stock, if he used the same shooting and editing techniques that he used with "Bedhead" he could make a feature film for $7,000. (By this time, he had already made nearly thirty short narrative films.) He checked himself in for more drug clinical trials (with ruled index cards, notepad, and a copy of Stephen King's *The Dead Zone*) to earn part of the money (Gallardo also contributed) to make the film, and, with a borrowed Arriflex 16mm, Rodriguez and Gallardo went south of the border to make a film. The idea was to make a film to sell to the Spanish-language video market; to make an inexpensive feature length film that he could, as he remarks, "quietly fail on, and learn from my mistakes" (*Rebel* 4). With only fourteen days of borrowed time on the Arriflex, they went straight to Ciudad Acuña where Gallardo had family connections and where they might piggyback off of resources available by Alfonso Arau's crew, who were filming *Like Water for Chocolate*.

At a fever-pitched pace, Rodriguez shot *El Mariachi* in just shy of fourteen days (as it turned out, the Arriflex was needed back on day 13) and for the budgeted $7,000. After much hard work editing and synching the sound, he was ready to peddle his wares in LA. Rodriguez recounts this part of the story much better than I could in *Rebel Without a Crew*, but suffice it to say that pounding pavement didn't lead to the result he'd hoped for. Rodriguez didn't sell *El Mariachi* to the Spanish video market. As Ramírez Berg states, "his plan failed because *El Mariachi* was too good" ("A Teaser before the Show" ix). Indeed, not expecting much after he dropped off his short film "Bedhead" and a two-minute trailer for *El Mariachi* with the International Creative Management talent agency, they called him back. By April 1992 Robert Newman, Rodriguez's agent, had used it to lasso a film deal with Columbia: the $7-million budgeted follow-up, *Desperado*, along with national distribution of *El Mariachi*. (See Macor *Chainsaws*.) In *Rebel* Rodriguez remarks, "The main reason was that I wanted to make a modestly budgeted Hollywood picture with a Latino action hero, something I'd always wanted to see in movies since I was a kid" (194). After a $100,000 investment in a 35mm blowup of *El Mariachi*, it picked up awards at the Sundance Film Festival and other film fests and then grossed $5 million as a mainstream release; it went on to make an additional $1.5 million with its English-dubbed VHS version that sold in the video market.

Not only has *El Mariachi* been credited with energizing the indie-film director scene of the 1990s but its cultural, historical, and aesthetic importance is such that it has recently been added to the National Film Registry of the Library of Congress. Moreover, for Latinos in U.S. film, as Ramírez Berg states, "There had never been a prodigious Latino talent like Robert in the Hollywood system—someone who wrote, directed, co-produced, edited, recorded and edited the sound, edited the music, and acted as cinematographer and camera operator on his first film. This was an unprecedented and unexpected kind of Latino filmmaker, a Mexican American combination of Orson Welles and Steven Spielberg" ("A Teaser before the Show" x).

Matters of Mind, Borders, and Borderlands

Robert Rodriguez's corpus is extensive. He works within—and against—film genres and character types. He comforts audiences. He also turns upside down and inside out audience expectation. The chapters collected here begin to open our eyes to the manifold ways in which Rodriguez's films operate both internally (plot, character, event) as well as externally (audience perception, thought, and feeling). I have not included a chapter on his more studio-straitjacketed film, *The Faculty* (1998). Brought in as a hired hand of sorts by the Weinstein brothers to save a runaway train (delays, rewrites, and much more led to the film's hemorrhaging of money), the producer and studio constraints made it very difficult for Rodriguez to realize his creative vision in this film. The film is discussed further in the final piece to this volume, "Five Amigos Crisscross Borders on a Road Trip with Rodriguez," as well as at length in my book *The Cinema of Robert Rodriguez.*

I have created three main rubrics to contain chapters that seek to explore, respectively, these internal and external aspects of his films. "Matters of Mind and Media" includes two chapters that use the research in psychology (psychoanalytic and cognitive) to shed light on how Rodriguez's films complicate Latin identity as well as how they succeed in making new audiences' preconceptions of the world. The second grouping of chapters, "Narrative Theory, Cognitive Science, and *Sin City*: A Case Study," offers tools and models of analysis in the study of Rodriguez's and Frank Miller's (credited as codirector) film re-creation of a comic book. And the third section, "Aesthetic and Ontological Border Crossings and Borderlands," includes four chapters that consider how Rodriguez innovatively conveys content in his films that critique fixed notions of Latino identity and experience as well as open eyes to racial injustices. The fourth and final section, "It's a Wrap," contains two chapters that round out the volume by attending to Rodriguez's connection to Quentin Tarantino as well as discussing at greater length and in a polyphonic manner films of Rodriguez that were mentioned earlier in the volume but not fully fleshed out.

In many ways, however, these are pedagogically imposed divisions. As the chapters evince, while some might be more oriented toward questions of form and audience reception (perception, cognition, and emotion) and others more toward content (plot, character, and event), individually and taken as a whole they remind us that the actual experience of the films is of a gestalt whereby form and content are inseparable. The chapters also variously situate the films in time and place—the sociohistorical and regional contexts of their making, distribution, and reception.

The volume opens with Sue J. Kim's consideration of both Rodriguez's youth-oriented films such as *Shorts* and *Sharkboy and Lavagirl* as well as his adult-oriented action films such as *El Mariachi* and *Machete*. Rather than see these sets of films in opposition to one another as many do, in "From *El Mariachi* till *Spy Kids*? A Cognitive Approach" Kim reveals how they "invoke social-political issues, such as immigration and multiracial families." For Kim these films destabilize preconceptions of generic convention, stereotype, and filmmaking agent: "Who can tell the stories. . . ? What even constitutes a movie?" Moreover, she considers how these films ask audiences to parse (or chunk) meaning-making units in ways that lead us to think of new ways of existing in the world.

In a more close-up focus on the *Spy Kids* films Phillip Serrato attends to the evolution of the character Juni (Daryl Sabara). In his chapter "You've Come a Long Way, Booger Breath: Juni Cortez Grows Up in the *Spy Kids* Films," Serrato analyzes how Juni grows from boy to man during the decade in which all four of Rodriguez's *Spy Kids* films were released. Building on the insights from psychoanalytic and postcolonial theory, Serrato considers how issues of Latinidad, sexuality, and gender play into Juni's development from a sense of self as incomplete to a sense of self experienced as a whole. However, his nuanced analysis also reveals just how Rodriguez gives a gendered twist that shakes upside down this masculine whole. Ultimately, Serrato argues that the *Spy Kids* films in toto at once construct and then dismantle socially constructed expectations concerning (Latino) masculinity.

The next series of chapters deliberately focus on one film, *Sin City*, as a scholarly and pedagogical test case of sorts: it allows for teachers, scholars, and lay readers to see how different approaches to the same primary text can throw light on and enrich our understanding of the same film artifact. Each of the three chapters, then, shows that various formal aspects of Rodriguez's and Miller's film *Sin City* trigger certain kinds of responses—including the response of appreciation and awe. As an introduction to the kind of nuanced analysis one can accomplish with the tools of film narrative theory and advances in the cognitive sciences, Patrick Colm Hogan's "Painterly Cinema: Three Minutes of *Sin City*" offers a detailed analysis of the opening three-minute sequence, "The Customer Is Always Right." For Hogan, Rodriguez participates in and extends what he identifies as a painterly cinematic tradition—that tradition in world cinema whereby directors would take, as their referential model, painting. Rodriguez is a painterly filmmaker who uses the graphic novel as his referential canvas. Hogan's understanding of how we process "lateral inhibition" in visual perception and attentional orientation, among other neuroanatomical processes, allows him to enrich our sense of how Rodriguez creates painterly cinematic art that triggers specific emotional and ethical responses. For Hogan, Rodriguez's *Sin City* enhances "story emotion and artifact emotion—particularly, aesthetic emotion" in ways that take audiences out of the habitual and humdrum and into the new and vital. Emily R. Anderson's "*Sin City*, Style, and the Status of Noir" follows Hogan's chapter. She establishes clear differences between the audiovisual storytelling format of film and that of the visual–verbal of graphic novel to show just how Rodriguez/Miller succeed in re-creating (or remediating, her word) a story that we identify clearly with the original graphic novel but that is innovatively new as a film. After careful consideration of how Rodriguez's choice of lens and use of computer-generated images (CGI), green screen, and postproduction animatic technology allows him to create the drawn look of the film, she then turns to a discussion of how the film differs from the graphic novel. If Rodriguez were to have translated Miller literally, she concludes, "he would be forsaking everything that is valuable in the remediation. Instead, he locates his film in the history of the medium with the constant references to film production and conventions, conventions he flouts or adheres to in unmotivated succession." Wrapping up this section, Erin E. Eighan's "*Sin City*, Hybrid Media, and a Cognitive Narratology of Multimodality" attends to how the genesis of the film from graphic novel leads to a making of a hybrid film that "bridges the continuous motion of film with the panels and gutters of comics, the human face with caricature, the sound with silence." Eighan considers the difficulty of moving from one medium to the other, especially as it concerns the narrative effects of episodic sequencing and serialization. Turning to the research on dual coding theory (DCT) that reveals how we process two functionally distinct mental systems, Eighan determines how the film embraces instead a composite, polyphonic structure and sensibility that triggers "multiple sensory modalities and cognitive systems" in the audience.

Christopher González's "Intertextploitation and Post-Post-Latinidad in *Planet Terror*" opens the second group of chapters—those that more centrally consider how elements of content and form in Rodriguez's films ask audiences to think and feel differently about matters of ethnic, racial, and national identity and belonging. Rodriguez clearly situates *Planet Terror* in the sci-fi horror genre storytelling mode. However, González demonstrates how the two key elements that bookend the story—the faux-trailer for *Machete* at the beginning and the image of the Mayan pyramid of Tulum, Mexico, that closes the film—ask that audiences *re-view* (in their minds) the story with Latinos in mind. For González, Rodriguez adds significantly to the sci-fi horror genre, whereby the crossings of humans into monstrous others function as social critique (race dynamics of Us vs. Them no longer hold). Moreover, that Rodriguez ends the film with Cherry leading an ad hoc tribe of humans to Tulum offers audiences the possibility of apprehending a new space of inclusion—a space of "post-post-Latinidad." This, for González, "presents viewers with the possibility of transferring a similar empathetic response for real people—people they know little to nothing about—to real human beings who otherwise might only register as statistics on a CNN ticker at the bottom of their television set." Enrique García's *"Planet Terror* Redux: Miscegenation and Family Apocalypse" also attends to this nascent post-post-Latinidad present in *Planet Terror.* Using as his springboard his students' surprise with teaching *Planet Terror* as part of U.S. Latino cinema, he offers a nuanced analysis to defend this choice. For García, the crossings of genres (romance with sci-fi and horror, for instance) and ontologies (transmogrification of human into monster) represent the collapse of the traditional family structure (Latino or otherwise) built on insularity, isolation, and a general fear of racial mixing. García considers how the film works much like the blaxploitation films of the 1970s—and character El Wray is Rodriguez's *badass*—that brought awareness to sociopolitical issues such as racial oppression. Zachary Ingle's chapter, "The Border Crossed Us: *Machete* and the Latino Threat Narrative," takes as its focus another of Rodriguez's B-flick, exploitation-styled films: *Machete.* And like García does with *Planet Terror,* Ingle considers how the style and the content of *Machete* situate it within a blaxploitation cinematic tradition (as well as that of Cheech Marin's social satires) to shed critical light on the Latino threat narrative that weaves itself in and through Hollywood's drug traffic films, the news media's anti-immigrant hype, and immigration policy making. While *Machete* could be seen at first glance as a film that exploits the use of gratuitous violence to entertain, for Ingle a second glance reveals it to be a powerfully political and earnest film that offers audiences a salient critique of racist ideologies.

James J. Donahue's "The Development of Social Minds in the 'Mexico Trilogy'" explores how the films *El Mariachi* (1992), *Desperado* (1995), and *Once Upon a Time in Mexico* (2003) not only turn upside down Hollywood's stereotypes of the mariachi as source of entertainment—not just as musician, but in most cases as the comic buffoon—but also explore how he develops from "a loner to an integral part of a larger social unit." In a careful analysis of Rodriguez's use of eye-line match, lens, and angle (especially the close-up) Donahue unpacks how the formal structures along with the content convey this development from isolation into a sense of self as integral to the collective. In the first two films in the trilogy Rodriguez uses eye-line matching and extreme close-ups to convey the sense of his isolation yet with a potential for connection (or intermentality) with others. In an analysis of how Rodriguez chooses to exclude certain film techniques as well as to include others, like the final image of El Mariachi wearing a Mexican flag as a sash across his chest, Donahue demonstrates how the figure of El Mariachi realizes his social (or intermental) potentiality.

The final section brings the volume to a close with two wide-reaching critical exploratory pieces: in "Tarantino & Rodriguez: A Paradigm," Ilan Stavans provides the Latino lens of *lo cursi* through which to engage with Rodriguez's films, overturning misconceptions that he's somehow lowbrow and in bad taste whereas Tarantino is highbrow and intellectual. And, in "Five Amigos Crisscross Borders on a Road Trip with Rodriguez," Christopher González, Sue J. Kim, and myself, along with two new voices heretofore not present in the volume, Samuel Saldívar and Camilla Fojas, share ideas and insights that were either not covered or only glossed briefly in the chapters themselves. They include discussion of the late embrace of Rodriguez within the scholarly community; how his films complicate notions of Latinidad—or *Latino-ness*; genre bending and questions of art and industry; his rejection of the studio system; his controversial use of non-union crews; and issues of gender and ethnic representations in his films, including especially *From Dusk till Dawn*. On this road trip, these collective scholarly minds tie up many questions and issues that arise when thinking deeply about Rodriguez. And, like the volume as a whole, they also open up new avenues of exploration.

The volume wraps with Alvaro Rodriguez's eloquent "Postproduction in Robert Rodriguez's 'Post-Post-Latinidad': An Afterword." Alvaro invites us to join him on a journey that began for him when sitting in the back of a pickup in 1980 with his older cousin, Robert Rodriguez. He offers what I would call a flash fiction Künstlerroman (a fancy word for a narrative that tells of the education of an artist). Alvaro tells of his coming of age as a short story author and screenwriter as it intertwines with Rodriguez's journey in the creating of his cinema of possibilities.

Taken in its parts *and* as a whole, the aim of *Critical Approaches to the Films of Robert Rodriguez* is to open the doors wide for teachers, scholars, film students, filmmakers, and laypersons to understand deeply and widely Rodriguez's films as well as his techniques of filmmaking generally. It aims to open more doors to all variety of attentive and innovative approaches—multimodal, cognitive, affective, intertextploitational—to future studies of the multifaceted film world of Robert Rodriguez.

MATTERS OF MIND AND MEDIA

CHAPTER 1

From *El Mariachi* till *Spy Kids*?
A Cognitive Approach

SUE J. KIM

What happens on a cognitive level to keep people self-contained and willing to accept their subjugation rather than engage in the panic of a fight-or-flight response, where you lash out to protect your life and the lives of your loved ones at all costs or, alternatively, when you decide to pursue a more sustained strategy of resistance? . . . Does the conviction of hope by one or a few cause a synaptic shift in the brains of others so that they rise against their own parasympathetic suppression and spring to action, inhibiting the amygdala's fear and the paralysis that can result?

ARTURO J. ALDAMA, "FEAR AND ACTION: A COGNITIVE APPROACH
TO TEACHING *CHILDREN OF MEN*" (2011, 158)

As for my powers, I've learned that responsibility should be applied with them, and I'll never abuse them like I did today ever, ever again.

REBECCA, "BEDHEAD" (1991)

In his meditation on teaching Alfonso Cuarón's *Children of Men* (2006), Arturo J. Aldama ponders the relationship between cognition and ideology in engaging with films in a political world. Although the gulf between cognitive studies, or studies of the brain and mind, and cultural studies, where much of academic ideological analysis and critique takes place, is still great, an increasing number of scholars are addressing the kinds of questions that A. J. Aldama raises here. Or, to put it in the terms of Rebecca, the heroine of Rodriguez's early short "Bedhead," what is the relationship between our cognitive "powers," or capabilities and capacities, and our social and moral responsibilities to one another? Such questions can help us think about the corpus of filmmaker Robert Rodriguez. Rodriguez's ultraviolent exploitation homages, such as *El Mariachi*

(1991) and *Machete* (2010), seem to contrast sharply with his family-friendly fare, such as the *Spy Kids* series; as Aaron Hill of *The Village Voice* puts it, "Robert Rodriguez works in exactly two filmmaking modes: fast, cheap, genre violence (the *El Mariachi* trilogy, *Sin City*, *Planet Terror*) and fast, cheap, CGI-overloaded family adventure (the *Spy Kids* trilogy, *The Adventures of Sharkboy and Lavagirl 3-D*)." But in this chapter, I argue that cognitive approaches to film can help identify surprising resonances among Rodriguez's films, explaining their appeal and shedding light on their ideological dimensions.

Rodriguez is an indie film hero for breaking into the movie business with his independent film, *El Mariachi*, famously made for $7,000. The film, which he had intended for the straight-to-video Spanish-language audience, ended up winning the Audience Award at the Sundance Film Festival in 1993. Since then, he is, as one critic describes him, "arguably the most successful Latino director ever to work in Hollywood" (Berg 241).[1] While some critics have seen an assimilationist trend in his late 1990s/2000s Hollywood productions, other critics and Rodriguez himself see his films as subversive, particularly in terms of race and immigration.[2] Rodriguez tells the story of being told to Anglo-ize *El Mariachi*, and he discusses his own ambivalence about the negotiations he had to make on *Desperado*.[3] Nevertheless, many of his films either explicitly (*El Mariachi*, *Machete*) or implicitly (*Spy Kids*) invoke social–political issues, such as immigration and multiracial families. He is also largely credited with launching the Hollywood careers of Antonio Banderas (Spanish) and Salma Hayek (Chicana/Latina), and many of his cast and production crews straddle Hollywood and Spanish-language cinema (via Texas). His films are hardly unproblematic, but in a largely culturally and ethnically homogenous film industry, both in front of and behind the camera, his success is noteworthy. While I do not claim that Rodriguez's films constitute some kind of progressive call to arms, I do want to explore what Rodriguez's films can show us about the relationships between cognition (including emotions), art, and ideology.

I will first examine some of the ways that watching (and making) films involves basic cognitive processes that also are deeply embedded in—conditioned by while also reinforcing—sociopolitical contexts; Rodriguez's films both draw on and slightly shift the conventional ways in which our minds use films as "problem-solving tools," thus possibly shifting our relationships to those contexts. In the second part of this chapter, after examining some approaches to cognition and emotion in film, I discuss some of the ways in which Rodriguez's movies suggest that aesthetic form and historical context can play a significant role in what Ed S. Tan calls "film as an emotion machine."[4]

"Tools for Thinking": Chunking, Typification, and Cause-and-Effect

From its mid-century origins, which primarily saw the brain as a computer-like input/output logic machine, cognitive studies—particularly those branches attempting to meld the sciences, social science, and humanities—have moved towards explorations of brain *and* mind as complex, multivalent things that are historical, social, and embodied.[5] In other words, while we can identify shared or basic cognitive functions and capacities, in the real world, actual thinking and being works in complicated ways, which is why considerations such as an unequal distribution of resources within and between nations need ultimately to be part of understanding how our minds function.

Put simply, many scholars have moved beyond seeing cognition as simply an individual phenomenon. Although specific cognitive approaches range from the primarily neurobiological to those emphasizing social relations, and while methodologically we often have to isolate particular processes and patterns of thought to identify and study them, "postcognitivists" understand that cognition cannot really be separated from social relations (Herman, "Re-Minding Modernism" 257). Thus, rather than thinking of cognition as a wholly individual process—what James Wertsch calls "individualistic reductionism" (qtd. in Herman, "Stories" 168)—we can think of cognition as actually "mediated action" ("Stories" 168). David Herman, Alan Palmer, and others argue that we should see the mind as "distributed," understanding cognition not as "a wholly internal process unfolding within the minds of solitary, autonomous, and de-situated cognizers," but rather as a "transindividual activity distributed across groups functioning in specific contexts" (Herman, "Storytelling" 319). That is, cognition involves dynamic processes *within* an individual (emotion and reason, physiology and mind) and *beyond* the individual, who is in constant interaction with environment and history.[6]

Narratives of all kinds play an important role in shaping and mediating cognition. Herman writes, "Narrative, arguably, is at once a vehicle for and target of such distributed cognition, which is *enabled* by the shared construction and revision of stories, but which also *eventuates* in the fashioning and refashioning of accounts of how the world is, might be, or should be" ("Stories" 184). Cognitive approaches to film examine how and why viewers understand and become invested in a story-world through the specific medium of cinema.[7] Although some cognitive processes are similar to, for example, processing real-life events and/or reading books (e.g., attributing underlying states of mind to the actions of others, or "mind reading"), viewers process and react to films on a variety of different levels unique to the medium. Not only does film use visuals and sound, but also by now film has as many generic conventions and norms as other art forms and modes of discourse. Even experimental films constitute a genre with norms (e.g., fans of David Lynch might have been more puzzled if *Mulholland Drive* had concluded by answering all the questions and tying up all the loose ends).

Herman argues that stories themselves serve as important vehicles for thought itself, or "tools for thinking" (163–164); they train and re-train the brain to process information in a variety of socially impacted ways. In this chapter, I focus on three of the "problem-solving activities" that Herman discusses: (1) "'chunking' experience into workable segments"; (2) "managing problems with the 'typification' of phenomena"; and (3) "imputing causal relations between events" ("Stories" 172).[8] The latter two are specific instances of the first, but each particular cognitive process can be distinguished. I will explain briefly how each of these cognitive processes work and discuss them in relation to Rodriguez's films, examining how these analytics can help us understand what is happening in the films *and* how the films can challenge and further refine our models of cognitive processes, which in the real world are inseparable from politics. In other words, we can better understand the cognitive processes involved by examining not only the content of the films, but also their form and the historical contexts that they refer to and draw upon.

First, "chunking" is the basic cognitive process of separating "phenomenal reality into classifiable, knowable, and operable units," of "extract[ing] from the stream of experience a delimited set of participants, states, actions, and events and structures into a coherent whole what might otherwise be reabsorbed back into the atelic and unbounded process of time's passing" (Herman, "Stories" 174). We "chunk" in a variety of ways—temporally, visually, generically, modally, functionally, and so forth. One basic instance of chunking is reading English; I read and even write the words on this page not letter by letter (as I did when I was first learning to read) but word by word. My brain has been trained to chunk the individual letters and spaces into words as recognizable units; this "prechunking" enables me to process and recall information faster. If, however, I come across the word "DIEWELTISALLESWASDER-

FALLIST," I stop in my tracks; my brain has not been trained to automatically process such a conglomeration of letters. For the same reasons, most people can recall song lyrics (chunked into verses and choruses, linked to music and often rhyming) more readily than free-verse poetry.

Herman argues that stories themselves are ways of chunking, both as a whole and in various ways within the story. He writes,

> [N]arrative affords representational tools for addressing the problem of how to chunk the ongoing stream of experience into bounded, cognizable, and thus usable structures. Stories organize experience by enabling people to select from among the total set of sequentially and concurrently available inputs; preprocess those inputs into internally differentiated chunks with . . . a beginning, middle, and end; and then use those temporally structured segments as a basis for further cognitive operations on new experiential inputs. ("Stories" 173)[9]

Excellent (and entertaining) examples of chunking can be found early in *El Mariachi*. In the director's commentary, Rodriguez gleefully explains some of the shortcuts they had to use due to lack of money. In the first jail scene, they simply cast the female guard who worked at the jail because it saved them the trouble of finding a real actress. They used a wheelchair borrowed from the hospital for a dolly shot (they had to hurry because the hospital needed it back). Rodriguez discusses how one of the actors, a local ranch hand, appears several times in the movie, in different disguises, as "bad guys" who are killed because of the dearth of actors. He points out a continuity problem in which, in one shot, the female guard's hair is tied up, and then in a following shot, her hair is down: "This was one of those things where we knew that this movie was going to be cut so fast no one was going to notice things. So you'll see that I take a lot of shortcuts. . . . [It] made me realize we can get away with a lot of things" (Robert Rodriguez). The first gunfight in a bar serves as a kind of case study in low-budget filmmaking. Rodriguez details how they filled condoms with homemade dyed syrup and strapped them to the actors' bodies. When the actors are shot, he points out how, if viewers pause the DVD, they can actually see the weight-lifting belt holding the homemade squibs to the actor's chest. The entire director's commentary, during which Rodriguez talks nonstop, serves as a kind of "how-to" manual on low-budget filmmaking.[10] In other words, Rodriguez was able to make a film on a shoestring budget by drawing on the fact that our brains have been conditioned to chunk a series of film shots into a coherent narrative whole, with consistent characters (or different ones, in the case of the ranch hand playing multiple bad guys) and plot developments, despite the fact that the filmmakers could not afford proper actors, special effects, equipment, or even a dolly.

But in other ways, Rodriguez's films "chunk" slightly differently from mainstream Hollywood or even many indie films in their form and content. That is, the films cannot use wholly idiosyncratic standards; then they would be unintelligible. But the films do make use of existing pieces to put together works that play exuberantly with conventions. One key way that Rodriguez's films are unique is *visual*; even the critics of Rodriguez's plot structuring ability acknowledge that his films have great cinematic verve. As Roger Ebert writes of *Once Upon a Time in Mexico*, Rodriguez is more interested in "great shots" and "camera work, which includes a lot of shots that are about themselves," rather than "a coherent story." Rodriguez "chunks" less by realism of the content than by the fun of cinematic form (shots, visuals, editing/juxtaposition). For instance, the opening scenes of *Spy Kids 3* combine the conventions of film noir with a children's movie. We first hear slow jazz music playing over several establishing shots of an empty water park, recalling both the opening scenes of *The Maltese Falcon* (shots of Sam Spade's San Francisco) as well as the water park that featured prominently in *Spy Kids 2*. A high-angle shot (camera pointing downward) then shows litter (a brochure for "Agua Park") and dead leaves on the ground, and a trench-coated figure walks over the leaves as the wind blows. Then we hear the voice-over by Juni Cortez (played by Daryl Sabara), a typical trait of film noir, using a pseudo-hard-boiled tone, examining the brochure (translating the agua as "water"), Juni says, "Cute. But I wasn't here for cute. I was here because I'd gotten a call for my regular fee. $4.99." He then describes himself as an "ex-secret agent," who'd been "burned by the agency," and is now a "Private Eye" or "P.I." Juni then approaches a well-dressed (i.e., like a 1950s femme fatale) little girl (a very young Selena Gomez) who appears to be his client, and they speak to each other, although without making eye contact. This scene, which appears to us as one continuous unit, is a combination of disparate filmic conventions; in other words, individual film shots, music, lighting, dialogue, and other elements are "chunked" together into one apparently continuous scene while at the same time disrupting our usual categorizations and expectations. The ridiculousness of this conglomeration is what makes the scene amusing. For instance, when Juni describes himself as a detective, he makes a face of surprise; he looks down and calls himself a "gumshoe" at the very moment we see his shoe stuck in gum on the ground. Both "gumshoes" are appropriate to the genre (film noir and kiddie flick), but it is the combination that, using the term in the sense of the Russian formalists, "defamiliarizes" the conventions of both genres by mixing them unexpectedly together. Once we see such a combination of verbal and visual puns, moreover, we are partly conditioned to expect further, similarly silly chunkings.

Such recombinations and revisions lead us to another specific type of chunking that Herman refers to as "typification." We not only group things together (e.g., letters into words), but we also come to *expect* certain groupings, norms, and outcomes. Drawing on Alfred Schutz, Herman outlines the concept of typification, which serves a "broad variety of cognitive tasks—from the organization of objects into classes and members-of-classes, to the learning of the lexical and syntactic patterns of a language, to the ascription of motives to others during social interaction. . . . The constant feature across all these tasks is the expectation-creating modes of preprocessing that typification affords" ("Stories" 179). In other words, typification is a kind of shorthand we use (usually collectively and socially informed) for interpreting the world, which creates expectations and norms.[11] For instance, we expect some conflict to arise early in a film (typical script for both adult action and children's films). Since such norms are historically and socially conditioned, the issue of "typification" is not just an abstract mental function but can be an arena of political and cultural contestation.

As such, Herman and others argue that narratives play a crucial role in both creating and revising typifications. He writes, "stories provide tools for solving the problem of how to balance expectations against outcomes, general patterns against particular instances—in short, the typical against the actual" ("Stories" 179). Stories not only shape what we see as normal and expected (forms of chunking to interpret the world) but also help account for things that do *not* fit into the norm. Herman writes, "Stories fill the breach when typification fails. . . . narrative is a means of redressing problems that arise when anticipated similar experiences do not materialize" ("Stories" 180).[12] Furthermore, stories not only help explain deviations from typification; they also can *challenge* existing typifications and can thereby lead to new conventions and narratives, or new chunkings and prototypes.[13] Herman writes, "the narrative representation of anomalous or atypical events can in turn reshape a culture's or community's sense of what is normal or typical, and thereby help build new models for understanding the world" ("Stories" 179). Stories can serve "retypifying" (building new norms) as well as "metatypifying" functions (question the bases for existing models and norms); that is, they may account for anomalies as well as question the basis upon which norms and prototypes are formed (179).[14]

Rodriguez's films challenge typification in a number of ways related to form, content, and context. Most obviously, his films feature minorities (primarily Latinos), women, and children. Although the mere presence of people of color is hardly a revolutionary idea, the film (and television) industry still suffers from a shameful lack of minorities and women in front of and behind the camera. (See Charles Ramírez Berg's *Latino Images in Film*.) Rodriguez's films feature mixed-race families (the *Spy Kids* series), Latino/as as both principal protagonists and antagonists (as opposed to the usual peripheral drug dealer or domestic worker), and women/girls as action heroes. Despite popular discussions of postfeminism and a "postracial" society, these are all things that we still do not see very often in most films.[15] In shows like *Law & Order* and even the otherwise superlative *Breaking Bad*, Latino/as usually appear as depthless drug dealers and criminals (or service workers). Although many of Rodriguez's female characters in the adult films are hypersexualized (in accordance with genre conventions), many of his prominent female characters in the children's films are not: Carmen (Alexa Vega) and Ingrid Cortez (Carla Gugino), Demetra, Gerti Giggles, Lavagirl, Marissa Electricidad, and Marissa Wilson. In *Shorts*, although the protagonist, Toby Thompson (Jimmy Bennett), is a white male, the film also features the great Helvetica Black (played by Jolie Vanier, with a ridiculously catchy theme song) as the main antagonist/protagonist.[16] Another of my favorite scenes comes from early in *Spy Kids 4D*, when very pregnant spy Marissa Wilson (Jessica Alba), in hot pursuit of a villain, struggles to slide over the hood of a car. That is certainly not something we see every day.

The form of Rodriguez's films also questions the generally realist bent of Hollywood (and many indie) films by incorporating a myriad of forms. Rodriguez incorporates not only the formal elements of B-films (quick cuts, fast dialogue, outsized action) but also the production ethic (fast and cheap). He uses elements of exploitation films (e.g., sexploitation and Mexploitation in *Machete*); *narcotraficante* films, a Mexican police genre that was widely popular in Spanish-speaking film markets during the 1980s (Berg 226–227); spaghetti westerns (the *Mariachi* trilogy); video games (*Spy Kids 3-D*); graphic novels (*Sin City*); and cartoons. *Spy Kids 4D* even included "aromascope" (i.e., in the tradition of "Smell-O-Vision") in theaters. Behind the camera—or about the camera itself—Rodriguez also works to revise what we expect as norms. Rodriguez was one of the first proponents of digital filmmaking, which is cheaper and more accessible to anyone with a good computer and the right software. He cofounded Troublemaker Studios (originally Los Hooligans Productions) with producer (and former spouse) Elizabeth Avellán and introduced U.S. audiences to Salma Hayek, two of the few (but growing number of) women—let alone Latinas—with clout in the U.S. film industry.[17]

Rodriguez's filmic universe challenges the dominant view of the world, not only in including minorities and women on-screen and beyond, but also in the form of the films: fans of pop culture and the immature, trashy, and tasteless are all included in this universe. As Pierre Bourdieu wrote, "Taste classifies, and it classifies the classifier" (6); Rodriguez's films question the "metatypification" between high art and trash. At the same time, however, it is not just the atypicality of his films that makes his movies appealing. Rather, the particular combination of elements is what makes his films entertaining and interesting—for example, Latina Jessica Alba playing a pregnant spy in a scene that tweaks the conventions of action films (sliding needlessly over the hood of a car) in a children's film that incorporates not only cartoonish elements (a talking dog! voiced by Ricky Gervais!) but also *smell*. Rodriguez's films are, again, not necessarily revolutionary, but since what we see as typical or even possible is shaped in part by stories, narrative changes—even and especially in popular culture—can be linked to changes in how and even what we can think. What does a hero or villain look like? Who can be a film producer or director (i.e., who can tell the stories)? What even constitutes a movie? Because such typifications *matter*, revisions to the expected types are central to changing how we think about the possibilities of our world.

Another form of chunking, cause and effect, involves joining objects and events together over time. As Herman writes, "One of the hallmarks of narrative is its linking of phenomena into causal-chronological wholes; stories provide structure for connecting otherwise isolated data into elements of episodes or scenes" ("Stories" 170). The links between scenes and events do not have to be explicitly explained for us to attribute causal connections. Stories not only rely on our ability to relate cause and effect but also train us to link them together; thus, our "predisposition to find causal links between states, actions, and events in a sequentially presented way" is a form of cognitive "chunking" that is ingrained in us via stories in a social environment ("Stories" 176). Put another way, cause and effect is a heuristic for interpreting the series of words and events (in the case of film), visuals, and sounds that are presented to us.

Rodriguez's films play with our usual expectations of cause and effect, and they offer alternative cause-and-effect relationships. For instance, not only are the events in *Shorts* not presented chronologically, they are not even really linked by cause and effect (just the journey of the rainbow-colored wishing rock). This looseness of cause and effect has led some to critique Rodriguez; for instance, the plot of *Once Upon a Time in Mexico* has been described as "a maze" and "a convolution" (Travers, *Once*, and Winter, respectively, although Hartlaub describes the plot as "clever"). A. O. Scott of the *New York Times* writes that although *Once Upon a Time in Mexico* displays Rodriguez's "inventive eye," "ability to infuse digital video, so often flat and grainy, with uncommon depth and luster," and action sequences of "eye-popping flair," "[t]he only thing missing is a coherent story—or even, for that matter, an interesting idea for one." But the plots and emotional responses to the films are not limited to what happens *in* the story; as I will discuss in the next section, a good deal of the investment in the films comes less from investment in the characters as "real" (although they are not, however, wholly ironic) and more from the form (references to and play with generic conventions and technical innovations) and the cultural contexts (status of minorities, women, genre, and tastefulness/tastelessness) in which the films function.

For instance, despite the flawed logic of the plots of many of the children's films, I prefer them to the adult action films because they are interested in identifying the *causes* for the antagonists' evildoing. Granted, the insights are not often earth-shattering: *Spy Kids'* Floop just wants to make a truly inventive, quality TV show; *Spy Kids 2*'s Gary and Gerti Giggles just want their father's approval and attention, as does Helvetica Black in *Shorts*; in *Spy Kids 3-D*, the Toymaker wants forgiveness; in *Sharkboy and Lavagirl*, Minus wants better dreams; and in *Spy Kids 4D*, the Time Keeper just wants people to treasure the time they have with their families. Nevertheless, the recuperative plotlines for the villains suggest that addressable reasons exist for their discontent and antagonism. Similarly, the adult films—primarily the *Mexico* trilogy and *Machete*—show that immigration, the drug trade, and U.S. political, commercial, and cultural neo-imperialism affect everyone—white and minority, male and female, young and old, on both sides of the U.S.–Mexican border (as opposed to being a menace by foreign others or domestic criminal elements). Albeit stylized (and arguably exploitative), the stories that Rodriguez tells go beyond the great white wall of Hollywood. That is, if the ways that we make cause-and-effect links are conditioned *in part* by fictional stories, then the predominant narratives we see from Hollywood and on television tell us that minorities and others (the poor, women, criminals) are simply villainous and/or inscrutable, and we might not even realize different causes and effects exist.

In these ways, Rodriguez's films' storyworlds combine "outsider" film genres and "outsider" politics, particularly on issues of race, in ways that both draw on existing ways of chunking, typification, and linking cause and effect, as well as prod us to think in slightly different ways. As ethnic studies and feminist film critics have been pointing out for years, the stereotypes and ideological messages we receive from films wreak serious damage. Understanding these processes in terms of how our minds function helps explain *why* ideological conditioning works, *how* we can change them, and why the work of a particular filmmaker, such as Rodriguez, appeals to various audiences.

Film Emotions as Fiction, Artifact, and Context

Just as cognition is not wholly individual, emotion (as linked to and even part of cognition) is also not separable from social relations and history.[18] In cognitive psychology, as Patrick Colm Hogan and others have discussed, appraisal theory is a predominant approach to emotions. In classical appraisal theories, "emotion results from a type of evaluation in which one judges the implications of a certain situation," usually in relation to achieving some goal, and the emotion helps us to organize information and decide on actions (Hogan, *Cognitive Science* 140–141). In terms of film, the viewer may experience emotions that arise from identification with a character (usually the protagonist) and/or from the viewer's "preferred outcome" for the character (Hogan, *Cognitive Science* 149); for example, I am angry when the protagonist suffers an injustice and happy when he or she overcomes obstacles to achieve a goal. Many further distinctions come into play; for instance, Frijda argues that action outcomes are part of appraisal while Ortony and others claim that action responses are not necessary for an appraisal that leads to emotion. Other researchers have discussed the role of memory and empathy in viewers' reactions.[19] While the details of such approaches vary, appraisal theory arises out of understanding reason and emotion not as mutually exclusive processes, but rather complexly interwoven processes that occur in the brain and the body.[20]

In examining emotion-as-appraisal in film, Ed Tan distinguishes between what he calls "fiction emotions" and "artifact emotions." *Fiction emotions* are emotions evoked by the viewer's immersion in the film storyworld, while *artifact emotions* are elicited by the experience of the film as an intentionally constructed art object. Tan argues that fiction emotions arise out of the "diegetic effect," which is the viewer's "experience of the fictional world as the environment" and "the illusion of being present in the fictional world" (52). Of course, we know what we are watching is not real, and as film scholars we also know that film is not a neutral or nonmediated medium. Nevertheless, Tan argues that the primary emotional impact of film for most viewers stems from the viewer's investment in the characters and events in the "fictional world" or "storyworld." He summarizes the diegetic effect's influence on emotion: "the situational meaning structure in film viewing is related primarily to the situation in the fictional world. . . . Viewers experience the fictional events as if they were happening all around them; the events appear to be real, concrete, and taking place in the here and now" (Tan 53).

Thus, the element of "appraisal" in film viewers' emotions functions similarly to but slightly different from appraisal about one's own goals, situations, and so forth. As film viewers, we do not believe these events are really taking place; rather, we experience "witness emotions," in which the film viewer feels emotions based on the achievement or obstruction of goals for the protagonist(s). These usually are not as strong as real-world emotions, but they may be, depending on the particular issues, values, and emotions at work. Oatley notes that the appeal of fictional story derives both from the excitation of our emotions and our immunity from harm. He writes, "In the theory of sympathetic emotions, our enjoyment of a fictional story derives from entering a narrative world in which we feel for those who suffer certain events. But we're immunized from harmful effects of the events on our own person or on loved ones. By following the story, we achieve the satisfaction of narrative closure" (Oatley 160). Thus even fear and anxiety are pleasurable experiences because the viewer experiences tension and resolution without risking anything (which again is part of the appeal).

But Tan also goes on to describe artifact emotions, which arise from the viewer's experience of the artfulness of the film, such as pleasure in a swirling camera shot or musical soundtrack. He writes, "[T]he traditional feature film makes it clear to the audience that there is an editorial intelligence at work . . . , who has carefully ordered the events that they are viewing. As soon as they are aware, no matter how fleetingly, of the operation of that intelligence, they are in that instant aware of the film as artifact" (65). Because he focuses on realist film, for Tan artifact emotions are usually negative, indicating an aberration that indicates a break in the illusion (e.g., a love scene has gone on too long or a boom microphone accidentally enters the frame). Tan argues that these two levels of emotional responses—fiction emotions and artifact emotions—work together dynamically to create interest, which Tan (following Frijda) identifies as an emotion. So even though he touches on the role of film as artifact, his account focuses on fiction emotions.

Drawing on but departing slightly from Tan's conclusions, Greg Smith argues that film works to elicit emotion by creating "mood," which thereby conditions the viewer to experience more intense, briefer emotions proper, which in turn help to sustain the overall mood. Smith calls this understanding the "mood-cue approach." Smith describes "moods" as "a longer-lasting but less forceful emotional state with an orienting function that encourages us to express a particular group of emotions" (38). According to Smith, this filmic mood-cue approach works in two stages. First, "emotion cues" at the beginning of a film create an "emotional orientation" toward the film as a whole; then the body of the film supplies a "periodic diet of brief emotional moments. . . . to sustain a mood" (44). This general mood interacts with the stronger, punctual emotions throughout the film to produce the viewer's emotional experience. Smith continues, "Filmic cues that can provide emotional information include facial expressions, figure movement, dialogue, vocal expression and tone, costume, sound, music, lighting, mise-en-scène, set design, editing, camera. . . . , depth of field, character qualities and histories, and narrative situation" (43). In other words, Smith identifies a more fluid affective-orienting zone somewhat in between Tan's fiction and artifact emotions, and Smith accounts more for the formal elements of film in bringing about affective responses from viewers.

Bringing Tan's and Smith's approaches to emotion in film into conversation with Rodriguez's films illuminates similarities between his films and other considerations that impact film and emotion. As with many other feature films, Rodriguez's films offer a way for viewers to experience emotions without any real risk to themselves. But it would be difficult to say that the emotional impacts of Rodriguez's films arise more from the fiction emotions than the film as artifact. Rodriguez's films clearly indicate *both* that the characters are truly invested in their own storyworld (diegetic level) *while also* that viewers should take an ironic relation to the film. The mood cues in Rodriguez's films—dialogue, sound, composition, editing, camera angles, and so forth—exaggerate the formal and stylistic filmic elements to the extent that artifact emotions interact in complicated ways with fiction emotions. It is not that the fiction emotions do not matter—for instance, the characters do not break the fourth wall to indicate that they know their world is not real—but many viewers' emotional responses do not arise simply from investment in the fortunes of the protagonists and their struggles. This dynamic is as true in *Machete* as in *Spy Kids 3-D*.[21]

In fact, in many of Rodriguez's films, while the outcome is never really in doubt, the story is nevertheless important. The viewer's emotional investment in the narrative may not arise from the viewer's *immersion* in the storyworld so much as the narrative's reference to extratextual, real-world phenomena like racism, immigration/border issues, multiracial families, globalization, patriarchy/feminism, and so forth. For instance, viewers' reactions to *El Mariachi* and *Machete* register at the level of content (investment in the characters' world), form (self-conscious references to and ironic plays on cinematic predecessors), *and* context (e.g., the economic and cultural devastation wrought by the drug trade in Mexico and the right-wing anti-immigrant crusade). Such reaction is also applicable to films such as the *Spy Kids* series; although they do not refer as explicitly to highly charged political issues as *Machete*, we have young Latino protagonists, the mixed-race family, and the appearance of Rodriguez's frequent stars Antonio Banderas, Salma Hayek, and Danny Trejo.

We can see this particularly in relation to how violence works in the films. Like his sometimes collaborator Quentin Tarantino, Rodriguez is known for his use of hyperstylized violence. As F. L. Aldama has put it, Rodriguez is a "comic book director" ("*Adventures*"), drawing on techniques from B-movie grindhouse films, exploitation films, *narcotraficante* films, and action movies (ranging from Bruce Lee to Steven Seagal to Chow Yun-Fat), to depict various kinds of comic-book-like violence. Whether in *El Mariachi* or *Spy Kids*, the violence is so hyperstylized that it becomes denaturalized. As Claudia Puig writes of *Once Upon a Time in Mexico*, "Plenty of blood is shed, lots of powerful artillery is fired, and action sequences provide astounding car crashes and fiery explosions. But Rodriguez is such a visual stylist, and the violence is so cartoonish, that the flurry of whizzing bullets and growing pile of bodies is not as offensive as it might be."

For instance, the first gunfight in the bar in *El Mariachi*, discussed above, is serious for the characters, but viewers can react to it on a number of levels. The first is on the level of diegesis, or identifying with the characters. But some viewers—including myself—react to Rodriguez's budget filmmaking ingenuity as much as or even more than to the diegetic events. The relations between the films' stylized violence and the emotions that viewers experience are complicated and myriad. When I watch *El Mariachi* (and even more so Rodriguez's later films), I do not react to the violence in the same way as if I were actually being attacked or if I were witnessing real violence. I understand that the violence is "serious" for the characters at their diegetic level, but my relationship to violence in Rodriguez's films is complicated. I experience pleasure at Rodriguez's ingenuity in crafting the scene with little resources, and, given my critique of Hollywood, I also take pleasure from the context of the film (shot outside Hollywood for very little money, a model for other independent filmmakers). In other words, the hyperstylized violence can elicit complicated emotional responses that draw not only on the fiction and artifact emotions and mood cues, but also on various other intertextual and contextual elements. Political views, personal experiences, and aesthetic values all inform the reaction to the fiction and the form. Likewise, in the kids' films, much of the action sequences are digital; in *Shorts* or *Sharkboy and Lavagirl*, I experience amusement at visuals during the children's battles against Carbon Black (the children transform digitally into wasps, dung beetles, and other creatures) and against Mr. Electric. Diegetically, or in the storyworld, these battles are "real," but I do not feel any sense of threat or anxiety; rather, the presentations of worlds in which children can transform into bugs or in which children rule the ocean and lava are what engage and entertain.

Another example comes from a scene towards the end of *Machete*, which produces *some* kinds of emotions but not quite in the ways that Tan and Smith have outlined. In the film, Machete is a former Mexican *federale*, who retires after his wife is killed by a drug lord, Rogelio Torrez (Steven Seagal). Machete is hired to assassinate the virulently and violently anti-immigrant Senator John McLaughlin, played by Robert De Niro, although, as we find out, the supposed assassination is meant to actually frame Machete and help the Senator's political polls. Machete is aided by Luz, played by Michelle Rodriguez, who works with an immigrant aid movement known as "the Network." She uses a taco truck as cover for the Network. Luz may also be "Shé," the leader of the Network, who is planning an uprising against the anti-immigrant forces. We believe her to have died, having seen her shot in the eye earlier. But in this scene towards the end of the movie, Machete and the Mexican immigrants go head-to-head in a battle against the anti-immigrant border vigilantes at the latter's compound. During the over-the-top fight scene, a hospital ambulance zooms into the compound and a doctor and two buxom nurses, with extremely short skirts and high heels, burst out and mow down the vigilantes with machine guns. The back door of the ambulance then slowly opens as an electric guitar starts to play in the manner befitting a Charles Bronson film. Rodriguez, now clad in a black leather bra, pants, and an eye patch, emerges in slow motion from the ambulance. As she walks into the battle, the doctor asks her, "How's the eye?" and Rodriguez replies stoically, "What eye?"

From the beginning of the film, the mood cues clearly indicate an ironic distance from the events; *Machete* is an homage to *narcotraficante* films, Mexploitation and sexploitation films (in the tradition of Russ Meyer), vigilante films, grindhouse films—cheap B-movies churned out to appeal to a particular demographic and/or cash in on a particular cultural fad. But the film is also referring to extratextual issues that are very real, including anti-immigrant racism, labor exploitation, and Machiavellian political manipulation of these issues. Some viewers' emotional response to the film may be informed by the desire for resistance and punishment against the anti-immigrant forces; other viewers may feel repelled that Rodriguez is using these issues for a commercial film; and some viewers may be ambivalently divided between both feelings. Some viewers may simply be aroused by the sexy nurses and Luz's incredible belly-baring leather outfit while others may be bored by the lack of character development. In other words, our response exceeds the level of fiction emotions (what happens to Machete and Luz against the racist anti-immigrants) but is not limited to the level of film as artifact. Our reactions, emotional and otherwise, are conditioned by myriad other social–political, historical, and aesthetic considerations.

By the same token, the end of *Spy Kids 3-D* evokes emotions that are not limited to the diegesis. The Toymaker, played by Sylvester Stallone, had been banished to cyberspace by the OSS (Organization of Super Spies) for his previous crimes; having escaped, he now attacks a real city using an army of robots. All the previous characters from the previous *Spy Kids* films show up to help fight the robots, including parents Ingrid (Carla Gugino) and Gregorio Cortez (Antonio Banderas), grandmother Helga Avellan (Holland Taylor), Uncle Machete (Danny Trejo), "Uncle" Felix (Cheech Marin), mad scientist Romero (Steve Buscemi), amusement park owner Dinky Winks (Bill Paxton), and former villains Floop (Alan Cumming), Minion (Tony Shalhoub), and Donnagon Giggles (Mike Judge), along with his wife Francesca Giggles (Salma Hayek) and children Gerti and Gary Giggles. After a CGI-enhanced fight scene, one giant robot remains, controlled by the Toymaker, and Carmen and Juni Cortez's wheelchair-bound grandfather Valentin Avellan, played by

Ricardo Montalbán, enters the robot for a final showdown. But instead of a grand battle, Valentin tells the Toymaker that although he (the Toymaker) lashes out due to guilt and fear of retribution for putting Valentin in the wheelchair many years ago, "Now, let me tell you all the good things that came of it: humility, spirituality, understanding. You've been living in fear of me all these years, but I've only been searching for you so I could tell you that I forgive you." Valentin then persuades the Toymaker to forgive *himself*, and the Toymaker calls off the giant robot. As Valentin and the Toymaker emerge in peace, Donnagon asks, "So, wait a minute. Who won?" Valentin responds, "It's not whether you win or lose," and the Toymaker concludes, "It's how you play the game." The film ends with all the characters—heroes, villains, and secondary characters—joining in a paean to (extended) family.

Some of the emotions evoked by this scene derive from the story; despite the CGI "violence," everybody ends up friends, inviting warm and fuzzy feelings. But part of the response arises from extradiegetic elements, particularly the high caliber of actors, all appearing in this comic strip film. Antonio Banderas mugs it up and appears to be having a great time, as he does throughout the first three *Spy Kids* films; this element of sublime ridiculousness, in conjunction with the no-stakes, digital cartoon "violence" and unexpected cameos by famous actors, elicits affective responses—amusement, interest, perhaps puzzlement or irritation. Disability also constitutes a context; audiences may respond positively or negatively to Valentin's recasting of being wheelchair-bound as a strength.

In these ways, Rodriguez's films suggest that there are more dimensions to emotional experience than those outlined by Tan and Smith, although their insights are also operative and useful. Viewers' reactions to a film like *Machete*, despite and perhaps because of its status as ironic homage to all kinds of exploitation films (border films, sexploitation films, violence, etc.), may trouble the distinction between "witness emotions" and emotions-for-oneself, as well as between "fiction emotions" and "artifact emotions." If one is an immigrant, then racial profiling, incarceration, and/or deportation may not be abstract dangers, *even if* the events in the film are recognized as fictional and not threatening. Likewise, if one is a child, the sense of powerlessness in an enigmatic and sometimes dangerous and/or painful adult world may not be a fiction, even if the child recognizes that the film's storyworld is not real. Furthermore, *Spy Kids 3-D* appeals to viewers through the visuals as much as the story, and it may tickle some adult viewers for additional extratextual reasons (Ricardo Montalbán! Sylvester Stallone!?). Viewers' responses may be historical in a number of senses; individual memories of past events can haunt and inform emotions in the present, and also collective memories and experiences can shape feelings about a narrative (positively or negatively). Political and historical events may inform emotional responses to a film, but so can filmic history, particularly Rodriguez's films that ostentatiously refer to styles and genres of film. And these considerations may interact in a variety of ways; for example, Rodriguez's recurrent use of actors Salma Hayek and Danny Trejo, even in films without such overt political references (such as *Spy Kids*), refers intertextually to his other films that do deal explicitly with border issues *and* refers beyond the films not only to the political issues in general, but also to Rodriguez, Hayek, and Trejo's professed political stances (particularly on immigration). Our sense of the director impacts our response to the film with respect to not just our sense of Rodriguez as auteur, but also of his sociohistorical location and that of his casts and crews.[22]

Examining the range of possible cognitive and emotional operations involved in Rodriguez's films troubles individualist assumptions about how we think and feel, and it can suggest further directions for research into the dynamics of cognition, emotion, diegetic content, cinematic form, and context. If stories constitute tools for thinking, and stories are culturally and historically shaped, then the cognitive processes involved in storytelling (or films) can be arenas of ideological contestation. Likewise, feelings are historically situated, political processes that operate even while interacting with the most seemingly childish or "tasteless" films. To paraphrase how Rebecca, the protagonist of Rodriguez's early short film "Bedhead," puts it, we all have cognitive powers of thinking and feeling in a historically shaped, social–political world, and in telling our stories—which include scholarly accounts—we can strive to use them responsibly towards a better world.

Notes

Earlier versions of this chapter were presented at the March 2012 International Conference on Narrative in Las Vegas, Nevada, and in the American Studies I.D.E.A. working group at the University of Massachusetts, Lowell, in April 2012. I thank all the participants for their helpful feedback.

1. In 2005, Rodriguez codirected with Frank Miller the film adaptation of Miller's graphic novel *Sin City*. Rodriguez has also collaborated a number of times with Quentin Tarantino, first in the genre-bending *From Dusk till Dawn* (1996) and then in the *Planet Terror* portion of the *Grindhouse* homage (2007). In this

chapter, I focus on Rodriguez's solo-directed films (many of which he also produces, writes, edits, and writes/plays music for).

2. For further debates on the politics of Rodriguez's films, see Ramírez Berg (*Latino Images in Film*); Cameron; Flanagan; Leen; and Torres.

3. See chapter 10, interview with Rodriguez, in Ramírez Berg (*Latino Images in Film*).

4. Whereas psychoanalytic approaches to film have been predominant in film studies, recent decades have seen the flourishing of alternative approaches to film, particularly in relation to the cognitive sciences and psychology. For an introduction to some central issues, see Stam and Miller; for the most tendentious exchanges, see Bordwell and Carroll as well as Žižek.

5. For more sources on the history of cognitive studies, see F. L. Aldama, *Toward*; Hogan, *Cognitive Science*; Herman, *Story Logic*; G. A. Miller; Richardson and Spolsky; and Zunshine, *Introduction to Cognitive Cultural Studies*.

6. See also Hogan, *Cognitive Science*, chapter 2, for more on the "cognitive architecture" that cognitivists work to figure out and situate.

7. David Herman defines "storyworld" as "mental models of who did what to and with whom, when, where, why, and in what fashion in the world to which recipients relocate—or make a deictic shift—as they work to comprehend a narrative" (*Story Logic* 5). This term has come into use in narrative theory because it attempts to account for multiple dimensions, not just temporal order; Herman writes, "In trying to make sense of a narrative, interpreters attempt to reconstruct not just what happened . . . but also the surrounding context or environment embedded existents, their attributes, and the actions and events in which they are more or less centrally involved" (*Story Logic* 13–14).

8. The other two that Herman discusses in "Stories as a Tool for Thinking" are "sequencing" and "distributing intelligence across groups" (172).

9. Even stories not using normal temporal progression use some form of "chunking"—thematically, associatively, etc. But such texts tend to be more challenging to most readers precisely because non-conventional narratives challenge the "chunking" patterns of conventional narratives.

10. Rodriguez has a series of "Ten Minute Film School" clips on his various DVD releases in which he discusses other techniques for low-budget filmmaking.

11. Typification is a broader concept that can also include "prototypes." A "prototype" is a "a sort of concretization of the schema with all default values in place" (58). A schema is a "hierarchy of principles defining a lexical term" (Hogan, *The Mind and Its Stories* 57); in other words, a schema is the essential requirements for a thing, its definition. But because prototypes "vary with context" (we always encounter them in some context), Hogan adds that what we actually encounter are "prototype effects," rather than pure prototypes. So, for instance, a "schema" for a cat may be a small, domesticated mammal that walks on all four legs and has soft fur, whiskers, and retractable claws. The prototype for a cat is the image of a cat that pops into your head when you hear the word or that may appear as an icon for your desktop—or rather, these are "prototype effects," because we always encounter the expectation/norm in *some* context. Furthermore, the prototypes and schema are obviously open to revision; there exist cats without fur, without claws, without whiskers, and without all four legs, and yet we would still classify them as

cats. Hogan (*The Mind and Its Stories*) and Herman ("Stories") argue that stories help us both create and revise such norms and expectations.

12. In fact, nontypicality is arguably what makes a story worth telling. If I tell you that my cat coughed up a hair ball, neither of us would consider this story very riveting; if, however, I tell you that my cat coughed up a hair ball made of *gold*—that would be a "tellable" story.

13. For instance, the Russian formalists' account of automatization and defamiliarization of narrative forms is itself a kind of narrative that helps to account for innovations in literary form. Once we understand their account of the "evolution" of literary forms, nontypical narratives may become less abnormal and, in fact, can become conventional themselves.

14. Herman's example is an oral story about a shape-shifter; the story questions the boundaries between human and animal, as well as natural and supernatural.

15. For further discussion of the lack of women and minorities in films (and television), see Goldberg; Johnson; Martins and Harrison; and Sarkeesian, among many others.

16. The whiteness of Toby Thompson's family can perhaps be read as critique of white upper-middle-class obsession with techno-consumerism.

17. Avellán was inducted into the Texas Film Hall of Fame in 2007 as the first recipient of the Ann Richards Award and has gone on to produce films on her own (*Internet Movie*).

18. Physiological processes form part of the equation, but as F. L. Aldama argues: "[N]o matter how personal emotions are as bodily experience and subjective feeling, they are also interpersonal and social. Emotions are part and parcel of the social tissue in that they are present in the way people connect with each other and treat each other as members of society and, more generally, the human race. They join and attach individuals, they separate and antagonize them, and they function as a social tool" (F. A. Aldama, "Putting" 137–138). Attempting to mediate between, on the one hand, wholly universalist, physiological, and/or ahistorical accounts of emotions and, on the other hand, culturally relativist and/or strict constructivist accounts of emotion, David Herman theorizes "emotionologies," or "the collective emotional standards of a culture as opposed to the experience of emotion itself" ("Storytelling" 322). Narratives do not just emerge from existing cultural emotionologies; they also serve to instill, shape, and police those emotional understandings (324–325).

19. Appraisal is not the only model and not without controversy, but the debate is too complex to explore here. For further information, see Dagleish and Power; Evans and Cruse; Frijda; Lane and Nadel; and Ortony, Clore, and Collins.

20. The many debates over the definitions and delineations between different kinds and intensities of emotion are too many to get into here. For instance, Brian Massumi distinguishes between affect, which is "unformed and unstructured," and emotions, which have "function and meaning" (260), whereas Frijda defines "emotions" as a motivational state linked to appraisal and action (*The Emotions*). For the purposes of this chapter, I use a broad definition of "emotion" to refer to any affective reaction to film.

21. Despite the special effects, Rodriguez's alien/horror/teen flick *The Faculty* (1998) is arguably one of the most self-consciously stylized of his films; on the sur-

face, it appears to be a simple aliens-take-over-a-high-school film. Yet discussions of the film, by professional reviewers as well as fans, involve a range of intertextual and contextual considerations, ranging from comparisons to Rodriguez's previous films as well as the lack of Latino characters/actors (except Salma Hayek as a school nurse).

22. That we do not do so as often with white male directors suggests that the continuing unmarked privileged term still often serves as the norm.

CHAPTER 2

You've Come a Long Way, Booger Breath: Juni Cortez Grows Up in the *Spy Kids* Films

PHILLIP SERRATO

Robert Rodriguez brings to the silver screen the character Juni Cortez (Daryl Sabara) in his *Spy Kids* series of films, *Spy Kids* (2001), *Spy Kids 2: Island of Lost Dreams* (2002), *Spy Kids 3-D: Game Over* (2003), and *Spy Kids: All The Time in the World* (2011). With this character, audiences witness the development of boy to man both as character and as actor. Initially, the boy Juni struggles to arrive at a confident sense of self. Feelings of inferiority, isolation, and abjection besiege him for most of the original trilogy and devastate his dignity and self-esteem.[1] By the end of the third film, however, audiences see a boy who has negotiated the assorted challenges that had previously made his childhood a particularly stressful experience. Upon his successful completion of the mission assigned to him in this film, Juni emerges with a respectability that had formerly eluded him. Most recently, the appearance of Juni as an adult in *Spy Kids: All the Time in the World* seems to round out the dramatization of his transformation from an abject little boy to an accomplished man. In this fourth installment, Juni is introduced as embodying the self-confidence, emotional invulnerability, and professional distinction typically associated with—and expected of—mature masculinity.

At first glance, the transformation of Juni over the course of the series seems to leave intact dominant ideals of masculinity. The trajectory of the films seems to privilege his development into an accomplished and respected young man. But in the fourth film it eventually emerges (in classic Robert Rodriguez fashion) that appearances are not what they seem. By the end of the fourth film, normative masculinity turns out to be more elusive, illusory, and undesirable than one might realize. In effect, what had, in the span of the original trilogy, been a fantasy of a disempowered boy's rise to prominence, empowerment, and "proper" masculinity gives way to skepticism about this fantasy and a destabilization of the masculine ideals that it entails.

Up from Abjection

The first *Spy Kids* installment introduces audiences to Gregorio and Ingrid Cortez (Antonio Banderas and Carla Gugino) and their children, Carmen (Alexa Vega) and Juni. According to a backstory provided in the form of a bedtime tale that Ingrid tells the children at the start of the film, Gregorio and Ingrid once worked for opposing spy agencies. When, by a twist of fate, each is assigned to assassinate the other, they end up falling in love. Of course they marry, and when they do, they retire from spy work so they can focus their energies on raising their children. Amidst the relative doldrums of domesticity, the two accept a mission that requires them to venture to the castle of Fegan Floop (Alan Cumming), the host of the popular children's television program *Floop's Fooglies*. Floop, it turns out, is working on the side as a contractor for Mr. Lisp (Robert Patrick), a villain who has hired Floop to create a robot army that will help him take over the world. Apparently, a number of spies from the OSS spy agency have tried to foil Floop's work only to end up captured by Floop and transformed into one of his Fooglies, the bizarre characters who serve as Floop's sidekicks on his show. When Gregorio and Ingrid return to action to stop Floop and Lisp and rescue the captured agents, they too are caught and detained by Floop. It then befalls Juni and his big sister to travel to Floop's island and save their parents. While the circumstances within which Carmen and Juni find themselves set the stage for the possible maturation and empowerment of both characters, the film is primarily organized around Juni's development of courage and self-reliance.

The empowerment that Juni exhibits by the end of this first film constitutes a dramatic change from his condition at the start. In the film's opening sequence, viewers find him in the bathroom, a space intrinsically associated—especially in childhood—with shame and the abject. With a dejected expression that bespeaks a compromised self-esteem, Juni stands before a mirror applying drops of medicine to the numerous warts that dot his fingers (see figure 1). Clearly, the eruptions on his fingers signify for him his abjection vis-à-vis his apparent aberration from normative, implicitly hygienic embodiment. That he is standing in front of a mirror and contemplating his image while he tends to his fingers is a crucial detail;

Figure 1. In *Spy Kids* (2001), Juni worries about his warts.

the crafting of the mise-en-scène clearly plays on psychoanalytic presumptions of the integral role of processes of mirroring in identity formation. Specifically, as Juni's eyes toggle between his fingers and his visage in the mirror, he is denied the narcissistic pleasure that Jacques Lacan describes in his discussion of the mirror stage. In Lacan's formulation,

> The fact is that the total form of the body by which the subject anticipates in a mirage the maturation of his power is given to him only as *Gestalt*, that is to say, in an exteriority in which this form is certainly more constituent than constituted, but in which it appears to him above all in a contrasting size . . . that fixes it and in a symmetry that inverts it, in contrast with the turbulent movements that the subject feels are animating him. (2)

Lacan posits here that the (child) subject's encounter with his or her specular image enables a coherent, and therefore pleasurable, sense of self. By smoothing over the emotional "turbulence" that otherwise complicates the child subject's experience and obstructs the development of an integrated sense of self, the flatness or superficiality of the specular image that he or she encounters provides a refreshingly stable template and means for self-recognition and self-constitution. The trouble for Juni, though, is that the body that he sees in the mirror is not nicely bounded and coherent and does not allow for the resolution of his emotional turbulence. Instead, the image he encounters does nothing more than reanimate the emotional turbulence that torments him because all it does is remind him of his own imperfection and inadequacy.

Consequently, rather than witness Juni's indulgence of narcissistic pleasure, audiences see illustrated Julia Kristeva's complication of narcissism:

> Even before being *like*, "I" am not but do *separate, reject, abject*. Abjection, with a meaning broadened to take in subjective diachrony, *is a precondition of narcissism*. It is coexistent with it and causes it to be permanently brittle. The more or less beautiful image in which I behold or recognize myself rests upon an abjection that sunders it as soon as repression, the constant watchman, is relaxed. (13)

Narcissism eludes Juni because the immediacy of his warts makes the repression of his own abjection impossible. Along these lines, Juni cannot perform the "separation, rejection, or abjection" that Kristeva mentions because he has no *other* against which to define himself. Instead, he remains mired in what Kristeva calls "the abjection of self" (5). According to Kristeva, the abject

> is experienced at the peak of its strength when the subject, weary of fruitless attempts to identify with something on the outside, finds the impossible within; when it finds that the impossible constitutes its very *being*, that it *is* none other than abject. . . . There is nothing like the abjection of self to show that all abjection is in fact recognition of the want on which any being, meaning, language, or desire is founded. (5)

In the case of Juni, the incompleteness and imperfection that he sees in the mirror produces an encounter—or reencounter—with "want," which ultimately underwrites his experience of his own abjection.

The gendered implications of Juni's abjection compound his shame and humiliation. In Juni's mind, a correlation between nervousness, sweaty hands, and warts leads him to regret that his warts attest to an unacceptable emotional weakness on his part. Granted, his understanding of the causes of warts is inaccurate, but the fact remains that for him his warts signify a deficiency that situates him at a distance from proper masculinity. Symbolically, the pastel colors of the bandages that he wraps around his medicine-treated fingers underscore his alienated relationship to normative masculinity. Since these colors are stereotypically inconsistent with masculinity, his bandages effectively reflect and reinforce the imbrication of his abjection and his apparent gender failure. Interestingly, Juni's sensitivity to the gendered implications of his abjection reveals itself in the strategy he utilizes to surmount his condition. While contemplating his image in the mirror, he decides to imagine himself anew. To this end, he first removes his fingers from view, which allows for the momentary repression of his abjection. He then raises his chin, puffs out his chest, and warps his lips into a slight snarl in an effort to perform a more aggressive persona. Evidently, he wants—both in terms of desire and lack—"proper" masculinity.

The posturing that Juni tries on also constitutes an imaginary strategy for standing up to the various others who have instilled in him the inferiority that haunts him. First, his mother and sister emerge as key antagonists. In both relationships, Juni chafes against the females' authority over him as well as their potential to humiliate him. For example, when his mother reminds him in the opening sequence to brush his teeth before bed (and thus not be abject), the boy brusquely replies, "I am, I am," in a manner intended to neutralize her power over him.[2] Shortly thereafter, when Ingrid asks to check Juni's bandaged fingers, he refuses, tucking his hands behind his back so as to limit her ability to reinforce the shame that he already feels. Carmen, meanwhile, poses an even greater threat to the boy's self-esteem due to the merciless disdain with which she treats him for most of the film. By continuously hurling names at him such as "scaredy-cat," "little twerp," and "butterfingers," she not only infantilizes and ridicules him, but also contributes to his painful feelings of alienation from his own family.

Given the conflicts that arise with his mother and sister, a very conventional—and very problematic—stage seems to be set for Juni to recover his dignity via an assertion of himself over and against the feminine. This, of course, would rehearse the all-too-familiar edict that a boy's assumption of normative masculinity depends on his repudiation and domination of the feminine. But soon enough viewers learn that females are not the only sources of distress for him. In a private conversation between Ingrid and Gregorio about problems that the children are having at school, Ingrid reveals to Gregorio, "And those school friends Juni talks about? No such beasts. It turns out the other kids pick on him. He has no friends." Accordingly, the only time we see Juni at school, a boy approaches him and, in response to the bandages on Juni's fingers, taunts, "Hey, it's the mummy. Nice looking bandages, mummy."[3] To no avail, Juni protests, "Just stop it, man." The bully continues to force himself on Juni, however, by proclaiming, "When I'm talking to you, you listen," which reduces Juni to a painfully belittled position. Once he finally makes his way into the school building, Juni sits alone, obviously disgraced, only to overhear Carmen pass by and complain to the several friends who flank her, "I even have to share a room with him because he's afraid of being alone." Unsurprisingly, Carmen's remark leaves Juni even more depressed and looking more and more like the kind of anguished and withdrawn boy depicted by boy-crisis psychologists such as Dan Kindlon and Michael Thompson (142–143).[4]

Given the loneliness and low self-esteem from which Juni suffers both at home and at school, the appeal for him of *Floop's Fooglies* makes sense. Aesthetically reminiscent of recent children's fare such as *Teletubbies*, *Boobah*, and *Yo Gabba Gabba!*, *Floop's Fooglies* is a hypercolorful program that features its host performing songs and delivering messages of encouragement to his young viewers. In one musical number, for instance, Floop promises,

> It's a cruel, cruel world
> All you little boys and girls
> And some mean nasty people
> Want to have you for their supper
> But if you follow me
> You can all be free!
> FREE!
> You can all be free!

With lyrics such as these and exhortations such as "Always remember, whatever you do, believe in yourself. Your dreams will come true," it is no wonder that watching the show brings a smile to Juni's face. As removed as he is, Floop constitutes the only source of inspiration, validation, and consolation available to Juni. Not to be overlooked, the presence of the Fooglies on the show reinforces for Juni the appeal of Floop. The Fooglies are the gibberish-speaking, rather monstrous-looking cast of sidekicks who participate in the program's on-screen shenanigans. Floop's apparent willingness to befriend these otherwise hideous creatures convinces Juni that Floop is someone who takes in social outcasts and misfits. Consequently, when Juni overhears Carmen's rant about having to share a room with him, he says to the Floop action figure in his hand, "What's so special about being a Cortez? I wish I could go away to your world, Floop. You'd be my friend." As far as Juni is concerned, the presence of the Fooglies on

Floop's show suggests that Floop might be inclined to befriend alienated and unloved little boys, too.

The opportunity for Juni to transcend his shame and alienation arises once Gregorio and Ingrid are captured on their spy mission and he and Carmen must rescue them. The first indication of a bolder, more empowered Juni appears when the children find their way to the workshop of their estranged uncle, Machete (Danny Trejo). Machete, the children discover, is a spy gadget designer who has not seen his brother Gregorio in years because of an unspecified falling out between the two. Due to his strained relationship with his brother, when Carmen and Juni track down Machete and ask for his help, he refuses. This puts the children in the position of having to take matters into their own hands. Subsequently, in the middle of the night Carmen and Juni steal away in one of their uncle's mini-planes. Notably, when the hour arrives for them to make their escape, Carmen, with a glow stick in her hand to light her way, approaches Juni's bed and asks, "Ready?" In response, the boy who had previously been an emblem of fear confidently states, "Let's go," at which point he unveils from beneath his pillow his own glow stick. In a rather blatant dramatization of Juni's emerging claim to normative (phallic) masculinity—and its corollaries of power, courage, and confidence—Juni's stick is markedly longer than Carmen's. Obviously, the visual suggestion is that Juni is indeed not just ready to meet the demands of their mission, but readier than Carmen. Unfortunately, among other things, this suggestion of a competition (which Juni eventually wins) between Carmen and Juni over phallic mettle inaugurates a dynamic in which Juni's progression toward masculine integrity and distinction occurs alongside the incremental disempowerment and subordination of his sister.

In a key moment during the flight, Juni definitively turns the tables of humiliation on his sister and turns a crucial corner in his Entwicklungsroman, or process of growth and maturation. As one would expect, neither of the children knows how to operate Machete's mini-plane. Nonetheless, with Juni at the controls while she fumbles with the instruction sheet, Carmen hurls a slew of insults at her brother, including "meathead," "warthog," and "booger breath." On this occasion, however, rather than internalize and capitulate to Carmen's verbal abuse, Juni repeatedly cautions her, "I'm warning you," and, "Stop it, or I'll call you names." Brimming with confidence, Carmen sharply asserts, "Go ahead. You got nothing on me." To Carmen's surprise, the boy does prove to have something on her; eventually he shuts her up (and thus down) by calling her "diaper lady." Immediately Carmen ceases and asks, "How long have you known?" which confirms to Juni and the audience that her little brother has managed to out-humiliate her by reducing her to an especially infantile and abject condition. Importantly, the confirmation from Carmen that she is indeed the "diaper lady" overturns any presumption the audience might have carried that Juni wets the bed. In an earlier scene that shows Ingrid and Gregorio in captivity, Gregorio worries aloud about the ability of the children to fend for themselves, complaining, "They still wear diapers." In a cryptic manner, Ingrid insists, "Only one is in diapers and only at night. It's not that unusual, OK?" With Juni previously established as the more juvenile, more abject of the siblings, it is easy for the audience at this earlier point to jump to the conclusion that he is the bed-wetter. Once it emerges during the plane ride that in fact Carmen, and not Juni, wets the bed, Juni begins recovering, at his sister's expense, some dignity and power for himself.

Juni's new potential to be more than just an abject little brother is realized once the siblings arrive on Floop's island and Juni finds himself left to his own devices. As the children snoop around Floop's castle in search of their parents, Carmen stumbles through a trapdoor. When she falls and cries out, "Find mom and dad," Juni assumes sole responsibility for completing the mission. In turn, the opportunity arises for him to find the courage, confidence, and self-reliance that he has hitherto lacked. The fact that this development coincides with the removal of Carmen from the narrative underscores her status as an obstacle to his development. Upon her removal, Juni proves himself capable of fending for himself and overcoming obstacles. He finds Floop, convinces him to reprogram the robot children he has made to be good, and frees both Carmen and his parents. In the process, he extricates himself from his initial condition of abjection.

Self-Differentiation, Self-Determination, and the Consolidation of Selfhood

Whereas the first *Spy Kids* film depicts Juni's negotiation of his inferiority complex, *Spy Kids 2* presents Juni as an emerging adolescent who increasingly asserts an autonomous sense of self via the self-conscious differentiation of himself from others. The film revolves around the efforts of Carmen and Juni—both of whom are now officially recognized Level 2 OSS agents—to recover the Transmooker device, a small, indescribably powerful apparatus that in the wrong hands could (somehow) mean the takeover—or even the end—of the world. Although the fate of the world hinges on the recovery of the Transmooker, the recovery of the device is also a means for Juni to restore his good name and professional integrity, both of which have been blemished by Gary Giggles (Matt O'Leary), a rival spy kid who early in the film unfairly blames Juni for the theft of the device. By the end of the film, Juni restores his good name and professional integrity by helping to save the world from domination by Donnagon Giggles (Mike Judge, Rodriguez's fellow Austinite and film director), Gary's father and the newly appointed director of the OSS. Donnagon, it turns out, orchestrated the Transmooker heist. By the end of the film, Donnagon is thwarted, but above all else, viewers see Juni embody an autonomy that, interestingly, somewhat resists popular formulations of masculinity.

At the start of the second film Juni immediately displays his newfound maturity. It begins with Alexandra (Taylor Momsen), the daughter of the president of the United States, causing a stir at the Troublemaker theme park by climbing onto the ledge of the Juggler thrill ride. With the Transmooker device in her hand, she demands personal time with her absent father. Recognizing a need for the special talents of Carmen and Juni, Secret Service agents on the ground radio for the assistance of the siblings. Apparently, Carmen and Juni have been enjoying themselves at the amusement park. When they appear, they are wearing propeller hats and eating cotton candy. As soon as the realization that they need to work sets in, they toss aside the trappings of childhood fun and jump into action. That Juni springs into action without hesitation attests in particular to his courage and confidence. As Carmen attempts to shut down the ride from the control box, Juni climbs, with the aid of some Spiderman-like gloves, to the top of the ride where he exhibits an ability to listen carefully to Alexandra and explain, in a noticeably measured manner, why she should come down from the ledge. With a combination of wisdom and consolation, as well as the promise that as a Level 2 agent—which he proves by flashing his clearly marked badge—he has the power to force her father to meet with her, he talks her down and ends the crisis.

Certainly, Juni's possession of a Level 2 badge carries a host of implications. Foremost, it documents his entry into the prestigious echelons of the OSS. Given the usual standing of children as "marginalized mites in an outsized world of towering adults" (Griswold 53), Juni wields a power not typically accorded to children. Such power is additionally in action at the banquet shortly after the theme park incident when Juni asks Alexandra to dance. When he approaches the girl, she says she cannot dance because of the horde of overprotective agents that encircles her. As soon as he flashes his Level 2 badge and instructs the towering agents, "OK now, break it up," the agents part and he has his dance with the girl. With the work of Kaja Silverman in mind, we might go so far as to read Juni's Level 2 badge as a phallic signifier. Admittedly, discussions of the phallus and phallic symbols can quickly become overwrought and tiresome, but Silverman's work opens up some potentially insightful interpretative avenues for conceptualizing the privilege and prestige that Juni has accessed. Discussing the social stakes involved in the symbolic equation (or collapse) of the penis and phallus—chief among them the enablement and maintenance of patriarchal primacy—Silverman points out that biological maleness does not automatically guarantee patriarchal privilege or power. For some males, she notes, "Oppression experienced in relation to class, race, ethnicity, age, and other ideologically determined 'handicaps' . . . poses obstacles in the way of a phallic identification" (47). In the first *Spy Kids*, various elements, including age as well as embodiment, work against Juni and preclude both ego integration and phallic identification (which according to the logic of Juni's portrayal are conterminous). As seen in the scene with the glow sticks, though, the film drives toward the resolution of the various handicaps that haunt him, including his alienation from normative, phallic masculinity. The Level 2 badge that he flashes at the start of *Spy Kids 2* symbolically confirms that he has indeed attained phallic masculinity and all of the honors and privileges appertaining thereto, which in Silverman's formulation include "power . . . and wholeness" (Silverman 388).

While Juni thus seems, with Level 2 badge in hand, to have made significant progress in his advancement toward normative masculinity, the introduction of Gary Giggles in this sequel threatens to unravel everything he has attained. Gary functions as an ego ideal incarnate, and as such he carries the potential to induce anew inferiority and humiliation in Juni. Gary is tall, blond, slim, and overall well-groomed and good-looking, which stands in contrast to Juni's stout build. In fact, as registered by Carmen's interest in him, Gary has sex appeal. Moreover, Juni discovers at various points that Gary has superior spy gadgets. Bearing in mind Gary's mantra that "An agent is only as good as his gadgets," Juni finds himself wrestling with gadget envy. Snide remarks by Gary about Juni's bulging "gut" and "big head" only reinforce the former's antagonistic role.

At the hands of Gary, Juni quickly comes to experience the loss of the distinction and integrity that he has accomplished. At the aforementioned OSS banquet, the waiters—who are actually Donnagon Giggles's henchmen—slip a sleeping potion into the champagne. When the adult OSS figures doze off in the middle of dinner, the waiters pilfer the Transmooker out of the president's coat pocket and attempt to make a getaway. Since the sleeping potion is slipped into the champagne, however, the spy kids—who are too young to drink champagne—remain awake and attempt to thwart the escape. In the course of the ensuing scuffle, Juni recovers the device, but motivated by a desire for glory, Gary struggles with Juni for possession of it. At the end of a tussle during which Gary derisively calls Juni "squirt" and "carrottop," the Transmooker flies out of both of their hands and into the grasp of a waiter, who along with the others manages to make an escape. When the adults reawaken, Gary unfairly fingers Juni as responsible for the loss of the device, at which point all eyes zero in on Juni. Significantly, as the scorned object of a critical gaze, he again occupies a condition of "otherness, subordination, and expulsion" (46), which Linda Kauffman succinctly describes as characteristic of abjection.

Blamed for what happens, Juni loses his job with the OSS, and with it, he loses his professional distinction as well as a measure of personal pride. Symbolically, the deposal of Juni culminates with the replacement of his Spy Kid of the Year photo by one of Gary. Gary also claims a superior phallic standing vis-à-vis the conferral of a coveted Level 1 badge. Yet as the film proceeds, rather than let the apparent superiority of Gary hold sway over him and induce in him an existential crisis, Juni disidentifies from his rival in a process that ultimately facilitates the consolidation—rather than the decimation—of selfhood. From the beginning of the film, Juni clearly resents Gary not only as an ego ideal that haunts him, but as a negative example of the person he wants to be. For this reason, when Carmen shows signs of a crush on Gary, Juni intervenes, "You like him and believe him? Gary's a bad guy, Carmen." When Carmen responds, "I know that. I think I can change him," Juni's mature perspective is reinforced (and the girl's status is further compromised via her figuration as stereotypically obstinate and naive).

Juni's differentiation of himself from Gary comes into especially sharp focus when he, Carmen, Gary, and Gary's sister, Gerty (Emily Osment), discuss Donnagon's involvement in the theft of the device. Unwilling to be critical of his father, Gary simply proclaims, "He has his reasons. That's what being a good spy is all about. Trust no one." When Gary proceeds to quote from the *How to Be a Spy* handbook, "A good spy makes no binding commitments with family or friends," Juni forcefully interrupts, "Well I don't believe that, do you?" In this moment in which Gary uncritically promulgates the legitimacy of both his father and the spy handbook, Juni distinguishes himself as someone who thinks for himself.

By the end of the film, the restoration of Juni is accomplished with the discovery and foiling of Donnagon. In acknowledgment of his efforts, Alexandra, acting on behalf of the president, offers Juni a Level 1 badge. He declines, however, telling her, "No, thanks. I'm leaving the OSS. I've seen what it takes to be a top spy, and I think I can be better use to the world by just being the best . . . me." Through this response, Juni effectively deconstructs what Kerry Mallan identifies as the phallic fantasy. As discussed by Mallan, the phallic fantasy is an ideal that "[privileges] the phallus and its relations of dominance and submission" (151). As such, its governing principle is that males should aspire toward social power and prestige. Importantly, Mallan notes that this fantasy has the effect of "clos[ing] off other possibilities for male and female ways of being" (151). A valuable opportunity for "challenging dominant modes of patriarchal masculinity" (Mallan 151) arises at the end of *Spy Kids 2*, though, as Juni effectively shuns the popular ideals promised in Alexandra's offer. When Alexandra presses, "But what about all the cool gadgets?," which can simultaneously be read as an appeal to a juvenile fascination with toys as well as an offer of phallic masculinity, Juni assuredly removes an elastic band from his wrist and corrects her, "I got the best gadget right here. Use number one—a stylish bracelet," at which point he puts the band around her wrist in a mature gesture of friendship.[5]

The Boy Becomes "The Guy"

Besides featuring one of Rodriguez's less clear story lines, *Spy Kids 3-D* provides a fraught resolution for Juni's Entwicklungsroman and so leaves unrealized the promise and potential that arises at the end of *Spy Kids 2*. At the start of this installment, Juni narrates that he has cut ties with the OSS and is working as a private detective. He relates, "I'd been burned by the agency, the OSS. So I left. . . . I handle my own assignments now." Accordingly, we see him field phone calls from the OSS and insist, "Look, I'm no longer an agent. I can't help you. Whatever it is, it's your problem. Leave me alone." When he receives a call from Devlin (George Clooney), a former director of the OSS who is now president of the United States, Juni appears poised to issue yet another rejection. Devlin calls, however, to inform Juni that Carmen is trapped in *Game Over*, a virtual reality game that is actually a sinister ploy concocted by the Gamemaker (Sylvester

Stallone) to (somehow) take over the world. In an effort to stop this new villain, the OSS sent Carmen into the game, but she has been caught and is being held inside. As soon as he finds out what has happened, Juni sets aside his bitterness and decides to cooperate with the agency this one time. Once inside the game, Juni encounters a group of beta testers who (mis)take him to be The Guy, a savior figure prophesied to be able to beat the game. In the role of The Guy, it befalls Juni to lead the beta testers through the game as well as find his sister.

The fact that Juni must navigate the unfamiliar landscape of the game and learn the rules that govern this realm reflects the ways that adolescence can be a baffling and frustrating time in life when one struggles to figure out and accommodate oneself to the adult world. As such, it can also be a time when one feels isolated and alienated. An especially important aspect of adolescence is captured when the beta testers assume that Juni is The Guy. Such a slippage results in a host of expectations for Juni that parallel the gender-specific expectations faced by adolescent boys making their way toward manhood. As The Guy, Juni is expected to be a courageous leader who knows how to win the game and thus claim the "untold riches, toys, and prizes beyond your wildest dreams" that allegedly await anyone who can defeat Level 5, the game's highest level. In its own way, such a narrative arrangement deftly points toward the fact that today's boys are expected to fearlessly, and without any guidance, negotiate adolescence and come out from the other side as winners who can lay claim to the material and social prizes that purportedly await them if they assume their proper gender role.

An important critique of such a predicament for adolescent boys is embedded in Juni's unpreparedness for the role of The Guy as well as his hesitancy to be thrust into it. Such a portrayal resonates with William Pollack's contention that today's boys must grow up "too abruptly, with too little preparation for what lies in store, too little emotional support, not enough opportunity to express their feelings, and often with no option of going back or changing course" (xxii). Notably, Pollack's remark about boys having no option of going back or changing course is literalized in the stipulation that Juni must either win the game or face a Game Over (which carries a set of consequences that are never clearly specified but seem to be rather ominous). The audience also sees this during the Mega Race that Juni must complete to get through Level 2. According to the Gamemaker's instructions, "There are no rules at this game except win at all costs," which could just as well describe how adolescence works for boys in the real world of contemporary capitalism. When, to the terror of Juni, the Gamemaker announces, "The race will begin . . . now!" and he rapidly counts down, "1-2-3, GO!," a compelling metaphor for the way that boys find themselves mercilessly tracked into normative masculinity takes shape.

All the while, we must note that Juni has been pushed into the role of The Guy simply because of his physical resemblance to the silhouette of the figure in a promotional billboard for the game. When Juni chances to step in front of this billboard, one of the beta testers notices the resemblance between him and the empty outline of The Guy and exclaims, "Hold onto your joysticks, boys. I think we got him." That the only image that exists of The Guy is an empty silhouette critiques dominant formulations of masculinity by suggesting that they are fundamentally empty and constructed ideals. Moreover, these are ideals that have been contrived and circulated by mass media. The fact that the distinguishing feature of this figure known as "The Guy" is nothing more than a silhouette also suggests that anyone with the "right" body could be The Guy or be expected to be him. Such is precisely the reason Juni ends up pushed into the role, and it is also the manner by which contemporary boys end up compelled to live up to popular definitions of masculinity. In this day and age, to be born with a boy's body results in the imposition of a demanding and specific set of expectations.

The gap between the role of The Guy and Juni's willingness and ability to fulfill the role encourages a consideration of the psychopathic, constructed nature of normative masculinity. As Silverman notes, moments in which a male "fails" to embody normative masculinity always carry the potential to "expose masculinity as a masquerade" (47) as opposed to a natural condition or corollary of being male (or, more specifically, of having a male body). As audiences bear witness to Juni's lack of readiness for a role and identity that he has no inclination or preparation to assume, they can reconsider the gender norms to which boys are held. It is particularly interesting that the basis on which Juni fits the silhouette of The Guy is not even his real body but the suit of armor that he wears inside the game. Foremost, that a suit of armor is put upon Juni upon his entry into the game develops the allegorical significance of the game by symbolically representing the presumptions of strength and invulnerability that are placed onto boys without their assent or even their realization. Suddenly they find themselves cast into the game of contemporary capitalism encased in a suit of presumptions that become the basis for a host of personal and social expectations to which they must measure up. Along these lines, the imposition of the suit of armor on Juni happens to bring to mind Judith Halberstam's comment that masculinity in Hollywood action films, a popular venue for the codification and promotion of popular masculine ideals, "is primarily prosthetic and [usually] has little if anything to do with biological maleness and signifies more often as a technical special effect" (3). As a socially constructed set of presumptions and expectations that solidify and circulate in mass media, masculinity, as it is popularly known, can indeed be conceptualized as a "technical special effect" that, like the armor foisted onto Juni via the technology of the game, is superimposed onto real boys.

The exposure of masculinity as a technical special effect continues in *Spy Kids 3-D* through the unveiling of the true character of the different boys that Juni encounters inside the game. First, when Juni finds a set of shortcuts, which are a violation of the rules of *Game Over*, he finds himself face to face with the Programmerz, an intimidating pair of young men who threaten Juni with automatic termination. It is revealed, however, that beneath their tough exterior the Programmerz are nothing more than "computer nerds." Similarly, the savvy and smooth beta testers who initially rejected and challenged Juni are revealed at the end of the film to be rather unimpressive boys. In what is tantamount to a parade of shame, the three boys are escorted into the OSS lab where the now-reformed Donnagon Giggles is debriefing Juni and Carmen. At the sight of the three boys, a stunned Juni utters, "Hey, wait a second. What happened to Francis the Brain, and Arnold the Strong, and Mr. Cool?" Once the three acknowledge that they really are not as smart, strong, or cool as they pretended with the aid of the technical effects available to them in the world of the game, Juni exclaims, "Reality check!" The potent implication is that the legitimacy of the images and definitions that circulate in our technologically advanced media culture and serve as touchstones for gender normativity must be reevaluated and recalibrated against the real nature of real boys.

Ironically, however, alongside such a critically valuable implication, *Spy Kids 3-D* ends up reiterating some of the pillars of normative masculinity. This occurs after the exposure of the true identities of the three beta testers and one of them asks Juni, "So, who are you in the real world?" At this exact moment, Francesca Giggles—Donnagon's wife and the agent overseeing the *Game Over* operation—appears and addresses Juni, "Special Agent Cortez, we need you." While Juni plays down the scene by insisting, "I'm just Juni Cortez," he clearly remains endowed with a privilege, prestige, and power that distinguish him from the humiliation of the three other boys. Indeed, we can say that Juni finally has abject others over and against whom he can (finally) assert his own normative, phallic masculinity. All of this effectively rounds out not just the fantasy of the boy's extrication from abjection and humiliation, but the selfsame phallic ` fantasy that appeared to be subjected to deconstruction at the end of *Spy Kids 2*. The casting of Salma Hayek—an actress renowned for her sex appeal—for the role of Francesca Giggles only amplifies the fantasy element of the scene and its normative implications. Through Francesca's apparent deferral to the professional status (and literal stature) of Juni, the petite woman becomes the culminating means by which the film, in a distinctive swerve from the critically promising ending of *Spy Kids 2*, confers phallic masculinity on Juni.

My, How You've Grown

The sight of a child actor or actress as an adult can be a bit startling. After, for example, seeing a film such as *Home Alone* countless times or watching several seasons' worth of television programs like *Full House* and *Family Matters*, audiences might have figures such as Macaulay Culkin, Mary-Kate and Ashley Olsen, and Jaleel White fixed in their minds as children. To suddenly see these same performers as adults can consequently be an uncanny experience. In all likelihood, the appearance of Sabara in the *Spy Kids* franchise reboot, *Spy Kids: All the Time in the World*, had the same effect for viewers accustomed to seeing him as little Juni.[6] In this fourth film, audiences see Juni as a grown man characterized not only by poise and self-assuredness, but also sex appeal and sexual confidence.

To be sure, Juni and Carmen are not the focus of this film, which centers on the efforts of the OSS to track down the Time Keeper, a character who has in his possession the Armageddon Device. Also known as the Wells Experiment, this device has the capacity (somehow) to usher in the end of the world by accelerating the passage of time to the point of its expiration. With a crisis afoot, the OSS first calls upon Juni and Carmen's aunt, Marissa (Jessica Alba), who has been in retirement, to tend to her new marriage, her new stepchildren, and her newborn baby. When Marissa gets involved, so, too, through twists of the plot, do her three children. As the urgency of the situation with the Time Keeper deepens, the agency also calls upon Carmen and then, as its most desperate move, Juni. Above all else, the return of Juni—both to the OSS and to the *Spy Kids* series—allows audiences to see, if not marvel over, the impressive man he has become.

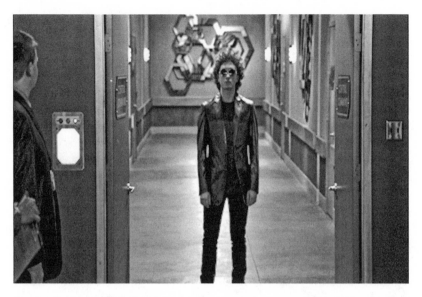

Figure 2. In *Spy Kids 4D* (2011), Juni makes a grand entrance at the OSS.

In no uncertain terms the introduction of Juni frames him as someone worthy of admiration. At a briefing of OSS personnel on ongoing efforts to catch the Time Keeper, agency chief Danger D'Amo (Jeremy Piven) informs everyone, "The fate of the world is on the line here. That's why I am calling upon one of our most valued and skilled operatives." At this point, the camera cuts to Carmen, who, standing amongst the others in attendance, begins shifting her weight in anticipation of a moment of pride. When the chief indeed announces the name of "Agent Cortez," Carmen even begins to humbly yet happily wave at everyone. Seconds later, however, one pronoun upends the moment for her as D'Amo continues, "He has even come out of retirement to help us." With Carmen thusly deflated, the eyes of both OSS personnel and the audience cut to a double door, behind which stands Juni Cortez, all grown up. As the doors open to reveal him, details of the mise-en-scène combine to fetishize him (see figure 2). A more aggressive, electric rock version of the familiar *Spy Kids* theme song begins playing, ratcheting up the energy and the excitement of this unveiling. All the while Juni stands at the center of the screen, allowing OSS personnel and the audience to dwell upon him for a few moments. As Juni is thus fawned over by the gaze of the other (whereas previously he was the scorned object of the gaze of the other), a wisp of air from some unidentified source kicks in to caress him, lifting locks of the curly red hair, the likes of which Gary Giggles once ridiculed. His black leather jacket and mirror sunglasses amplify the coolness he exudes while the responses of others in the room not only add to his aura but cue the audience to respond similarly. When the doors first open, a collective "Ooh" is exhaled. As Juni then struts into the room, one male, unable to bridle his excitement, pumps his fist and grunts, "Yeah!" providing a moment of masculine approbation far removed from the bullying to which Juni was once subjected.

Finally, when Juni takes his place next to Carmen, the facial expressions and body language of two nearby women betray that they clearly like what they see in him. In the process, the humiliation and inadequacy that Juni once embodied ends up completely overturned. Of course, this fetishism of Juni really does nothing less than reinscribe the valorization of a man's attainment of social, professional, and even sexual prominence.

As occurs in the original trilogy, we see an inversely proportional correlation between the status of Juni and Carmen. This first takes shape when Juni, and not Carmen, turns out to be the Agent Cortez that the OSS most needs to save the world from the Time Keeper. Later, Juni assumes even more importance when it befalls him to lead the fight against the Time Keeper, who turns out to have been D'Amo all along. When D'Amo uses a specialized watch to freeze in their tracks all OSS agents, Juni is the only one not frozen. Evidently, the freeze takes effect through the agents' badges, but since, in a fit of spite and jealousy, Carmen threw Juni's badge in the trash, Juni does not have one. Consequently, he remains unaffected by D'Amo's freeze. With Carmen and Marissa frozen by his side, Juni mulls his options and decides to activate Marissa's stepchildren, Rebecca (Rowan Blanchard) and Cecil (Mason Cook), as spy kids. Besides assuming and flexing this leadership and power, he provides the encouragement and wise counsel that the children need to accept their mission. With a plan set in motion, Juni proceeds to unfreeze Marissa, but before he does the same for Carmen, he decides to subject her to a little humiliation. He poses her with her finger in her nose and takes a picture, which once again aligns her with abjection while he assumes a place above it. Shortly thereafter Carmen's alignment with humiliation and abjection are reiterated when, following Carmen's lead, Juni, Marissa, and Carmen fall into one of D'Amo's traps. Frustrated, Juni complains to his sister, "Real smooth, diaper lady," which reminds audiences of the secret about Carmen that was revealed in the first film. When Carmen tries to explain, "I was just following my instincts," Juni underscores her alignment with abjection with the retort, "Well, your in-stinks!"

Nonetheless, after commanding a very masculinized respect in different ways, including through the assertion of his superiority over Carmen, Juni's status ends up revealed as rather fraught. Moments after Juni's "diaper lady" and "in-stinks" quips, Carmen asks her brother, "Where have you been all these years?" to which a suddenly self-conscious Juni can only confess, "I tried to strike out on my own, and I struck out." At once, Juni's professional success—and the respectability that such distinction entails in capitalist society—emerges as a facade. Additional critical pressure is applied to the coolness that Juni seems to embody when Carmen tells him, "But mom and dad left the family business to the both of us," and Juni acknowledges, "I guess I thought it wasn't cool to keep working with my sister." As Carmen proceeds to correct him, "It's what would have made you cool," Juni pauses to reconsider what he had previously believed (which models for the audience the reconsideration they ought to perform, too). Further deconstruction of Juni's bravado takes place when Carmen, Juni, and Marissa confront D'Amo and he wonders, "How did you get out of my sand trap?" Quickly and boldly Juni is first to reply, "With my bare hands," only to be trumped by Carmen pointing out, "Actually, it was my atomic lipstick."

Notably, the exposure of Juni's actual alienation from ideal masculinity occurs with a subtlety that somewhat softens his fall from the perch he had occupied. We do not see, for example, Carmen gloat over or delight in the truth that comes out. This seems calculated to avoid stigmatizing any failure or inability to live up to dominant ideals. The object of this narrative development appears more to be the sort of "cognitive clarification" (in this case on masculine ideals and expectations) that George Szanto cites as characteristic of dialectical propaganda as opposed to the manufacture or renewal of individual or interpersonal conflict.[7] With the exposure of Juni occurring under such terms, the film drives toward the undermining of the masculine ideals that it (and the series) had seemed to be privileging.

In the end, the shift in perspective on masculine achievement, autonomy, and power unfolds more fully when Carmen and Juni announce their decision to relaunch the OSS's Spy Kids program. Among other things, in this collaboration Juni sets aside not only the gendered valorization of individual success, but also his aversion to cooperating and otherwise coexisting with his sister, who in the past functioned, like his mother, as a threat to his emerging masculine ego. Now reconciled to the illusory, impractical, and ultimately undesirable nature of popular ideals of masculinity as well as at peace with the feminine, Juni appears ready to move into the future as part of a community organized around the greater safety of the world around him.

Overall the handling of Juni across the *Spy Kids* series (so far) reflects competing impulses that yield mixed messages. At the very least, the fourth film ends on a critically productive note. Ideally, if there is a fifth film, the handling of not only Juni but also Cecil, as well as the teams of Carmen and Juni and Rebecca and Cecil, will build upon and actualize the critical maturity and potential that comes and goes in the course of the series and that shows itself, with nice promise, at the end of the fourth film.

Notes

1. Such a portrayal of Juni in the earlier films resonates with contemporaneous concerns about the emotional and psychological vulnerability of boys. In the 1990s and into the twenty-first century, books such as *Real Boys* (1998) by William Pollack, *Raising Boys* (1998) by Steve Biddulph, and *Raising Cain* (1999) by Dan Kindlon and Michael Thompson exhorted parents and teachers to tend to the emotional and psychological welfare of boys. As suggested by subtitles such as "Rescuing Our Sons from the Myths of Boyhood," "Why Boys Are Different— And How to Help Them Become Happy and Well-Balanced Men," and "Protecting the Emotional Life of Boys," these texts dispute presumptions that boys are intrinsically resilient and tough individuals. In a distinctively alarmist manner, in fact, they depict contemporary boys as profoundly distressed by experiences with loneliness, bullying, and oppressive gender expectations.

2. The psychodynamics of abjection delineated by Kristeva are interestingly relevant to Juni's relationship to his mother. For instance, Kristeva's postulation that "The abject confronts us . . . with the earliest attempts to release the hold of the *maternal* entity" (13) enables the idea that Juni's warts betoken the threat of a feminine subsumption of his emerging masculine self. Elaborating on the primal threat posed by the maternal to the developing ego, Kristeva adds, "The abject shatters the wall of repression and its judgments. It takes the ego back to its source on the abominable limits from which, in order to be, the ego has broken away" (15). Bearing this in mind, we might say that when Juni brushes off his mother, he attempts to keep at bay *"the constant risk of falling back under the sway of a power* [i.e., the maternal] *as securing as it is stifling"* (Kristeva 13).

3. Incidentally, the denigration of Juni as a mummy dovetails with Kristeva's assertion that "The corpse . . . is the utmost of abjection" (4).

4. For critical overviews and commentaries on recent boy-crisis books, see Kidd, Wannamaker, and Anderson and Accomando.

5. This gesture becomes even more significant if we recall an earlier moment in the film when, bearing new gadgets, Machete proudly presents to Carmen and Juni an innovation he calls Machete's Elastic Wonder, which Carmen flatly calls

out as nothing more than a simple rubber band. When Machete counters that it has "999 uses, and the important thing is that you have to figure out what those uses are," Juni, with one around his wrist and a beaming smile on his face, happily agrees, "He's right. Use number one: a stylish bracelet." In response, Carmen, seemingly disgusted by her brother and his idea, announces, "Use number two," at which point she pulls back on her Elastic Wonder and painfully snaps the boy on the shoulder. As much as this scene resembles a simple instance of opportunistic sadism on the part of Carmen, one might also read it as a moment in which Juni faces discipline and punishment for exhibiting improper masculinity. After all, according to dominant definitions of masculinity, boys are not supposed to exhibit an interest in adornments or style. When Juni reiterates at the end of *Spy Kids 2* his preference for using an elastic band as a stylish bracelet, he encounters neither discipline nor punishment. The implication is that Juni has attained a position of individuality that is now respected by others (and that is thereby legitimated by the film). Of course, this gesture simultaneously points toward the boy's entry into the heterosexual economy, which happens to render it not completely inconsistent with dominant expectations/demands for maturing boys, too.

6. The same could also be said of Sabara's role as the hardened vato, Julio, in Rodriguez's *Machete* (2010), which was released a year before the fourth *Spy Kids* film.

7. In *Theater and Propaganda*, Szanto delineates three types of propaganda: agitation propaganda, dialectical propaganda, and integration propaganda. He suggests that dialectical propaganda "attempts to demystify . . . by depicting . . . the basic elements which comprise a confused social or historical situation" (75). The aim, he points out, is "to depict, for its audience, circumstances not previously understood. It will demystify relationships between individuals and institutions . . . so as to show, first, the nature of . . . social laws, and second, to demonstrate methods by which human beings can control both themselves and their institutions" (76). The description of such a critical dynamic seems applicable to the portrayal in the fourth film of Juni's relationship to dominant ideals of masculinity.

NARRATIVE THEORY, COGNITIVE SCIENCE, AND *SIN CITY*: A CASE STUDY

CHAPTER 3

Painterly Cinema: Three Minutes of *Sin City*

PATRICK COLM HOGAN

Sin City begins with a three-minute sequence that is an aesthetic gem—arguably the finest segment of the film. Indeed, the sequence is a work of art in itself, independent of the larger context. In keeping with this, it was shot before the film was even begun. Rodriguez used it to recruit the collaboration of actors such as Bruce Willis and the creator of *Sin City* graphic novels, Frank Miller. The supplementary material on the DVD of the film includes their testimony to the appeal of this brief sequence.

Specifically, this opening mini-narrative involves a careful visual aesthetic. In part, that visual aesthetic is an imitation of graphic fiction. One way of examining the film would be to treat these mimetic properties in detail, particularly in relation to Frank Miller's work. However, in the following pages, I will, instead, examine these three minutes of film in relation to larger patterns, on the one hand, and as particular to an autonomous work, on the other.

As to the larger patterns, what Rodriguez has done fits into a category that is much broader than adaptations of Frank Miller. Specifically, some movies take up a noncinematic visual art as a model, often to produce a distinct visual style. (For more on the different degrees to which art may inspire film, some extending beyond style to narrative, see Anthony Fragola's essay "Art as a Source of Imagistic Generator for Narrative.") Typically, this visual art has been painting, though it might also be sculpture, tapestry, video games—or graphic fiction. Given this breadth, one might refer to such films as "visual art" cinema. However, that appears to suggest that cinema itself is not a visual art. I will therefore refer to such films as "painterly" cinema.

The following discussion will first sketch the opening of *Sin City*, giving a basic interpretation and appreciation of that segment of the film.

Subsequent sections will outline varieties of painterly cinema and some of its usual functions. The final section will return to the three minutes of Rodriguez's film, examining the extent to which he takes up the usual ways of using visual art and the standard reasons for such usage. It should therefore serve to enhance the initial interpretation and to explain some of the initial appreciation.

A Very Short Film on Love and Death

The sequence begins with the ambient sound of a city, prominently a wailing siren in the distance, paralleled by the nondiegetic wailing of a saxophone. The meandering and spare quality of the music suggests film noir and such genres as "hard-boiled" detective stories. (For more on the film noir quality of the work, see Mark Bould's *Film Noir*.) The connection is significant primarily due to the often highly stylized nature of such genres, particularly in their language. We find that stylization in the voice-over, which is characterized by poetic devices, without employing "poetic" diction. Thus the first line of the voice-over, delivered by a man's voice, is "She shivers in the wind like the last leaf on a dying tree." The use of a simile is already suggestive of poetry. Moreover, the image involves foreshadowing (as we learn when the woman in question dies at the end of the sequence). Perhaps more strikingly, the line employs standard devices of sound patterning, notably alliteration ("She shivers," "like the last leaf") and assonance ("She . . . leaf . . . tree," "shivers in the wind," "like . . . dying").

More significantly for present purposes, this poetical treatment of the speech is matched, in fact intensified, by the visuals. The sequence is shot in black and white with extremely high contrast that makes shadows—most importantly, "attached" shadows on the character's faces and bodies—stark. It has something like the effect of enhancing "lateral inhibition" in visual perception. When we see the world, some visual receptors are strongly activated. In order to produce a more defined and clearly patterned image of the world, closely related receptors are suppressed in the course of perception (see Solso 61–72). In effect, Rodriguez's high contrast black-and-white photography intensifies the results of that definition enhancement. At the same time, the extensive darkness suggests a series of contexts, presumably triggering emotional memories in viewers. Initially, these memories would most obviously be either threatening (darkness as danger) or romantic/sexual (darkness as intimacy). As we will see, both are relevant.

The distinctive qualities of the visuals are not confined to high contrast. Two other features are particularly important. First, contour enhancement is extended by the use of rim lighting (e.g., around the edges of a character's face) and the tracing of other lines (such as the streaks of light Rodriguez uses to represent rain). Second, the scene is not entirely black and white. There is highly selective use of color. Specifically, there are two colors—prominently red, but also, briefly, green. We will consider the function of these colors below. However, at the very least, it is obvious that they serve to select segments of the visual field for attentional orientation (cf. Belton 62). We may also guess that they have some sort of emotional or thematic resonance.

Narratively, the story begins with a young woman walking out onto a large balcony. We see her from behind. In the stark silver and white of the cityscape before her, the red of her dress is striking. The attached shadows contour her spine extending down the plunging, open back of the dress, and the curves of her hips. Here, the red suggests passion, perhaps passion that is out of place in the otherwise dispassionate city. A voice-over, a man's voice, delivers the line quoted above—"She shivers in the wind like the last leaf on a dying tree." We see her dress rippling in the breeze and how she grasps herself around her bare shoulders in the silvery light, which may now seem cold, almost ice-like. The conjunction of the sensuous walk and the red dress with the breeze, the cold, and the ominous commentary brings together the narrative concerns of love and death. Later, the red dress will not be a signal of passion but will recall instead a pool of spilled blood (a point noted by Belton [62]).

The camera cuts to the other side of the balcony railing. Now, we are facing the woman. We see the shadows molding her shoulders and breasts in the low neckline of the red dress. We see her red lips. All this intensifies the sexuality of the scene. Behind her, a man is approaching. The inside of the building is brilliantly lit, and diffuse clouds of light billow out from the glass doors. It is almost heavenly. However, the man is in darkness. He explains that he lets her hear his footsteps. The point of this communication is that we, the viewers, should not be anxious. He is not sneaking up on her. He explains that "She only goes stiff for a moment." On first viewing, the line suggests just the anticipation of some sort of encounter, perhaps one that is sexual or romantic. By the end of the sequence, however, we realize that she has anticipated her own death. She experienced a moment of fear, followed by reconciliation. He offers her a cigarette. Initially, it appears to be a come-on. Afterward, it recalls the last cigarette of someone condemned to death.

The following dialogue seems like a scripted pick up, though there is some ambiguity as to whether or how well these two know one another. The man compliments the woman's face, figure, and voice. However, he stresses her eyes and what he sees in them. Just before he starts speaking about her eyes, her irises begin to shine green and jewel-like. Again, the effect of color in the monochrome context is powerful. The color green also hints at jealousy—"the green-eyed monster," as Shakespeare's Iago has it, in a famous phrase (II.ii.166)—and perhaps a story as to just what has led the woman to her present state. Specifically, she has hired an assassin, though (contrary to the usual script) not one to kill a cheating lover.

The man describes the "crazy calm" that he sees in the woman's eyes. As he speaks, she faces away from him, out over the city, into the camera. Her eyes are unnaturally wide and unblinking. When she turns back to him, they are brimming over with tears. The reference to "crazy calm" suggests both passion and resolve. The tears are consistent with the passion. The fact that no tears fall is consistent with the resolve. We only come to understand what the resolve is at the end of the sequence. Retrospectively, the ending also explains why the tears well up. They suggest her realization of her own death. The man explains that there is something that she must face, but she does not want to face it alone. She agrees—that is the moment when her eyes fill.

Before the ending, all this appears largely romantic. In keeping with this, the following shots show the man and woman kissing and the voice-over explains that he would protect her, take her far away, because he loves her. As the voice-over recounts this, we see the man's lips move, forming the words, "I love you."

The visual features of this part are still more striking and extreme than those we have seen up to this point. First, it begins to rain and the rain is marked by long silvery streaks in the air. Then, when they kiss, there is a cut to two white figures embracing before the white railing of a balcony (see figure 3). This is a black/white-reversed silhouette (a recurring technique in Miller). However, in the background, the buildings are still black and the windows are still white. Thus the black/white reversal occurs only in the foreground. In some ways, this shift simply extends and complicates the intensified contrast of the entire sequence. But here the white is genuine white, a lack of color, not the silver that is prominent elsewhere. It is somehow linked with her being "weightless" (as the man explains)

Figure 3. The assassin's kiss—a black/white-reversed silhouette from the opening of *Sin City.*

and with a sort of unreality in the kiss and the emotions it expresses. In keeping with this, it is the shot that is most visually similar to the means of representation found in graphic fiction, where the pure white is simply the color of the blank page.

Unreality is suggested by another aspect of the shot as well. When the man approaches initially, the woman turns to face him. As he speaks, she turns away again. In both cases, Rodriguez is careful to match the action perfectly so that the continuity is seamless across cuts. This care in continuity is strikingly absent in the cut to the reverse silhouette and the cut back to "reality" out of the cartoonish silhouette. Specifically, in the initial cut, the couple is perpendicular to the railing when they kiss, but in the silhouette, they are parallel to the railing. In the subsequent cut, the woman's hand is clearly placed on the man's neck before the cut, but not after. Of course, this could simply be "cheating" on Rodriguez's part. However, his great care with continuity in other parts of the scene suggests, rather, that these discontinuities are somehow functional for him. Again, the most obvious function is in suggesting that the scene is in some respect unreal.

After the cut out from the silhouette, the man's face is largely dark, except for rim lighting giving its outline. There is a soft fill light on the woman's face, so that it is not in darkness. Again, this could give the man's face particularly a sense of intimacy or of threat. As he says that he will save her and confesses his love, it appears to be the former. But just after he says that he loves her, there is a gunshot, visually stressed by an almost imperceptible cut to and from white. This cut to white recalls the kiss and contributes to the ambiguity of the woman's death. We now see the man as a threat. However, the threat is inseparable from intimacy—a point emphasized by the voice-over characterization of the gunshot, modified by a silencer, as a "whisper," just what the couple had been exchanging. In death, she collapses into him. He explains that he holds her "close until she's gone." He has, in a sense, taken her far away, as he promised.

Subsequently, we are given an overhead shot. Her red dress spreads out over part of the balcony like a pool of blood. The man looks up amid the silvery strands of rain. He explains that he will "never know what she was running from." At this point, the viewer is uncertain, not only of the woman's dilemma, but of the man's motivation for the murder. Then comes the "punch line," ironic but also poignant. He explains that he will cash her check in the morning. She has hired an assassin for her own death.

Kinds of Painterly Cinema

Again, painterly cinema uses visual art to create a distinctive visual style. The distinctiveness commonly derives from a school or period of painting. However, it may take other forms as well, such as the general means available for visual representation in a medium (e.g., painting or graphic fiction). Rodriguez most obviously draws on graphic fiction at two levels—the level of the particular work (Miller's *Sin City*) and the level of the medium. These various forms are part of a continuum.

Specifically, we may distinguish a range of degrees to which cinema may be seen as painterly. At the minimal end, we find works that incorporate allusions to works of visual art—particular works or broader schools. These are marginal cases. Here, we may further distinguish between isolated allusions and more systematic or continuous allusiveness. Generally, isolated allusions would not be adequate to make a work painterly. As the use of allusion is extended, becoming more integrated into the visual aesthetics of the work, the work becomes more painterly in style. In keeping with this, isolated allusion is commonly highly salient, even obtrusive, and reliant upon connection with a specific source (e.g., a particular, well-known painting). In contrast, continuing allusiveness is likely to be less foregrounded and to be less tied to specific sources.

Ongoing allusiveness clearly approaches the use of visual art as a model for the film. Indeed, the two are continuous with one another. Modeling may or may not forego particular allusions. But in either case the allusions are not the distinctive, painterly feature of the work. Insofar as specific allusions enter into the work, they serve as instances of more enduring properties—for example, properties of the school of painting at issue. Thus, in both ongoing allusiveness and modeling, a painterly film incorporates some features of the visual art source into the fabric of the film itself—again, commonly into the visual style. This careful fashioning of the visual style tends to mark such works as more or less *stylized*. That is to say that "modeled" painterly films (as we might call them) commonly constrain their stylistic choices so as to make stylistic features more salient, more likely to draw attentional focus, more likely to be the objects of interpretation, and so on. Typically, allusive works tend to be less stylized in this sense than modeled works, or they may be stylized more locally, in sections that are more continuously allusive.

Here, it is valuable to draw a further distinction. As already noted, isolated allusions are often highly salient, even obtrusive. Ongoing allusiveness and modeling tend to be more moderately salient. Sometimes, however, stylistic features of allusive or modeled works become highly salient. This is particularly likely when stylistic choices are to some degree inconsistent with principles of realistic representation. Indeed, the obtrusiveness of particular allusions often derives from the unrealistic quality of the allusion—the high improbability that, for example, a real scene would form itself into the particular configuration of a famous painting. When allusiveness or modeling makes style obtrusively unrealistic, then we may refer to the work, not as stylized, but as *mannerist*.

Since the discussion has been rather abstract, we might pause for a moment to illustrate some of these points. Consider, for example, Luis Buñuel's *Viridiana*. In that film, a young woman decides to help some beggars. At one point, the beggars are having a feast and they form themselves into the configuration of da Vinci's *Last Supper*. The image was clearly intended to stand out and does stand out. It is, of course, an allusion to a painting. However, the film as a whole is not something we would call *painterly*.

In contrast, we might consider Deepa Mehta's *Water*. This film treats the condition of widows in early twentieth-century India. Even if widowed at a very young age, women were expected not to remarry. The central story concerns one young widow, Kalyani, who falls in love with a young man, Narayan. Violating social taboos, she goes to meet him in the middle of the night. He waits for her, playing his flute. Mehta stages and photographs the scene in such a way as to recall visual representations of the nighttime meetings between Rādhā and Kṛṣṇa. (Critics such as Thomas Caldwell have pointed to the importance of Kṛṣṇa references. However, they do not seem to have recognized the specifically iconographic resonances; Fincina Hopgood, for instance, sees the source of the film's visuals in Satyajit Ray [145].) Kṛṣṇa was the incarnation of the great god, Viṣṇu. Rādhā was his devotee. Though married to someone else, Rādhā's one true love was Kṛṣṇa. When Kṛṣṇa called to her with the sound of his flute, she would come to him, whatever the time. Moments of this story and other aspects of Kṛṣṇa iconography were famously represented in paintings and other visual media that Mehta clearly seeks to recall for the viewer in this sequence. There may or may not be allusions to specific paintings in this scene. However, the function of the allusiveness does not rely on an identification of specific sources. What is important is the broad connection. In keeping with this, the connection is not obtrusive, though it is evident and likely to draw the attentional focus of viewers familiar with the earlier works at issue. Note, however, that this *allusiveness* is localized in the film, which does not develop such distinctive stylistic features consistently.

In contrast with both the preceding cases, Eric Rohmer's *Die Marquise von O* . . . is a paradigmatically modeled work. In this film, Rohmer consistently draws on neoclassical painting for his visual style (if a "neoclassical style" inflected with a "protoromantic sensibility," as Dalle Vacche puts it [9]). The use of neoclassical models is clear in many details, ranging from the placement of the figures to the folds of the curtains. In this case, the modeling is consistent from the beginning of the film to the end. As with *Water*, there may be allusions to particular paintings in the course of the film. Indeed, in this case, there certainly are, as Dalle Vacche shows. However, the operation of the modeling does not rely on such allusions.

Simply due to its extent, the visual style of Rohmer's film is somewhat more salient. However, it does not violate principles of realism, at least in any obvious way. Thus the style does not demand the sort of attentional preoccupation that actually brings it into the storyworld as a form of explanation. In the Buñuel film, the viewer needs to self-consciously refer to da Vinci's painting in order to explain the scene of the beggars' feast. In contrast, the viewer does not need to refer to Rādhā/Kṛṣṇa paintings to explain any storyworld feature of *Water*; nor does he or she have to refer to neoclassical painting to explain any storyworld feature of *Die Marquise von O* . . . Thus both may be aptly characterized as stylized, rather than mannered. (*Viridiana* too is not mannered, but that is simply because the allusion at issue is too confined.)

We have seen that there is a, so to speak, subminimal case of painterly cinema in allusion, a minimal or transitional case in allusiveness, and a central case in modeling. The movement from allusion to allusiveness involves an expansion from a highly localized moment to larger and larger segments of the recipient or "target" work (i.e., the film). The movement from allusiveness to modeling involves an expansion of the "source" from particular works (such as da Vinci's *Last Supper*) to broader features of a school or period (such as neoclassicism). What we might call the "upper limit" of painterly cinema continues this trajectory. This limit is reached when the film (the target) is pervasively modeled on painting broadly (as source), incorporating features that range across movements and periods. Thus at the upper limit of painterly film, we have works that draw on very widespread properties of art for their visual aesthetic—such properties as the creation of perspective, the patterning of color, the formation of planes of depth. We may refer to these as works of *painterly sensibility*. Of course, in some sense all aesthetically sensitive films involve features of this sort (that is why this is a "limit" case). A film is painterly to the extent that its aesthetic sensibility in such features is particularly informed by painting or other visual arts.

It is more difficult to draw the line between painterly and nonpainterly film at the upper end of the continuum than at the lower end—though, in fact, at both ends there is no single cutoff point. Nonetheless, there are some relatively clear cases. One obvious instance is M. F. Husain's film, *Meenaxi*. Husain is perhaps the most renowned contemporary Indian painter. He has made two films. It is unsurprising that he would draw on his experience as a painter, his aesthetic sensibility as a painter, in making those films. Indeed, his reputation as a painter is likely to sensitize the viewer to painterly techniques in his cinematic work. These techniques range from the use of gauzy curtains to create a sense of depth in space, to the careful use of echoing colors, to great sensitivity to the source of light in a scene, to the use of mirrors in order to give multiple perspectives in a single shot. Of course, in most of these cases, one could equally find cinematic sources for the techniques. (The apparent exception is the use of curtains, which seems more specifically painterly.) But the precise use of mirrors, for example, often seems to recall painters more than filmmakers. For example, there are scenes in which a character's image appears in a mirror in the far background. This is more reminiscent of, for example, the distant mirror in Velázquez's *Las Meninas* than of the use of mirrors in most films.[1] Moreover, Husain's sensitivity to hues and saturations of color seems more characteristic of a painter than of the usually less nuanced use of color by filmmakers (e.g., in the development of some prominent color motif).[2]

Indeed, one might even argue that some innovative aspects of *Meenaxi*'s cinematography have one source in Husain's experience as a painter. For example, it is common for filmmakers to dolly in on a character as the emotion of the character or the interest in his or her speech intensifies. It is common to dolly out in order to reveal a broader context. However, in some scenes, Husain seems to dolly in and out simply to alter the viewer's perspective on the character. The pattern is, in that way, more reminiscent of a painter or viewer moving up to and then back away from a canvas. (Though Husain alters this by making the movement much more regular and rhythmic than it would be ordinarily.)

In some cases, Husain does violate principles of realism in his story. Indeed, he does so quite blatantly. However, these violations do not in general seem to rely on stylistic features. Thus this film too is stylized rather than manneristic. However, works of broad "painterly sensibility" (as we may call them) are no less open to mannerism than are works of modeling or allusiveness.

Functions of Painterly Techniques

Of course, none of these painterly techniques has any value or particular interest if it does not serve some function in the film. It is standard to distinguish two broad purposes for fictional art, one emotional, the other thematic. Specifically, films and other artworks, including paintings, are commonly produced with the purpose of fostering some emotional response and/or communicating some normative point, typically an ethical or political point. Any given element of a film has a function in the encompassing work to the extent that it contributes to the emotional impact or the thematic force of the work.

The allusion to da Vinci in *Viridiana* is likely to produce laughter in at least some viewers. Thus it has an emotional (comic) function. It also has thematic consequences. As with many works of art, the theme is not simple and equivocal. Thus it is not easy to state as a sort of Aesopian moral. However, there is clearly an ironic representation of Christian self-sacrifice in the film, and this scene contributes to that irony. (The scene has been interpreted variously. For a representative discussion, see Gutierrez-Albilla.)

Similar points apply to *Water*. The most obvious emotional consequences of Mehta's allusiveness in this film bear on what is called "artifact emotion." (On artifact emotion, please see Carl Plantinga and citations therein.) Artifact emotions are our responses to a work as the product of creative activity. To some extent, one may admire Mehta for successfully imitating Rādhā Kṛṣṇa iconography. Indeed, this is a common feature of painterly films. Successful works of this sort may involve technical achievements that inspire the respect of viewers. The point holds more clearly for Rohmer's imitation of neoclassical painting.

A more important form of artifact emotion, however, bears on the aesthetic qualities of style. Imitating another visual art form is not usually an end in itself. The value of the crossover in media is not primarily a matter of technical skill. Rather, the value of drawing on a very different source to alter a target is primarily in the degree to which the use of the source enhances the target's achievement of its own intrinsic goals. Thus the primary value of drawing on painting to alter film comes in the degree to which the final film satisfies the desiderata for film. Put differently, the value is in the creativity of the filmmaker. Creative cognition research suggests that creativity is enhanced by integration of knowledge across diverse areas that are not commonly integrated (see, for example, Martindale 252). In connection with this, one may argue that the brief section devoted to the nighttime meeting of Kalyani and Narayan is one of the most beautiful in Mehta's film. She has not only imitated Kṛṣṇa/Rādhā art. She has used it to create visually striking scenes.

In addition, there are consequences for the story emotions of the work (i.e., our emotions regarding the characters and events). As to character, a viewer's associations with the well-loved Rādhā come to be linked with Kalyani. For viewers familiar with the Kṛṣṇa/Rādhā stories—thus most Indian viewers—this is likely to enhance their affection for Kalyani. There is a similar effect on the emotional response to the event of the meeting.

As these emotional points suggest, the allusiveness in this film is thematic as well. Linking Kalyani with Rādhā means invoking perhaps the highest ideal of Hindu devotion in order to understand and evaluate the life of this widow. The (divinely guaranteed) rightness of Rādhā's love for Kṛṣṇa strongly suggests the rightness of Kalyani's love for Narayan. Moreover, in doing this, it strongly suggests that the ideal of absolute wifely devotion to a husband is false. Rādhā did not maintain that absolute devotion even while her husband was alive. It appears particularly perverse to require such absolute devotion in widows.

The complexity of function only increases as we move from allusiveness to modeling and from there to painterly sensibility. For reasons of space, I will not enter into this in detail. However, the pervasiveness of the neoclassical style in Rohmer's film potentially affects the viewer's artifact emotions, story emotions, and thematic inferences in a number of ways. Perhaps most interestingly, to a great extent the modeling seems to invite complex and equivocal, to some extent ambiguous and ambivalent, responses, except in the case of artifact emotion.

Specifically, the fundamental fact of the storyworld is that the main male protagonist (the Count) has, first, saved the Marquise from violent rape, then raped her himself, if nonviolently. (He had sexual relations with her when she was in a drugged sleep.) One fairly clear effect of neoclassical style is that it dignifies its characters. It elevates and to some extent perfects them. This dignity is, of course, precisely what is lacking in the events of the film. Indeed, the events of the film are highly indecorous. Neoclassical aesthetics and neoclassical style are, above all else, highly decorous. The framing of intimate and disgraceful actions in a dignified style tends to set aside their indecorous quality—and, of course, in this case the indecorous actions themselves are never directly represented. Put differently, the stylized and "elevated" visual narration of the film selects and construes story events in a particularly dignified and decorous way.

Complexity enters with the precise emotional response the film projects for the "implied viewer." One might argue that the film is, in effect, covering up rape and that it expects us to cheer for the happy union of the couple at the end. However, one might equally argue that there is an ironic distance between a visual narrator who dignifies the rape and the implied filmmaker. Specifically, one way of interpreting the film involves seeing the neoclassical representation of the events as, precisely, a way of avoiding disagreeable aspects of ordinary life. The suddenness of the "happy" ending may, indeed, suggest that we cannot take the representation entirely seriously. On the other hand, this does not mean that the film is a thematic condemnation of neoclassicism. The sheer visual beauty of the film, the great aesthetic appeal of its visual style, speaks against such a condemnation. Moreover, it is possible to see the decorousness of the film as precisely *not* whitewashing the sordid act, *not* taking it up to prettify it, but allowing its viciousness to be regulated only by the viewer's imagination. In other words, we need not take the visual narration (with its neoclassical style) to be dignifying the rape at all. Indeed, for some viewers, the dignity of the general representation may enhance rather than diminish the horror of the (decorously unrepresented) violation.

Moving beyond modeling, we find that in some ways the most complex case is that of painterly sensibility. However, in other ways it is the simplest. Here, there is no specific allusive or modeling source for painterly sensibility. Thus there is not necessarily any specific "extrinsic" information to bring into play in understanding and responding to the target work. (Of course, such films, like any other works, may use allusion, but that is not what defines their painterly sensibility.) For this reason, our interpretation of and response to a film specifically as a work of painterly sensibility is more unequivocally focused on the film itself. Perhaps unsurprisingly, the most striking visual feature of Husain's *Meenaxi* is its great and complex visual beauty. Indeed, the sensitivity to depth, light, texture, color patterning, and color variation is particularly complex because it is not guided by a specific school such as neoclassicism. For this reason, the patterns and types of interrelation can vary from scene to scene or shot to shot. Of course, they do not vary randomly. There are relations across scenes as well—relations that are part of the film's aesthetic sensibility. However, there is no straightforward way of characterizing the stylistic norms of the work in terms of a source (e.g., by saying that they are defined by a particular movement).

Thematic concerns too arise subtly out of the development of the work itself, rather than by reference to sources. Thus the painterly quality of the film contributes to thematic concerns of life as a sort of artificial and illusory creation, filled with symbol and paradox. However, it does so only because the narrative of the film explicitly treats these issues. The main story concerns a writer who is penning a new novel. Within this frame, there are two embedded stories, both representing the novelist's attempts at a narrative. In each case, there are complexities and ambiguities. Most strikingly, the novelist himself enters into one of his novels and discusses the story with one of his characters. In addition, Husain himself appears briefly in the frame story, which is itself marked by apparent paradoxes. In this context, Husain's treatment of the film's visual style as a sort of painting, or series of paintings—thus the very painterly depiction of the "real" storyworld—contributes to the theme of the illusory quality of life. (The theme is ultimately developed in terms of Sufi mysticism. I discuss film in relation to Sufism in *Affective Narratology*, especially pages 108–121.) In particular cases, specific painterly techniques may be interpreted in relation to this theme—for example, the use of diffuse light around Meenaxi herself, the layering of curtains suggestive of partial concealment, the use of mirrors (an important Sufi symbol), and so on.

Sin City as Painterly Cinema

The opening of *Sin City* includes all the elements of painterly cinema discussed above. These most obviously range from specific allusions to Frank Miller's work to broader modeling on graphic fiction more generally. Undoubtedly, many viewers have strong artifact emotions in response to the work, greatly admiring Rodriguez's ability to mimic the visual qualities of Miller's graphic fiction. Such admiration is also bound up with the more general use of modeling in the work. I suspect that many viewers think that he has done a remarkably good job of creating the visual experience of a graphic novel on screen.

However, for other viewers, what is remarkable about the film generally, and these three minutes in particular, is the way Rodriguez has enriched the visual style of the film, not the way he has mimicked something else. Indeed, the film is as striking for its difference from the visual style of graphic fiction as it is for its similarity to that style. The sense of shadow, depth, contour, lighting, color—these are all inspired by the limited options available to the graphic novelist. However, Rodriguez has transformed them by synthesizing them with cinema.

Consider a simple case. When the rain falls in the last shot, Rodriguez represents it as continually changing streaks of silvery light tumbling into puddles that splash tiny beads of water around the young woman's corpse. This takes up a common convention of graphic fiction—that lines represent motion. When the motion involves raindrops falling, then the lines are downward streaks in the sky. However, these streaks are simply static line segments that conventionally communicate an idea. They are as aesthetic as, say, the word "rain." In contrast, the continually altering traces of raindrops in the shimmering light, the movement surrounding the motionless corpse, serve at least potentially to enhance several emotional responses in the viewer. First, the changing light and texture of the rain are themselves aesthetically pleasing. Aesthetic pleasure is a far more consequential artifact emotion than mere admiration that he managed to imitate downward streaks for rain. Moreover, the contrast of motion with the woman's stillness increases the pathos of the scene, intensifying the story emotion.

Here, one might ask whether it would have been better simply to shoot the scene in an ordinary way with ordinary rain. We would still have the falling rain and the unmoving corpse. Here, I believe, another aspect of the modeling enters. Unlike the neoclassical sources used by Rohmer, the visual style of graphic fiction is blatantly nonrealistic. In keeping with this, Rodriguez greatly constrains the options for visual style and he does so in ways that clearly violate realism—or, rather, ways that violate expectations based on realism. The difference is important because it is the expectations that are crucial here. Insofar as our ordinary expectations are fulfilled, we are likely to not even notice objects or events. This is because we are *habituated* to normalcy. The point is well established in cognitive psychological and neurological research (on the attentional and emotional effects of habituation, see Frijda 318 and LeDoux 138, respectively). It also has a long history in literary theory (see Kant 80 and Shklovsky 741). Cognitive and neurological studies indicate that, as a stimulus is repeated, we respond less and less. The corpse in rain is, by now, so commonplace as to be unremarkable—or irritatingly trite, if noticed. It almost certainly has no great emotional impact. The small changes in the representation of a corpse in the rain in effect follow the Russian formalist instruction to dishabituate the viewer's perception and thus his or her response.

There are several things to say about deviations from expectation in this context. First, they illustrate the process of creativity resulting from the use of a distant source for problems faced in a target medium. In this case, graphic fiction is the source, and the problem is enhancing both story emotion and artifact emotion—particularly, aesthetic emotion—in film (here, for a death scene). This is precisely what we would expect from the creative cognition research noted earlier. The importance of expectancy deviation also indicates again that the artifact quality of the target work—the force of its visual style—cannot be attributed to the source alone. Features of graphic fiction that are, frankly, banal in their original context may become aesthetically powerful innovations when integrated into the target medium of film.

It is also important to note that the constraint on style and the violation of realistic expectation mean that *Sin City* is manneristic. Indeed, the style is continually foregrounded, such that the mannerism affects other possible forms of habituation, including those associated with film itself. Rodriguez's increase in visual contrast and his highly selective use of color both distinguish the work from standard black-and-white film. The use of color is particularly noteworthy in the case of the woman's eyes. The green color fades in and out in a way that mirrors the man's—and the viewer's—interest in the eyes rather than the objective properties themselves. Alternatively, they may represent a surge of feeling (perhaps recollected jealousy) in the woman. In any case, neither color nor black-and-white photography becomes a banal background of habitual normalcy here.

There is a further foregrounding of the nonrealistic quality with the clear violations of continuity in the cut to the kiss. Moreover, as already noted, that shot reverses silhouette coloring in the foreground, as if in a photographic negative, but maintains ordinary black/white relations in the background. This shot is the one that most closely approximates the visual properties of graphic fiction. However, even that is dishabituated by the use of relatively realistic rain in the near foreground (between the camera and the couple).

This enhanced dishabituation is related to the film's increase in other pattern-intensifying properties, such as increased contrast, which are themselves extensions of pattern-intensifying processes of human cognition, such as lateral inhibition. All this bears on the final aspect of the work, particularly these three minutes—its broad painterly sensibility. This goes beyond allusion or modeling to Rodriguez's larger sense of visual aesthetics and the emotional effects of style.

Before concluding, it is important to say something about the thematic suggestions of these three minutes. Though the main function of the section appears to be emotional, it is not entirely lacking in thematic resonances. The man is a sort of modern manifestation of the angel of death. The woman is a modernly icy version of the classic figure of despair. However, there is a sort of unreality about their relationship, about the comfort of the man's profession of love, about the apparent gullibility of the woman, whose red lips smile at his assurances. Both the modernity and the unreality are communicated not only by aspects of dialogue and action, thus the storyworld, but by the very features of style that we have been considering. The punch line, again, comes at the end when we learn that the exterminating angel is bought and paid for. In place of God, we have a check—a replacement that is, perhaps, not unlike the substitution of a bright red dress for blood.

Painterly cinema comprises films that draw on sources in other visual arts—prominently painting, but also sculpture, tapestry, mosaics, and so forth—particularly, though not exclusively, for stylistic features. Hints of painterly cinema may be found in localized *allusions* in which a filmmaker configures a shot or cluster of shots to recall a particular work of visual art. When such localized allusions are extended to scenes or larger units, we may speak of *allusiveness*. We may consider allusiveness to be a minimal condition for painterly cinema. When a filmmaker is consistently drawing on a period, movement, or other style larger than a single work, we may speak of *modeling*. Modeling is the prototypical case of painterly cinema. If we conceive of painterliness as a sort of arc, moving from allusion through allusiveness to modeling, we may see the upper limit of the trajectory in *painterly sensibility*. Allusiveness extends allusion from local to broader use in the target film. Modeling extends allusiveness from particular source works with their specific representational contents to distinctive styles of period, school, and so on. Painterly sensibility generalizes both the source and the target. It broadens the source to the entire range of that particular visual art (e.g., painting), independent of movement or period (as well as content or topic). Thus the filmmaker of painterly sensibility draws on a range of techniques and sensitivities available to painters, independent of their particular school. Works of painterly sensibility most often expand the scope of painterly quality to the entire target film as well (though this is also common in modeling).

In each case—allusion, allusiveness, modeling, and painterly sensibility—the use of features from other visual arts may serve thematic or emotional purposes and the emotional purposes may bear on the story or the aesthetics of the film as an artifact. In cases of modeling and painterly sensibility in particular, the relations between such source features and the target work's themes are likely to be to some extent ambiguous. Similarly, in these cases the relation between the source features and story emotions may be somewhat ambivalent. In contrast, the artifactual consequences of painterly techniques seem more often to conduce toward straightforward visual beauty, or perhaps sublimity, with relatively little ambivalence. This is linked with the creativity and dishabituation that tend to result from the integration of distant sources and targets.

The opening of *Sin City* comprises three exquisite minutes of painterly cinema. It manifests the allusiveness, modeling, and painterly sensibility that we associate with works that have sources in the traditional fine arts, though it draws on graphic fiction rather than painting. Moreover, it evidences the same degree of creativity in drawing on a distant medium. Finally, the result has the usual, complex thematic and emotional consequences—the latter bearing both on the story and on the visual style of the work. The consequences for artifact emotion—here bound up with mannerism and thus foregrounding of style—are perhaps the most significant, stressing as they do the operation of dishabituation in painterly cinema.

Notes

1. Indeed, Husain seems to be aware of this difference. In one scene, he places a mirror on a dining table in front of the main character, who is turned away from the camera and whose face therefore appears in the mirror. The placement makes no sense realistically and seems to function as a sort of parody of the common use of mirrors in film—a link enhanced by the fact that, at this time, Meenaxi is looking at him through small binoculars quite reminiscent of a director's loupe. Specifically, table mirrors are often used to solve practical problems (e.g., of filming a character who would be facing a wall or of filming two faces simultaneously when they would not be turned in the proper way). Here, there is obviously no practical problem since the scene could simply be shot from the other side of the table. Nor is there any story-based motivation for this mirror. It is simply a strange, obtrusive presence. In contrast, this scene also includes an unobtrusive mirror in the distant background. This mirror is particularly reminiscent of mirrors in painting. In keeping with this, it enhances the sense of space and gives us a different visual perspective on the characters. It may also suggest a sort of play with the audience's implied viewing position, as in the case of *Las Meninas*.

2. I should perhaps note that I am not criticizing filmmakers here. Filmmakers have to deal with many more variables in creating a work that includes multiple scenes and stretches over a couple of hours. Moreover, viewers—including filmmakers viewing their own film footage—cannot engage in the same lingering attention to the nuances of a film as they can to those of a painting. Thus we would not expect even highly sensitive filmmakers to apply the same fineness of attention to aspects of hue and saturation as we would expect from painters. This is one of the reasons why a painterly sensibility may be innovative in filmmaking, as in the case of Husain.

CHAPTER 4

Sin City, Style, and the Status of Noir

EMILY R. ANDERSON

When Robert Rodriguez's *Sin City* (2005) was released, critics, reviewers, and audiences alike hailed it as Frank Miller's graphic narrative brought to life.[1] The film succeeds in "recreating the very panels of the comic strip layouts," one reviewer writes (Alleva 21). Others describe it as "a scrupulously meticulous translation . . . of three of the graphic novels," "fetishistically faithful" to its source text (Fuller 13, Flagg). And in his history of comic form, Jared Gardner notes that it "painstakingly translates Miller's protagonists to the screen" (*Projections* 185). Rodriguez must have been pleased to hear it. When he first considered filming three of the books in Miller's *Sin City* series, he "wanted to translate [Miller] directly to the screen. And if you read his books," he suggests, "you see that he's already a director; he was just working with paper instead of a camera. I really wanted to emulate that in the movie and make the cinematic equivalent of his book" ("15 Minute"). Of course, before he was able to "translate" Miller's books, he had to get permission. Frank Miller was famously reluctant to allow anyone to adapt these stories, having suffered through the miserable experience of losing control over *RoboCop 2*. (For details on this and other aspects of the film's inception, see Brian Ashcraft and almost every other article written on *Sin City*.) But Rodriguez eventually persuaded him to watch one day's worth of tests, a day on which Rodriguez shot, edited, scored, and created effects for Miller's short story "The Customer Is Always Right"—as Patrick Colm Hogan discusses in detail herein. The result was a short that re-created much of what Miller had done on the page—the black-and-white tones, the high angles, and the dialogue. Miller was thrilled, and the short became the film's opening sequence.

Rodriguez works exclusively with digital cameras and shot *Sin City* almost entirely in front of a green screen. As a result, every background and almost every "set" is actually computer-generated imagery added in post-production. That is, much of the film is actually *drawn*, albeit with pixels instead of pens. In this sense, the film is much closer to a graphic narrative than any film shot on location or on a traditional soundstage could be. And when Rodriguez describes Miller as a director "working with paper instead of a camera," he suggests the ease with which a film's cinematography and editing can re-create many of Miller's panels, from their compositions to their angles to the implied movement between one panel and another. And it was through his use of corresponding compositions, angles, and edits, along with the drawings—the computer-generated imagery that constitutes most of the film's mise-en-scène—that Rodriguez was able to make the "cinematic equivalent" of Miller's books.[2]

It is no surprise that reviewers dwell on the similarities between Miller's and Rodriguez's texts, as the similarities are truly striking. Rodriguez essentially treated the comics as storyboards for his film, and as a result comparisons are easy to make. Most shots are framed, for example, according to the composition in Miller's panels. Near the beginning of the film, for instance, Marv (Mickey Rourke) spends a delightful evening with Goldie (Jaime King), and then wakes up in the morning next to her corpse. In one sequence, we get an overhead shot of Goldie on the bed and Marv sitting next to her, his hand on his head (see figure 4). The arrangement of lights, the window, the door, the bed, the Bible on

Figure 4. Frank Miller and Robert Rodriguez's film re-creation (in *Sin City*) of an overhead shot of Marv waking up next to a dead Goldie.

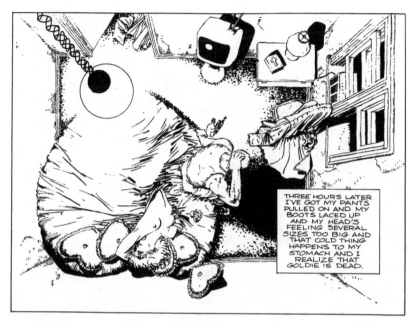

Figure 5. Frank Miller's original comic book panel from "The Hard Goodbye" of Marv awaking next to Goldie.

the table, and the actors' bodies is virtually identical to that in Miller's panel (see figure 5). Even the difference in aspect ratio between the images is smoothed over with the apparent use of a wider lens in the film, allowing the walls to take up more space in the frame. Rodriguez managed this similarity in framing and composition by comparing, on his monitor, the image he was capturing to the relevant panels in Miller's book. He could thus adjust the camera and actors to correspond to the panels. The footage then went to one of three special effects companies, in this case Hybride Technologies, that created the "sets," again based on Miller's panels. Just as similar are the film's dialogue and voice-overs, which come right out of the source text. In this example, we hear Marv in voice-over: "Three hours later and my head's feeling several sizes too big and that cold thing happens to my stomach, and I realize Goldie's dead"—a slightly abbreviated reading of the language in the panel.

Equally striking is the similarity between lighting in the two texts. Not only is the film mostly in black and white, for example, but the relationship between light and dark in Rodriguez's film parallels that seen in Miller's drawings. Typically, black-and-white films include dozens of shades of gray, differences in shading that allow an audience to differenti-

Figure 6. Frank Miller's original comic book panel from "That Yellow Bastard" of Nancy tied to a chair.

ate among the various objects on screen in a way that a two-tone image — actual black and white — would not. However, Rodriguez wanted to replicate as much of Miller's look as possible: "Another trick that Frank uses in his book that you can't really do photographically is, he gives everything an edge. This sort of realization early on convinced me that we'd have to make the movie in green screen . . . because then we could put lights anywhere, give [objects] the edge that's needed when you shoot black and white" ("15 Minute"). In other words, Rodriguez was able to light his actors, often using just a key light and a backlight, without regard for light spill — the light that would illuminate not only the actor but the set as well. Rodriguez wanted the set to remain dark, and because the "set" was merely a graphic created in postproduction, it could be as dark as he liked, as dark as in Miller's panels. The result is a film that, far more than most black-and-white films, is actually black and white, but that still manages to separate the figures from their environment. For example, a few minutes into the film we learn that an eleven-year-old girl, Nancy (Makenzie Vega), is about to be raped and murdered. At one point, she is tied to a chair in a large, dark room as one of her kidnappers enters. In Miller's panel, the background consists mostly of this kidnapper's shadow, and Nancy is drawn in white against it (see figure 6). Miller uses no shades of gray, no crosshatching to indicate another tone. He doesn't need to.

In the film (see figure 7), Rodriguez adjusts the composition of the image to accommodate his wider frame, but he still places Nancy in front of a black background. The key light is at her back, and the backlight separates her hair, chest, and lap from the background (though some of this is difficult to see in a reproduction). The absence of a fill light allows the areas of her body not outright bright to remain virtually black. On the other side of the frame is the digitally created shadow of Nancy's kidnapper, who appears to be standing in a well-lit room as he looks through the door at Nancy. Were this photographed on a traditional set, light spill from the key light at Nancy's back would make it impossible to see the kidnapper's shadow on the wall. We would see Nancy's shadow instead, and the rest of the wall would be fairly bright. Moreover, light from the room in which the kidnapper stands would act as a fill light for Nancy, illuminating the areas of her body that are here dark. But because the actual set is green screen, Rodriguez can put his key light wherever he likes and add whatever shadows he likes in postproduction. This relationship between light and shadow defies the laws of physics. That is, it is

Figure 7. Frank Miller and Robert Rodriguez's film re-creation (in *Sin City*) of Nancy tied to the chair.

possible only in art—through a pen, in Miller's case, or a computer, in Rodriguez's.

The similarities between the film and comic book are remarkable, so remarkable that critics seldom mention the ways in which the comic and the film differ. This oversight is explained in part by the fact that some differences go without saying; that is, of course the texts differ—one is a film and the other is a book. And indeed many differences can be attributed to the properties of the media, specifically differences in rate, relationships among frames, and channels. Rodriguez's film, for example, progresses at a rate of 24 frames, 24 separate pictures, per second. This rate is constant throughout the course of the film and beyond the viewer's control. The comic book reader, though, can linger over particular panels or read quickly if he or she can't stand the suspense.[3] On a particular page of "The Big Fat Kill," for example—a moment right before the final confrontation—the viewer has seven panels and eight speech balloons to inspect (see figure 8). How long that will take, it is impossible to say. The film, however, presents these same events, or rather the 960 corresponding frames, in 40 seconds, and that number will not vary depending on the viewer.

Similarly, the relationships among images in a film are fixed, but they are variable in a comic, most obviously in terms of sequence. A film moves from its first frame to its last. In a graphic narrative, the arrangement of panels can interrupt a traditional left-to-right, top-to-bottom reading. On this same page of the book, for example, Miller lays out the panels unconventionally. I have numbered them from one to seven in the order that seems to make the most sense, but the page is not at all committed to this order, the primary difficulty arising with where to go after panel three: to panel four at the left side of the page, clockwise to panel five, or some combination thereof. This difficulty does not inhibit comprehension, however, as only panels 3, 4, 6, and 7 must be read in sequence— Dwight demanding Gail's release (3), Manute accepting the terms (4), the delivery of Jackie Boy's head (6), and the subsequent standoff (7). The other three panels—two representing Becky's distress (1, 5) and one representing Gail's (2)—could occupy any position at all except the last. (The film, in fact, chooses the following sequence: 3, 2, 1, 5, 4, 6, 7.) The reader is thus free to choose any number of sequences, or perhaps to interpret the absence of a fixed sequence as an indicator of simultaneity. Furthermore, and in addition to sequence, the size of a panel and its position on the page can indicate timing, relative importance, or duration. In this example, Becky's panels (1, 5) are smaller than the rest but also overlapping them.

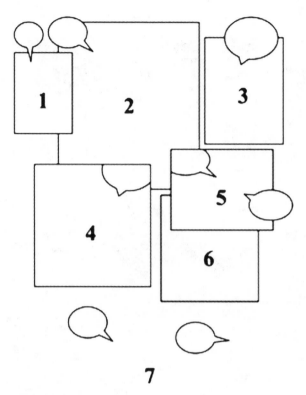

Figure 8. Dissection of a page layout from Frank Miller's "The Big Fat Kill."

Her warnings about Jackie Boy's head, warnings that could have saved Manute's life, are ignored even as she shouts over the conversations of the others to be heard. Film can signify in none of these ways, as every frame is the same size, in the same place on the screen, and in a fixed order.[4]

Similarly, comic panels can change shapes from one to the next, often unconventionally. One panel from "The Hard Goodbye," for example, takes the form of the word "BLAM!" (see figure 9). Only inside of the letters can we see the figure of a priest, falling backward as Marv shoots him in the head. What is remarkable about this panel is what its shape signifies: the shape of the letters lets us know that the gun has been fired, and the middle of the letter M cleaves the priest's head in two. Moreover, a tension exists here, as Luke Arnott argues, as in this panel "the word signifying the sound can either reproduce the temporal or the auditory features of its signified," when we see "blam" on the page in an instant or pronounce it to ourselves more slowly, "but never both at once" (385).

Figure 9. An example of Frank Miller's giving shape to panels in the form of letters that make words like "BLAM" (from "The Hard Goodbye").

The film, on the other hand, depicts the priest falling backward as Marv shoots him and as we hear the gunshot, but the screen itself does not assist in the representation of events.

Before we feel any sympathy for film and the limited ways in which it can signify, though, we must note that it has two channels at its disposal—the visual and the auditory—as opposed to the one visual channel available to graphic narratives. In the example above, the audience actually hears the gunshot in the film, as opposed to reading the word "blam," and the sound may surprise the viewer in a way that the panel cannot. Throughout the film, actors' line readings add nuance and subtlety to the characters, of course. And Miller himself has noted the benefits of sound. When Miller created Shellie, a barmaid who appears in all three stories, for example, he imagined that her voice cracked, but he couldn't think of a way to represent this sound on the page. When Brittany Murphy was cast as Shellie in the film, he was delighted to hear the crack in her voice, believing that it helped develop Shellie's character (Mitchell).

Scott McCloud has explored some of these differences between media. He defines comics as a "sequential art," a "[juxtaposition of] pictorial and other images in a deliberate sequence" (199). This is not to say that the sequence must be fixed, but that the juxtaposition of images is the way in which comics signify. Nowhere is this truer than in the gutter, the space between panels. Because the images themselves are static, even if they suggest motion, the action occurs in the reader's interpretation of what happens between them. According to McCloud, the gutter is a gap that must be closed, and closure, he argues, is the grammar of comics (67). Certainly, there are Iserian gaps in film as well—events not depicted or sequences difficult to interpret—but these gaps are not the very mechanism by which film signifies. Images in comics require the reader to do a great deal of interpretive work to make sense of the still images as a representation of action. (Not just action, actually. McCloud notes eleven kinds of change that a reader might imagine between one panel and the next.) Or as McCloud puts it, in comics "time and space are one and the same" whereas in film the passing of time usually resembles our experience of time in real life (100).[5] And the same is true of auditory data, which in film resembles the sounds we hear in the world, but which must be represented graphically in comics. Graphic narratives, McCloud argues, are thus "a medium where the audience is a willing and conscious collaborator and closure is the agent of change, time and motion" (65). In other words, Miller's text requires of its audience far more participation and interpretation than Rodriguez's does even to understand the story.

The differences above, between film and comic, thus arise from the differences in the material properties of the texts themselves. Rodriguez has said that he wanted to "make the cinematic equivalent of" Miller's books, but the texts can be equivalent only insofar as some properties can move from text to screen. Others, the film must give up. To this extent, the film and comic differ because their media differ. Another way to make this point would be to say that the film and the books necessarily generate different discourses. "Discourse," as Seymour Chatman tells us, is "the expression, the means by which the [story] is communicated" (19). And he goes on to divide discourse "into two subcomponents, the narrative form itself—the structure of narrative transmission—and its manifestation—its appearance in a specific materializing medium" (22). The narrative structure is essentially a communication model that describes entities between the real author and the real audience. This structure frequently parallels Gérard Genette's description of discourse as a combination of tense, mood, and voice—essentially the relationships between the story, narrating (the act of narrating), and narration, which Genette defines as "the signifier, statement, discourse or narrative text itself" (27). In other words, Chatman's text might communicate according to Genette's description of techniques. Genette's description, though, is largely specific to verbal narrative, while Chatman's structure may obtain in a variety of media. But the second of Chatman's components, "the *substance* of narrative expression" in a given medium, by which Chatman means the signs—the "words, drawings, or whatever"—will obviously vary according to medium (24, 23). A novel, for example, contains only words; a film contains words and pictures. Because different texts have different material properties, employ different kinds of signs, and adhere to different conventions, their discourses will *necessarily* be different. And this is the case no matter how ardently Rodriguez would like to translate Miller's books directly to the screen.

If translation is an overstatement, though, we can understand Rodriguez's desire to "[pull off] things that were stylistic signatures of Frank's books" as a desire to replicate Miller's work wherever he could ("15 Minute"). But if this is the case, it is particularly surprising to note the many differences between the two texts that are not to do with the media but in fact with choices Rodriguez makes. That is, the film and the comic use different signs, different images to tell the story. Miller's text, for example, frequently represents the characters and setting through abstract lines. Many images are hardly comprehensible out of context. Diagonal lines represent a rainstorm. A white blob on a black background represents a pool of blood. In many panels, there are only a few lines to suggest a background. In others, there is no background at all, just the characters. Rodriguez's film, on the other hand, uses human actors and a more realist mise-en-scène. Unlike the changes in rate, sequence, and channel, which inhere in the medium of film, these differences are unnecessary. Rodriguez could, for example, have created an animated film that merely added 150,000 images to Miller's and screened them at 24 per second. Such would be a "translation" across media in the truest sense. Instead, Rodriguez uses signs—here, actors and sets—overtly different from Miller's comic book.

Images of the actors in the film, even the actors' bodies, are altered to resemble those in Miller's drawings, but the actors are unmistakably human. For example, Bruce Willis had scars affixed to his forehead that resemble his character's scars in the comic, and an image of Hartigan on the screen may remind us of Miller's Hartigan. However, it is obviously an image *of* Bruce Willis. Similarly, many of the women in Miller's comic have proportions that would render them unable to stand of their own volition were they real people. In the film, the women's proportions are certainly compelling, but they are just as certainly human. Moreover, the "locations" in Rodriguez's film often appear to be real sets constructed on a studio's soundstage—a far cry from the spare images in Miller's drawings that often resemble what McCloud calls "the picture plane" (52). For example, when Hartigan punches Bob, who is trying to stop him from saving Nancy at the beginning of "That Yellow Bastard," diagonal lines suggest the pier on which they are standing, and the rest of the background consists of a few pillars and some wavy lines suggesting water. The diagonal lines of the pier are taken up again in the lines of the men's coats, the arrangement of the men and the pillars, the suggested trajectory of Hartigan's fist, and the very angle from which we see them. A very few lines, then, along with an efficient use of black-and-white space, represent not only the assault but instability and movement (see figure 10).

Rodriguez's representation of this moment is very different (see figure 11). Most obviously Bob (Michael Madsen) and Hartigan are represented by real actors, and not only are these actors obviously people, but they are people we might recognize from their previous work. The casting of Bruce Willis is especially significant, as he is known for playing tough, likeable cops with a code of honor, meaning that the casting of this particular human signifies. Moreover, the framing and angle accord with cinematic convention. This scene features standard two-shots, over-the-shoulder shots, and editing. Here, Hartigan is in the center of the frame, his punch forcing Bob out of it. The lines—created by the buildings, the lampposts, the actors' bodies, Hartigan's arm, and the direction in which it is moving—are horizontal and vertical, and the camera is at eye level. These are not the diagonal lines and high angle of Miller's panel, which suggest far more instability than does the scene in the film. Equally significant, though, is the mise-en-scène, which is far more detailed and realistic than Miller's. Hartigan and Bob are standing on the street in front of the pier, and the background is taken up with buildings, streetlights, and fog. And while the setting is stylized, it is detailed and reminiscent of the world we ourselves occupy.[6]

Figure 10. Frank Miller's original comic book panel from "That Yellow Bastard" with Hartigan punching Bob.

And this despite the fact that the "location" was actually *drawn*. With the exception of three sets—Kadie's bar, Shellie's apartment, and a hospital—all of the film's "sets" were created in postproduction. Rodriguez describes his early work on the film "as a test to . . . try out these more realistic backgrounds," backgrounds that "would fall somewhere between a stylized reality and the books that Frank had drawn." He goes on to describe a competition that developed among the three special effects companies that resulted in "images that were . . . a lot of times realistic when they didn't need to be," as each company tried to outdo the others ("15 Minute"). In fact, the decision to create a more realist mise-en-scène was driven by the use of real actors. Chris Olivia, a visual effects artist at Rodriguez's Troublemaker Studios, points out that "a comic-book film that's really graphic, pure blacks and whites, sounds good in theory, but as soon as you put an actor with shades of gray into the scene, it doesn't integrate well. So we found ourselves pushing the backgrounds toward a more realistic look" (qtd. in Robertson 46). While claiming to translate the comics, then, Rodriguez is actually adhering to a different set of criteria: these aspects of Rodriguez's film embrace a realist aesthetic that Miller eschews.[7]

These aspects of the film seem to work exactly against Miller's style. But then, perhaps style is more complex than aesthetic choices, more than just the characteristics of the signs? James Phelan has defined it, in reference to verbal narrative, as "those elements of a sentence or passage that would be lost in a paraphrase" (6). Dan Shen argues, again in terms of the verbal, that "'style' may be defined as 'the language aspect of how the story is presented.' Accordingly, 'stylistic features' will be understood as choices of *verbal* form or *verbal* techniques" (146). Examples might include diction, idiom, and syntax—features of language that one writer will use differently than another. What, then, for graphic narratives? Certainly, most graphic narratives contain language, which might be analyzed in terms of its style as productively as a novel's might. But Jared Gardner argues that style in comics is best understood as "the trace of the hand, the graphic enunciation that is the drawn line," which he describes as "roughly analogous to diction and syntax in narrative fiction" ("Storylines" 54, 57). Lines may be rough, fine, heavy, light, and the artist may use a variety of pencils and pens. In a similar vein, David Bordwell argues that filmic "'style' simply names the film's systematic use of cinematic devices . . .— mise-en-scène, cinematography, editing, and sound" (247). That is, a cer-

Figure 11. Miller and Rodriguez's film re-creation (in *Sin City*) of Hartigan punching Bob.

tain filmmaker's style might involve using dissolves instead of straight cuts, a high key-to-fill ratio, and lightning mixes.

These definitions suggest that style does not refer to a narrative's story or organization. To return to verbal narratives, a novel might tell a particular story in a particular way—leaving some events out, presenting others in flashbacks—but with sentences that are spare, eloquent, or convoluted. Spare, eloquent, or convoluted, then, would refer to the novel's style. As Dan Shen argues, "'narrative presentation' or 'how the story is told' consists of two aspects: one organizational and the other verbal, with a certain amount of overlap in between" (146). Shen's "organization" might better be called, as the Russian formalists have it, the *syuzhet*, which we can understand here as Genette's order, duration, and frequency—the order in which events are presented, the length of time the presentation takes, and the frequency with which a particular event is presented (or not). And David Bordwell makes a similar claim, in just these terms, about the distinction between style and *syuzhet* in film. In a particular instance, he writes,

> the syuzhet may require that two story events be cued as occurring simultaneously. The simultaneity may be denoted by crosscutting from one event to the other, by staging the two actions in depth, by use of split-screen techniques, or by the inclusion of particular objects in the setting (such as a television set broadcasting a "live" event). (250)

Whatever method the film employs will reflect a "stylistic choice" (250). As Shen's and Bordwell's emphasis on choice suggests, "style" most appropriately refers to those elements that are contingent when presenting a particular organization of a particular story. Much like a specific word choice in a novel, a specific shot transition in a film or a specific line in a panel *could have been different* without changing the story or its organization.

In this discussion of style, it becomes clear that Shen's aspects of presentation, "one organizational and the other verbal," are remarkably similar to Chatman's subcomponents of discourse, "the narrative form itself . . . and its manifestation—its appearance in a specific materializing medium" (22). And these distinctions are in turn similar to Bordwell's: "The conception of syuzhet avoids surface-phenomena distinctions (such as person, tense, metalanguage)," phenomena that belong to style, "and relies upon more supple principles basic to all narrative representation" (248). All three critics suggest that some element of presentation, dis-

course, or narration—its organization, narrative, or *syuzhet*—is independent of medium, and that another—its style or signs—is not. (See Pascal
Lefèvre and David Herman for other considerations of the aspects of discourse that might or might not be medium-specific.) And here is where
the problem lies: if style is a component of discourse (and let us for the
moment read "presentation" and "narration" as synonymous with "discourse"), does it refer to the signs themselves or to the predilections of
a particular artist when choosing signs? Or, to do more justice to Chatman, why might some critics describe what is medium-specific as style
while others might describe it as the mode of signification? Bordwell, in
fact, is closer here to Chatman than he is to Shen, as his understanding of
style includes Genette's mood and voice, which is largely beyond the purview of Shen's. And Lefèvre goes even further, conflating style and signs
when he claims that only style "can be directly perceived by the reader of
graphic narratives; [it] encompasses the lines and colors that form images
and the letters that form words and sentences" (15). However, if style and
material medium are inextricably linked, what would it mean for Rodriguez to translate Miller's style from one medium to another? One answer
might be found in the history of noir.

Whatever style might be, noir has a lot of it. As early as 1955, three
years before Orson Welles's *Touch of Evil* would mark the end of classic
noir, Raymond Borde and Étienne Chaumeton were trying to define what
other French critics had dubbed *les films noirs américains*. They described
this group of films as a historically contingent "series," that is, "a group
of motion pictures from one country sharing certain traits (style, atmo-
sphere, subject matter . . .) strongly enough to mark them unequivocally
and to give them, over time, an unmistakable character" (17). And the
traits in this case are "the moral ambivalence, the criminality, the complex
contradictions in motives and events [that] conspire to make the viewer
co-experience the anguish and insecurity which are the true emotions of
contemporary *film noir*" (25). Since then, critics have taken issue with
this definition, alternately describing noir as thematic, representing existential crisis, moral ambiguity, and subjectivity; as a kind of story, usually
of hard-boiled detectives, corrupt cops, and femmes fatales; or as a style,
specifically including low-key lighting, disorienting mise-en-scène, and
imbalanced composition.

Raymond Durgnat tries to find a middle ground, claiming that "noir"
indicates the presence of certain thematic motifs or a particular "tone."
Paul Schrader argues that "*film noir* is more interested in style than theme"
(63). And James Damico returns to the work of Borde and Chaumeton,

arguing that it is a genre—a category of films whose stories follow a particular model: a bitter man meets a "not-innocent" woman who, overtly or not, leads him to murder a second man to whom she is somehow attached; this murder usually leads the woman to betray the protagonist, and she is ultimately destroyed, often along with the man himself (103). Damico's description of story, though, is utterly devoid of what Place and Peterson identify as the hallmark of noir—its visual motifs: low-key lighting, key lights in unexpected places, night-for-night shooting, wide-angle lenses that create a greater depth of field, imbalanced compositions with a dearth of two- or three-shots, choker close-ups, high-angle shots, a lack of establishing shots, and sparing camera movement. The question seems to be, then, whether it is the story or the style that defines noir.

Frank Miller has stressed the influence of noir on his own work, and primarily in thematic terms: "*Film noir* is about inner darkness and the frightening scent of our souls. The darkness that is the noir of film noir is internal darkness; it's not external" (Siegel).[8] And this darkness besets every character in a noir story, including its protagonist: "The noir hero is a knight in blood caked armor. He's dirty and he does his best to deny the fact that he's a hero the whole time" (Mitchell). Miller's description of the "noir hero" characterizes his protagonists perfectly: Marv gives his life to avenge the death of a prostitute; Hartigan gives his life to protect the life of an exotic dancer; and Dwight (Clive Owen) risks his life to defend a gang of prostitutes; and along the way, they bring down corrupt cops, a cannibal cardinal, would-be rapists, a pedophile, and the mob. The primary differences between these stories and Damico's telling of the noir story is that the men, here, seem to resolve their existential moral crises, and their women never betray them. These differences reflect Miller's description of *Sin City* as, "first and foremost, a crime comic. It's a series of crime stories. Also a series of love stories set in a very, very dark world where nobility is hard to come by" (Mitchell). Miller's assigning the stories to the "crime" genre, far from distancing them from noir, points out their similarities to hard-boiled fiction—a noir staple.

Hard-boiled noir is a subgenre (if we can allow something that may not be a genre to have subgenres) derived from hard-boiled crime fiction. Much of this fiction appeared in *Black Mask* or similar pulp magazines, and the best of it was Dashiell Hammett's and Raymond Chandler's. These stories featured down-and-out detectives who are tough, urban, and comfortable with violence. There are dangerous women and plenty of booze, but in contrast to other subgenres of noir, their protagonists are usually on the right side of justice, if the wrong side of the law. In his comics, then, Miller is bringing noir back to its roots—to the page. Stories in *Black Mask*, for example, were frequently accompanied by an illustration of the characters. And much of Miller's language is straight out of these tales (Hartigan, for example, has a "bum ticker"). Whatever it may be worth, then, Miller himself seems to be reading noir as a genre.

Hard-boiled fiction was the basis for multiple films noir that appeared in the 1940s and 1950s—from Hammett's *The Maltese Falcon* to Chandler's *The Long Goodbye*—and this brings us back to Rodriguez. While any film based on Miller's books would be "noirish," *Sin City* is particularly interested in its status as a film noir. That is, it is acutely aware of cinematic history. There are several references to the methods of film production conventional in the 1940s and 1950s. As Mark Bould notes, for example, "when Hartigan drives to the waterfront to rescue young Nancy, he does so in front of a digitally created backdrop which looks like an old-fashioned back-projection" (113). This effect does "not claim to offer a more direct experience of the real but . . . a familiar and thus authenticating visual language or representation"—a cinematic representation, in other words (113–114). And this "visual language" operates throughout the film, as in the next scene when Hartigan fights his partner, Bob (see figure 11). In addition to its realist aesthetic and conventional angle, this scene includes buildings, bridges, and fog—all created on a computer in postproduction—that appear on-screen exactly as if they were a rear projection. That is, they are blurry, just as if the light projecting their images were diffused by the time it got to the screen. Moreover, the lampposts, the fire hydrant, and the street in the middle ground appear to be constructed on a soundstage. Conventionally, such a set would appear in front of the screen on which a larger background was projected, but because the set was real, it would be in much better focus. And that is just what we find here—the lampposts, hydrant, and street remain in focus. The scene appears to be shot with a wide-angle lens that can keep the entire soundstage in focus, if not the projection behind it. All of which is to say that in this scene the film goes to extraordinary lengths to appear as if it were made in the 1940s.

A much stranger reference to film production occurs when a dishonest cop (Jude Ciccolella) is trying to beat a false confession out of Hartigan. As the blood flies—dark red, against the black-and-white figures and background—a few drops appear to land on the camera lens (see figure 12). They splash onto the screen, coalesce, and then fade away. These drops of

Figure 12. Detail (from the film *Sin City*). Miller and Rodriguez's film shows drops of blood spattered on the camera lens.

blood were digitally created in postproduction, but it appears on-screen as if the camera were an actual player in the diegetic world. That is, the camera itself appears in the film. Similarly, and even more significant because it is ever present, is the use of color. Many objects on-screen are not in fact black and white but instead blue, green, or the aforementioned vibrant blood red. In the scene where Marv wakes up to find Goldie (see figure 4), for example, the heart-shaped bed is red, her hair is appropriately gold, and her skin is a washed-out peach. A particular prostitute, Becky, has preternaturally blue eyes. Dwight's shoes are red. Indeed, there are dozens of examples. Rodriguez managed these effects by shooting the film in color, converting the images to gray scale, and then adding back desaturated versions of the color or computer-generated replacements. The effect is striking. And the result is that the film is continuously drawing attention to itself as a film—a material object that underwent a variety of cinematographic transformations.[9]

These obvious transformations affect the viewer's relationship to the film. Normally, an audience interprets a (seemingly) photographic image as an actual representation of the world. However, a film that has obviously undergone extensive work in the digital intermediate (DI)—the process of digitally manipulating images to create special effects—thwarts this interpretation. John Belton argues that, in such films, viewers

know that the relationship of a digital image to what it is an image of involves forms and/or stages of mediation potentially far greater than those
involved in the typical photographic image. DI represents a perfect instance of such mediation—the mediation of image data during the postproduction process. For the most part, it is difficult for us to perceive this
manipulation. To the extent that digital imaging, in general, effectively
simulates photochemical imaging, it does not effect [*sic*] our psychology
of the image—that is, not until it becomes visible—as in spectacular digital special-effects sequences or in digital image break-up. (61)

And this is exactly what occurs in *Sin City*. Becky's blue eyes and Hartigan's blood on the lens prevent us from understanding the film as a representation of the real world because they require us to see the film, not
just as a material object, but as a *mediated* object. Remarkably, these references to mediation have exactly the same effect as Rodriguez's references
to studio techniques in the 1940s and 1950s. Both highlight the production of film, which the audience must now understand as artificial, that
is, as an artifact.

The film's insistence on its status as an artifact defines its relationship to
Miller's comics and to the history of film noir. In other words, Rodriguez
does to the films what Miller does to the hard-boiled stories of Hammett
and Chandler. Miller remediates these stories; more than adapting them,
he subjects them to the limits and possibility of another medium. And
were Rodriguez to "translate" Miller in the most limited sense—adding
150,000 drawings and screening them at 24 per second—he would be forsaking everything that is valuable in the remediation. Instead, he locates
his film in the history of the medium with the constant references to film
production and conventions, conventions he flouts or adheres to in unmotivated succession. Indeed, even the similarities between Rodriguez's
text and Miller's are experiments in what film is capable of—whether it
can violate the physical laws of light and shadow, for example, or of color
and tone. Noir, in Rodriguez's hands, is more than a style or a story. It is a
discourse, or a genre of discourse, that consists of a particular relationship
between a text's style and its structure. That is, it describes an organization
that any number of films might produce, but an organization deployed in
a particular way. Noir thus depends upon style, but "style" understood
to be the particular way in which the signs will obtain in the context of a
medium and its conventions.

Any consideration of style and discourse, then, must be a consideration
of the methods of signification in a particular medium. What a sign might

"mean" depends on what the medium is capable of. Drawings do not signify in films what they signify in comics, for example, nor does black and white signify in comics what it signifies in films. Similarly, neither rear projection nor phrases such as "bum ticker" signify now what they did in the 1940s. In his history of film noir, James Naremore argues that noir is "a kind of mediascape—a loosely related collection of perversely related motifs or scenarios that circulate through all the information technologies," and while he means media in the broadest possible sense, the characterization of noir as a relationship that circulates among media is apt (255). Particularly at this moment, as investigations of narrative tend toward the cognitive processes and contextual elements involved in its reception, we would do well to bear in mind the relationships that make up discourse. These relationships, however we may define them—but perhaps among medium, style, the object itself, and whatever histories and conventions come with them—are the real processes of signification. Among the many things Rodriguez has managed to do with *Sin City*, it turns out, is show us how far we have to go in attempting to explain it.

Notes

1. Throughout, I use "graphic narrative" and "comic" interchangeably. What I mean is a narrative text composed of still, drawn images, usually in conjunction with language.

2. I'm referring to the film as Rodriguez's despite the fact that Rodriguez and Miller are listed as codirectors. I do this in part because, while both men were on set throughout principal photography, Rodriguez appears to have worked more consistently with the actors. Moreover, he was the film's cinematographer and editor; he cowrote the score; and he supervised postproduction. See Barbara Robertson's description of Rodriguez's and Miller's respective roles in the film's production.

3. Genette's formula for working out duration—counting the number of pages devoted to a particular event—does not work particularly well for comics, as the panels can differ considerably. One page might have one large image and no text, for example, and the next might have eleven panels and several paragraphs of text.

4. Jared Gardner notes that DVDs often allow viewers to skip around, "essentially remixing the film as the viewer sees fit" (*Projections* 190). But though we need not look at images in scenes in a particular order, the medium of film encourages us to do so. See also Will Eisner's *Graphic Storytelling and Visual Narrative*.

5. As Kay O'Halloran notes, film uses "time sequences in a two-dimensional frame to represent our three-dimensional lived-in material experience of the world" (109). On the other hand, "graphic representation [in comics] does not

directly mimic our naïve perceptions of temporal reality," according to Neil Cohn (144).

6. Johannes Fehrle argues that, historically, "the medium of comics is closer to the 'marvelous' tradition (in Todorov's sense) than to the mimetic, realist tradition of the novel" (217). I would add, and of film.

7. "Realist," here, is different from "realistic." "Realist" refers to a fictional world that resembles our own, especially to the extent that it includes sensory details—in these cases, visual.

8. Christopher Pizzino argues that, in *Sin City*, Miller "perfects a noir aesthetic, one specific to the medium of comics, that rehearses its own generic limitations while still confirming the genre itself, and the medium through which it is expressed, as sufficient" (124).

9. One use of color in the film does mimic Miller's text. "That Yellow Bastard" is entirely in black and white with exception of the yellow Yellow Bastard. In these sections of the film, Rodriguez similarly adds a yellow tint to Roark Junior's character. Despite its coming from Miller, however, the effect is the same—it draws attention to the medium.

CHAPTER 5

Sin City, Hybrid Media, and a Cognitive Narratology of Multimodality

ERIN E. EIGHAN

The new millennium for cinema ushered in hoards of comic book adaptations—from the standard throes of DC and Marvel superhero comics like *X-Men* (2000) to Harvey Pekar's ode to the abject rust belt in *American Splendor* (2003). Adaptations transform the story of one medium into the discourse offerings of another. Directors of films like *X-Men* and *American Splendor* work within the filmic medium to re-create the story of a comic book. For *Sin City*, however, Robert Rodriguez wanted something different for the work of his medium—rather than merely *adapt* Frank Miller's *Sin City*, he wanted to *translate* it, form and all. In a "Behind the Scenes" interview, Rodriguez asked,

> How could they ever adapt it [the comic book series, *Sin City*]? It would just become a regular movie. . . . [I]nstead of trying to turn it into a movie, which would be terrible, let's take cinema and try to make it into this book. . . . I don't want to make Robert Rodriguez's *Sin City*. I want to make Frank Miller's *Sin City*.

For Rodriguez, story and discourse in the narrative of Frank Miller's *Sin City* were inseparable. Yet he was not convinced that Frank Miller's *Sin City* was necessarily bound to the singular medium of comics and the graphic narrative. In fact, of all narrative forms, film seemed to be the best candidate for a medium-specific translation of comics. For Rodriguez, the mediums of comics and film seemed to invite a formal crossover. "[T]he mediums really are very similar," he noted. "These are just snapshots of movement" ("Behind the Scenes"). He is certainly right, to a degree: both comics and film are constructed at base by segmented chunks of visual information. Yet, Rodriguez's project is more profound than this. *Sin City* actually pushes the bounds of the filmic medium to imitate the offerings of another. It becomes a hybridized medium—one that bridges the continuous motion of film with the panels and gutters of comics, the human face with caricature, the sound with silence.

In this chapter, I will explore the narratological effects of a hybrid medium in Rodriguez's *Sin City*. An argument like this has the potential to become overwhelmed if it were to attempt a complete articulation of each facet of hybridity—a project that film critics and popular audiences, alike, have already begun. Roger Ebert's review of the film, for example, recognizes how it "internalizes the harsh world of the Frank Miller *Sin City* comic books and processes it through computer effects, grotesque makeup, lurid costumes and dialogue that chops at the language of noir." In what follows, I will explore how Rodriguez's hybridized medium affects the serialization and episodicity of a narrative, the segmentation and sequencing of comics and film, and the integration of different narrative tracks. Most importantly, though, Rodriguez's *Sin City* is a highly theoretical project—or, at the very least, it inspires a new approach to theory. As a hybrid narrative that emphasizes medium-continuity and similarity, *Sin City* challenges the narratological principle of medium-specificity. Rodriguez's *Sin City* ultimately begs that narratologists consider a more unified narratological approach. I will offer one framework to do so: a cognitive approach to a unified narratology of the multimodal using Allan Paivio's dual coding theory (DCT). Just as Rodriguez effects changes to his medium, so too does he effect change to the critical reception of that medium. Accordingly, we begin with a word on the complexity of *Sin City*'s hybridization.

The Hybrid Medium

Rodriguez's hybridized medium was not merely visual—not just an aesthetic spectacle, though these elements are apparent from the first few moments of the film. Rodriguez was careful to hybridize as much of the comic's offerings as he could—a particularly difficult feat for Rodriguez. His *Sin City* had to somehow translate the serialization of Frank Miller's *Sin City* into a Hollywood blockbuster feature film. Miller's *Sin City* saga spans seven volumes or "yarns"—each comprising anywhere from five to thirteen issues—which develop the narrative of a single character at a time. The volumes are stand-alone vignettes, cross-sections of a whole. Together, they tell a larger story of a diseased and etherized Basin City from Miller's noir-ed imagination. In this way, *Sin City* is both episodic and serial. On the one hand, the seven separate volumes could exist independently of one another as separate episodes, focalizing on different characters in the same storyworld—whose lives at times intersect—but, when viewed together, do not necessarily comprise a single narrative arc. On the other hand, each volume consists of a serialized narrative that develops over the course of several issues. Like traditional "pulp" comics from the mid–twentieth century (and, to be sure, most serialized literature in this century and otherwise), serialization met the demands of popular consumption and a fickle market. The segmentation of narrative into these marketable chunks actually allowed for a kind of story continuity, narrative complexity, and storyworld building that longer, single-volume formats did not. This, however, left Rodriguez in a difficult position: how could he translate the narrative effects of episodicity and serialization into the standard feature-film format?

Rodriguez's *Sin City* would deviate from Hollywood convention in this regard. Rodriguez would stray from the typical comics adaptation, one easily compressible narrative thread of a comics series. Rather than producing a film with a unified narrative arc that spans a manageable two-and-a-half hours, Rodriguez would transform the feature-length film into a series of shorts stitched together by a unifying aesthetic and storyworld. In so doing, he actually hybridized the serialization of comics with the narrative coherence of popular American cinema. Part of honoring the *Sin City* universe was bowing to the natural breaks and continuities in the original, serialized format. He did not, however, follow the standard comics form of serialization—a sequential segmentation, bound to one storyline at a time. Each issue of "That Yellow Bastard," for example, followed one after the other from February 1996 to July 1996, until that story ended and "Daddy's Little Girl" began. Rodriguez, instead, translated comics serialization into a variation on the cinematic form of polyphony. In this way, he could translate the formal peculiarities of comics serialization into the language of feature film. Inclusive of a star-studded ensemble cast, Rodriguez's *Sin City* would take on the cinematic characteristics of a portmanteau or composite film—for a mass audience, a slightly more palatable version of polyphony than a purely episodic film (like Krzysztof Kieślowski's art films *Three Colors: Red* or *The Double Life of Véronique*).

As a composite film, Rodriguez stitched together four separate "yarns" within the *Sin City* series: a short story called "The Customer Is Always Right" from Frank Miller's *The Babe Wore Red and Other Stories*, "That

Yellow Bastard," "The Hard Goodbye," and "The Big Fat Kill." With the exception of the opening segment "The Customer Is Always Right," the rest of the film interweaves segments of yarns in the story sequencing. After the opening credits comes the first part of "That Yellow Bastard," interrupted by "The Hard Goodbye" and "The Big Fat Kill." However, Rodriguez still maintains the hard stop of Miller's episodic yarns. "The Hard Goodbye" and "The Big Fat Kill" are presented in their entirety, as separate volumes. Prior to the continuation of "That Yellow Bastard," roughly two-thirds of the way through the film, audience expectations are bound by an episodic format. But as Hartigan is resurrected in a hospital bed, audience expectations transition into those bound by a frame narrative. What was a purely episodic film becomes a composite film. By suspending narrative completion in one yarn, the film maintains a facade of narrative coherence: as the audience anticipates the continuation of "That Yellow Bastard" yarn, the other encompassed yarns retain a quality of narrative importance. They transform from functionally independent episodes to satellite story events—developing thematic elements and story-world ambiance—for the frame narrative's story arc.

You will notice that I carefully excerpted from that argument the anomaly of "The Customer Is Always Right." At three-and-a-half minutes, this "aesthetic gem" and example of "painterly cinema," as Patrick Colm Hogan puts it in his chapter in this volume, acts as a lyrical prelude to the film immediately before the opening credits roll. It is the quietest, most seductive version of the *Sin City* aesthetic, and it entices. Originally produced as their proof-of-concept footage, Rodriguez and Quentin Tarantino collaborated on the production of "The Customer Is Always Right" before anyone else had jumped on board, Frank Miller included. As already discussed by Patrick Hogan earlier in this volume, it was a test shot, a pitch to Miller and A-list Hollywood actors to show them how they would formally approach a comic-book-to-film translation. If nothing came of it, then Tarantino and Miller planned to let it exist as a short film, independent of anything else. And, as Emily R. Anderson remarks in her chapter in this volume, the stand-alone short was an instant success.

Miller initially had no interest in turning his comic books into film and ignored every request and inquiry that came his way from Rodriguez—until the test shot. "In a lot of ways, this movie is quite literally like having a dream come true," noted Miller after seeing what Tarantino and Rodriguez had accomplished ("Behind the Scenes"). Because it was originally designed to stand on its own if need be, "The Customer Is Always Right" as a prelude cues the audience to expect episodic segmentation. As a result, the initial formal blueprint accustoms the audience to narrative co-herence based not on story, but on discourse—not on *what* is told, but on *how* it is told. However, that expectation is turned on its head when we return to a thread of "The Customer Is Always Right" in the last scene of the film. After escaping the ruthless firefight between the mob-allied mer-cenaries and the warrior-women prostitutes of Old Town, Becky—the turncoat prostitute, lynchpin to the climactic battle—walks down a hos-pital corridor, recovering from her injuries, ready to leave. As the doors of an elevator open, she is greeted by The Lady-Killer, the Assassin in the film's prelude. The dance of prey and predator, so carefully construed in the prelude—a brooding voice-over, an offering of a cigarette, a flash of iris, a knowing look—is recited again. Becky's fate is sealed.

Crucially, this narrative decision diverges from Frank Miller's original series—and it does so to highlight the hybridized nature of Rodriguez's *Sin City*. According to Miller's "The Big Fat Kill," Becky should have died in the massive gunfight. Rodriguez's decision to reintroduce "The Cus-tomer Is Always Right" in this way complicates the audience's original understanding of it as a prelude, as episodic in nature. When part two of "The Customer Is Always Right" weaves into the story of "The Big Fat Kill," it bridges paratext (any material outside the story proper such as a story or chapter title, an epigraph, or a prelude, for instance) with narra-tive proper. What was once a functionally independent prelude now trans-forms into a frame narrative that revises the entire narrative coherence of the rest of the film. It becomes a microcosm of Rodriguez's hybridized form of serialization. In bringing a serial form to film, Rodriguez's *Sin City* transgresses both the cinematic and comic notions of narrative co-herence. In this hybridized medium, no longer can a single episode stand alone, as it could have in a traditional comics format, but it must come into contact with the episodes of the storyworld around it. It must hint at cause and effect; standard Hollywood blockbusters usually determine narrative coherence on the basis of story events. If not, then a blockbuster film must have some other facade of unification—some thematic consider-ation that cleanly wraps the cinematic experience into something singular and definite.

The unexpected transformation of "The Customer Is Always Right" into a frame that is woven directly into another episode of the narrative does just that. It makes dependent what was originally independent; it links the disparate pieces and creates narrative unity. But it also demands that the audience reconsider narrative unity. If the film begins and ends here, then what are the real kernels (fundamental) and satellites (ancillary) of *Sin City*'s story events? If one can no longer identify the kernels and satellites in *Sin City*, is it a single coherent narrative? Rather than creating a cinematic experience of a coherent and whole narrative, then, Rodriguez's hybridized medium created a cinematic experience of a coherent and whole *storyworld*. Each episode builds Miller's *Sin City* universe. Yet, it does so in a way that mimics narrative coherence. Rodriguez's hybridized version of serialization in cinema challenges the audience to construct narrative coherence in the fleshing out of a narrative world. As one instance of Rodriguez's hybridization, this illuminates the productive differences inherent in Rodriguez's transformed medium.

To focus on Rodriguez's hybrid serialization techniques is to say nothing about the most obvious of Rodriguez's project—the most forcibly seen and heard, the issue of the visual, verbal, and auditory narrative tracks across the film and comics mediums, for example. Yet, I have hoped to show how Rodriguez's hybridized project works in less obvious ways, that his form of hybridization is more complex than what one might initially notice. These are certainly not the only sites rich for investigation. Consider, for example, the issue of audience empathy across mediums or the cognitive reconstruction of complex characters based on their caricatured representations.[1] All of these elements deserve extended treatments in their own right. Ultimately, however, I wish to argue that Rodriguez's project is most interesting not in *how* it hybridizes, but in *what* that hybridization does and, especially, in what it asks of narrative scholars. As such, I turn to the most productive of these narrative translations: the issue of multimodality.

Multimodality and Dual Coding Theory

Both comics and film are multimodal mediums—that is to say, both engage multiple sensory modalities and cognitive systems. This is certainly not a novel concept. The whole comics criticism coterie since Will Eisner and Scott McCloud have characterized this phenomenon as an interaction between "text" and "image"—or as Eisner explains it, the "successful cross-breeding of illustration and prose" (*Comics* 8). Film theorists like Peter Verstraten, on the other hand, describe the filmic medium not as engaging text and image but *sound* and image. In either case, both mediums are multiply coded on different narrative tracks, and theorists are deeply invested in the concurrence of these narrative tracks in pursuit of a medium-specific narratology. By "medium-specific narratology," I take my cue here from Noël Carroll, who defines "medium-specificity" as the fundamental formal property of an artistic production that is both constrained by and exploitative of the representational and expressive parameters of its medium (*Philosophy* 35–37). As such, the medium-specificity hypothesis posits a normative framework for evaluating art based on its adherence to and manipulation of those parameters. In an early formulation of medium-specificity, Carroll explains,

> Art forms should not overlap in their effects, nor should they imitate each other. . . . [E]ach art form is assumed to have some range of effects that it discharges best or uniquely as a result of the structure of its physical medium. Each art form should be limited to exploiting this range of effects, which the nature of the medium dictates. ("Specificity" 7)

This raises a number of issues for Rodriguez's *Sin City*, in which Rodriguez had hoped to "take cinema and . . . make it into this book" ("Behind the Scenes"). He was not concerned with the differences between the film and comics mediums, but their similarities: how to mimic the formal qualities of comics, how to minimize medium-specificity in the translation of one art form into another. According to Carroll, this kind of medium imitation could only fall flat in its failure to embrace the unique expressions available to its own medium. In truth, though, Rodriguez is on to something here. There is a degree of concordance between the medium-specificity of film and the medium-specificity of comics. That is, they are both multimodal mediums. Rodriguez is in some way exploring the broader opportunities available to the multimodal narrative. Consequently, while the study of medium-specific narratologies is productive and necessary to an extent, Rodriguez's *Sin City* begs us to consider the relationship between similar mediums and offer an umbrella narratology specific to multimodal narrative productions. The resulting narratological project more closely approaches the goals of a cognitive narratology—to explain all narrative in terms of its production by, effects on, and processing through cognition generally.

To develop a cognitive narratology for specifically multimodal narratives, I turn to DCT, a theory of cognition that assumes two functionally distinct mental systems—a verbal and a nonverbal system—that operate in tandem to receive, process, store, activate, and synthesize various kinds of information. DCT's ultimate goal is to explain our meaning-making processes in all situations, including—most pertinent to our purposes—the meaning making in literacy (Sadoski and Paivio). At its most basic formulation, we make meaning not through language alone, but through various stores of mental imaging that access nonverbal memories that are coded in our sensory capacities. One system is "verbal and abstract," retrieving abstract information and processing it through a sequential system of language. The other is "imagistic and concrete," soliciting sensory information and processing it synchronously through mental imaging (11). Of the competing theories of cognition circling academic discussions, DCT is especially suited to multimodal narratives because they exploit the rejoining of these two cognitive systems in an aesthetic experience.

Since its inception in the 1970s by Allan Paivio, DCT offered an alternative to common coding theories of cognition that assumed that all cognitive processes ran through a common, abstract, representational code of, for example, propositional representations or nested data sets.[2] DCT, on the other hand, is rooted in the understanding that all cognition is inherently *embodied* cognition and, as such, is unique in its positing of two subsystems that correspond with the embodied condition. According to theories of embodied cognition, cognitive processes are grounded in the indissociable human being—the integrated mind and body in relation to the external world.[3] DCT understands that cognition is both shaped by and filtered through embodiment and so considers the way in which external perception is connected to mental representation. First, external stimuli are received through sensory modalities (i.e., visual, auditory, olfactory, gustatory, haptic, and proprioceptive). They are then coded in memory via the verbal and nonverbal systems. As received information filters through each system according to its kind, it then undergoes a series of transformations in higher-order cognitive processes as the two systems process verbal and nonverbal information in tandem.

Indeed, it is often necessary for the two systems to work together in what is called "referential processing," or "the activation of the nonverbal system by the verbal system [and vice versa]" as is the case when one verbalizes images or names objects (Paivio, *Mental* 69). Early research into lexical retrieval demonstrated a processing advantage of concrete over abstract concepts—and, consequently, the nonverbal over the verbal system—because they activate more semantic content and involve mental imaging (James; Whaley; Rubin; West and Holcomb; Levy-Drori and Henik). For example, "concrete language that evokes sensory images (e.g., *stained glass window*) is better understood and recalled than abstract language that has less access to images (e.g., *theory of semiotics*)" (Sadoski 189). Further research has indicated that the activation of both systems simultaneously will significantly strengthen the functionality of higher order cognitive processing—not just lexical retrieval, but meaning making and memory as well (Paivio, "Dual Coding"; Paivio, *Mental*; Paivio, *Imagery*; Sadoski and Paivio; Welcome et al.; Kounios and Holcomb; Lwin, Morrin, and Krishna). The greater the amount of information received and the more options for information retrieval, the faster the processing.

Both comics and film, as multimodal mediums, may have similar effects on cognition. Because both vigorously engage the verbal and nonverbal systems simultaneously, they both presumably have a greater impact on cognitive processes like memory formation and meaning-making. What is unclear, thus far, is precisely what other higher order cognitive processes (if any) are similarly effected and to what end. Thus far, researchers investigating DCT have primarily concerned themselves with the effects of multimodality on learning tasks like memory recall and semantic processing; however, narrative art does not entail these processes alone, nor is it necessarily concerned with knowledge accumulation per se. Meaning making in narrative art fundamentally engages aesthetic response and affect. Comics and film critics alike have yet to tap into the theoretical offerings of DCT, nor have the proponents of DCT turned to literature and the arts to expand their ground. However, I think the cross-pollination of the two is a productive endeavor. On the one hand, then, literary theorists, take note: DCT can be a powerful apparatus to approach cognitive narratological questions of multimodality. On the other hand, cognitive scientists, take note: cognitive processing of multimodal *aesthetic* objects like comics and film can be a rich ground for empirically investigating aesthetic response in a DCT framework.

Independently construed medium-specific narratologies of film and comics have actually obscured the depths and complexities of their cognitive effects. An unfortunate result of this isolationism: each camp of theorists fixates on a single piece of the cognitive puzzle. Where one camp inadvertently privileges cognitive *processing*, the other privileges *coding*. However, a unified theory of multimodal cognition needs to consider both cognitive processing and coding. By cognitive *processing* I mean the activation of mental representations—those internal forms of information that register as memories and allow meaning making to occur—within and between mental structures. Coding is the way in which the external world is captured in mental representations. So, for example, if one sees a picture of a gun (as one might in *Sin City*), the initial image is coded visually by the black-and-white markings on the page and processed synchronously—different elements are processed in parallel, simultaneously, such as the organization of panels, the bulging eyes of a victim, the contrasting white marking of blood, and so on; however, if one reads, "The cop grabbed his gun," the initial stimuli is also coded visually (as written text) but processed *sequentially* (as language).

Comics narratologists demarcate narrative tracks on the basis of cognitive processes alone, disregarding how the stimuli are encoded. If the cardinal distinction is between "text" and "image" for comics narratologists, then they consider the only difference of import to be the one between the sequential processing of linguistic data versus the synchronous processing of nonlinguistic data. Yet, this demarcation in and of itself does not entirely hold, as illustrated above, for linguistic data in comics is first and foremost presented visually. Written language is encoded by nonlinguistic, visual stimuli—namely recognizable patterns of ink strokes against a background. In this, the narratological distinction between "text" and "image" does not adequately account for the coding of multimodal narrative building blocks.

Film narratologists like Verstraten, on the other hand, depend on the differences in information *coding* rather than processing to demarcate narrative tracks in their accounts of multimodality. This approach privileges the information received through and encoded in various sensory modalities—or, as Verstraten calls them, the *visual* and the *auditive* narrative tracks. He goes so far as to claim that "the narrator on the visual track is essentially deaf to all sounds, just as the narrator on the auditive track is blind to all visual influences" (7). The film narrator—or perhaps, more precisely, the *editive* narrator—brings the two together in a unified, aesthetic whole. I use the term "editive narrator," here, in part to emphasize not the content of the narrative track (as the terms "visual narrator" and "auditive narrator" do), nor the resultant medium (as the term "filmic narrator" would), but the *function* of the narrative track. The editive narrator is not additive—it does not generate material—as the visual and auditive narrators are, but synthetic. To describe this narrator as the "filmic narrator" would be to privilege it as the primary narrator in film and overshadow the generative aspects of the visual and auditive narrators. The visual narrator, auditive narrator, and editive narrator work together to create a unified whole. Considered in this way, Verstraten's formulation of a film narratology actually parallels quite closely the cognitive processes in DCT. Two functionally independent systems code narrative material according to sensory perceptions and are then synthesized by a referential processing system. The visual and auditive narrative tracks are akin to coding systems while the editive narrative track is akin to a processing system.

However, Verstraten's film narratology does not map as cleanly onto cognitive theory as it would seem. Remember that Verstraten demarcates narrative tracks on the basis of coding difference alone—that is, how material is coded in sensory modalities—and that *these codes* are functionally independent. Not so in DCT. According to DCT, sensory modalities work in tandem to code external stimuli in the verbal and nonverbal mental systems. These two systems are functionally independent, but the sensory modalities are not. Sensory stimuli, though received through different physiological and neurological pathways, are processed synchronously. So, for example, the visual modality is not processed independently of the auditory modality. When one watches a film, the sensory experience is received by each sensory modality and perceived holistically; the coded information then activates the verbal and nonverbal systems as necessary. The verbal system will process language—coded visually and/or auditively—sequentially, and the nonverbal system will process its information synchronously. While the traditional text–image or visual–auditive distinctions may be productive for certain narratological questions, they are not sufficient frameworks for considering the narratological effects of multimodal mediums in toto. The differences to which other narratologies cling simplify the coordinative and synthetic project of multimodality. Thus, the goal of a cognitive narratology for multimodal mediums is to account for both the sensory coding of various modalities in conjunction with its mental processing in the two subsystems.

Implementing a Cognitive Framework

Practically speaking, what does this mean for narratologists? A new framework may be interesting as an exercise in narrative theory, but without a meaningful application, it remains distended from the purview of literary scholarship. A cognitive narratological account should not just tell us something about the way in which we think, but the way in which a particular text works and the cognitive productions it elicits. What can a DCT-integrated narrative theory tell us about *Sin City* that these competing narratologies cannot?

On the one hand, their approaches create exceptional difference where there is only minimal. Take, for example, the prime issue of narrative concealment and overload—the careful selection of collapsible and constru-able details in any narrative mode, but especially the multimodal mode. It is an issue that must consider the entirety of narrative presentation, not a single narrative track. Even comics theorists find their initial distinctions between text and image unnecessarily binding on this issue, yet they're not quite sure how to navigate it logically and consistently. For example, in an analysis of Chris Ware's *Jimmy Corrigan: The Smartest Kid on Earth*—a graphic narrative not for want of visual and verbal detail (to the point of postmodern excess)—Georgiana Banita argues that the density of Ware's text is a result of "iconography and other descriptive devices and linkages that stabilize fictional reality." For her, an "excess of narrative connec-tivity" is marked primarily by the density of detail, visual or linguistic, and not necessarily in relation to the other or in its specific formal presentation (183). Douglas Wolk, on the other hand, writes, "If comics are 'a picto-graphic language,' as Ware says, then they're meant to be read *fast*. Domi-nated by simple shapes and 'dead,' fixed-width lines, Ware's pages zoom along, slowed down only by tricky diagrammatic layouts and occasional indigestible blocks of tiny type" (355). The focus, for Wolk, is on the se-quential nature of processing. The narrative becomes too dense only when the traditionally sequential nature of panels and language is obscured to the point of synchronicity—the panels, the page, and the text in excess are received as a whole. Wolk's language hints at the real density of the over-whelmed page—a much simpler explanation—that both the juxtaposition of text and image in this way overtaxes the visual sensory modality.

At base, narrative excess in a multimodal medium is an issue of modality-specific interference. According to Sadoski and Paivio, modality-specific interference is a phenomenon in which "[a]ttempting to perform two dif-ferent tasks in one modality causes a disruption in one or both of the tasks, but performing two tasks in separate modalities does not interfere" (44). Thus, we listen to music while on a run without much distraction because the two are coded in separate modalities: one is auditory, the other motor. Similarly, in a study conducted by Richard E. Mayer and Roxana Moreno, participants showed greater comprehension in multimedia presentations when different modalities were used—a visual depiction accompanying an auditive narration, for example. In the same study, however, in partici-pants who viewed a unimodal multimedia presentation—a visual depic-tion accompanied by a written explanation, for example—comprehension was significantly poorer. Mayer and Moreno conclude, "Given the limited resource students have for visual information processing [that is, limi-tations on working memory], using a visual modality to present both pictorial and verbal information can create an overload situation for the learner" (313). Consider the "cocktail-party effect": in a room of crowded people with animated discussions to your left and right, it is difficult to pay strict attention to one conversation and not another. Performing two auditory tasks simultaneously disrupts the processing in one or both instances. As Sadoski and Paivio note, the same thing happens to a simultaneous processing of visual cues: "silent reading (visual task) may be disrupted by experiencing related visual images (visual task) at the same time" (44).

The most effective formal elements of Frank Miller's *Sin City* are not necessarily his sequencing techniques or the juxtaposition of text and image, but his characteristic concealment of visual information. The signature Frank Miller aesthetic rests on minimalization and subtraction. Miller works with a two-toned palette—simply black and white. When he uses color, it is a single, flat color like the yellow associated with "That Yellow Bastard." He doesn't work with the highlights and shadows of a natural light—his is an impossibly lit surface. Black and white instead serve to highlight and obscure narrative details to an affective end. When text appears, if at all, it appears minimally in small panels as negatives of the image. I think here of the appearance of text in "That Yellow Bastard" just as Hartigan goes unconscious on the dock after having been shot by his partner—a scene that spans a full nine pages, but that is composed of only eleven panels and nine text boxes of a simple sentence each (51–59). Each page minimizes distraction so as not to overload the reader's working memory in its visual mode. The very next two-page spread is a silent sequence: the police arrive on the scene and rush Hartigan away to a hospital for emergency, life-saving surgery. Much of the action is obscured in Miller's highlights and shadows. Miller pares back all unnecessary visual detail, leaving only the bare bones of narrative progress and affect. Hollowed scrubs, dark faceless forms, surround what must be—but cannot be seen—a surgical table. A pair of forceps and a spurt of blood stain the panel with darkness. In that illusion of forms and action, Miller leaves plenty of room for his reader's gap-filling process to make sense of the scene. Miller's aesthetic choice to minimize visual distraction, here, elicits a cognitive response from the reader—one that, according to Mayer and Moreno, could more efficiently undergo referential processing and, as a result, attain a deeper level of comprehension. As such, the most purely Miller-esque panels and pages render a narrative reality that is minimally representational, yet incredibly affective. That isn't to say that all of Miller's panels achieve the same effect. There are many instances in which the noir genre competes with his pure aesthetic, and the narrative succumbs to drawn-out monologues, densely packed speech bubbles, and complex panel layouts that can overwhelm the visual modality quite easily.

This is one instance in which Rodriguez's filmic medium could counteract the cognitive limitations of the comics medium. Film, with its auditory track, can translate written text into spoken word, effectively dividing the workload of one sensory modality's working memory into the working memories of two sensory modalities. Some of the most successful scenes in Rodriguez's *Sin City* were those that translated the written speech of an interior monologue into a filmic voice-over. As the Mayer and Moreno study suggests, this formal choice allows for greater comprehension and referential processing—the key meaning-making processes. Rodriguez's filmic medium can attend to the real spirit of Frank Miller's aesthetic in certain ways that the comics medium would otherwise make difficult. Frank Miller's comic is a purifying aesthetic that subtracts only those necessary narrative and affective elements for a cleaner, more engaged cognitive appreciation. Where one medium's modality-specific interference can inhibit the goals of the aesthetic, another medium's options can realign those goals.

However, Rodriguez's own medium still presents cognitive difficulties. He now faces the problem of overloading the auditory sensory modality. The film's auditory track can be effectively split into three working parts: the spoken word, the soundtrack, and the sound effects. A soundtrack runs nearly continuously throughout the film. As such, it runs the risk of modality-specific interference, especially during scenes in which auditory stimuli is near excess. Take, for example, the scene in which "deadly little Miho," an Old Town prostitute, attacks Jack and his boys after their aggressive pursuit of one of Miho's Old Town sisters, Becky. The Miller aesthetic is subjugated to a Hollywood spectacle—the action-packed, manic stimuli of a fight scene that Rodriguez's audience expects. A deluge of sound effects—roaring thunder, spurting blood, whizzing blades, slashing swords, smashing glass, and more—coupled with a soundtrack of berserk staccatos and blasts, certainly incites a spectacle, yes, but also a staggering overload of the auditory modality. In these instances, Rodriguez is most challenged by the competing forces in his hybridized medium and aesthetic is subsumed by spectacle. However, it is clear that Rodriguez is aware of this danger and does take steps to minimize its effects. Ambient noises, for instance, are curiously left out of film production, and the result is three-fold. First, it minimizes the transmission of unnecessary storyworld elements to embody the spirit of the Miller aesthetic—a purifying and paring down of narrative excess. Second, it mimics the narrative constraints of the comics medium in a kind of environmental vacuum, a world closed off by panels, and silent. Third, it lessens the possibility of overloading the auditory modality with superfluous information. In this way, Rodriguez's hybridized medium must carefully balance not only the aesthetic of Miller's *Sin City*, but its cognitive effects.

Robert Rodriguez has inspired this turn towards a unified multimodal theory because of his insistence on—and success in translating—the similarities between multimodal mediums. His hybridized medium upsets the delicate balance of Carroll's medium-specificity hypothesis and begs us to reconsider the relationship between comics narratology and filmic narratology. Yet Rodriguez seems only to conceptualize his work in relation to its urtext—the graphic novels of *Sin City*—but it is an urtext in its own right as a provocative artistic production in its expression through a newly rendered medium. As such, Rodriguez's *Sin City* calls to be studied by a new narrative theory that can appreciate both its relationship to other multimodal mediums as well as its specific manifestation of multimodality. While DCT has its own limitations—not addressing, for example, affect, which is a crucial part of cognition and meaning making—it does offer a place for us to start.

Notes

1. For scholarship on character construction and audience empathy in the comics and film genres, see Aldama ("Characters"), Baker, Mikkonen, and Plantinga. See, especially, Suzanne Keen's work on narrative empathy (*Empathy and the Novel*) generally, and later applied specifically to the graphic narrative. For a cognitive perspective, see scholarship on mirror neurons, the "shared manifold" hypothesis, and intersubjectivity in Vittorio Gallese's work ("Action Recognition"); Gaut; Goldberg, Harel, and Malach; Hasson et al.; Mar and Oatley; and Zunshine ("Theory of Mind" and *Why We Read Fiction*), especially theory of mind and its literary and artistic applications.

2. See Allan Paivio's *Imagery and Verbal Processes* for the earliest formulation of DCT. When it emerged, it was a highly controversial theory but has since found credence in a number of empirical psychological studies on language-learning, memory formation, literacy, comprehension, and creativity. See, for example, Kounios and Holcomb; Levy-Drori and Henik; Lwin, Morrin, and Krishna; Paivio, "Dual Coding"; Paivio, *Imagery*; Paivio, *Mental*; Sadoski and Paivio; Welcome et al.; West and Holcomb; and Whaley.

3. Paivio's articulation of a DCT actually preceded formal acceptance of theories of embodied cognition as we now know them, though Paivio's premises were quite similar. Not until the 1990s when Francisco Varela, Evan Thompson, and Eleanor Rosch published *The Embodied Mind: Cognitive Science and Human Experience* would the embodied cognition movement be catalyzed in its proper form. For more on embodied cognition, see Antonio Damasio's *Descartes' Error: Emotion, Reason and the Human Brain*, which was the first major work to make embodied cognition accessible outside of the scientific community.

AESTHETIC AND ONTOLOGICAL BORDER CROSSINGS AND BORDERLANDS

CHAPTER 6

Intertextploitation and Post-Post-Latinidad in *Planet Terror*

CHRISTOPHER GONZÁLEZ

The ancient pyramid structure is symbolic of its engineering strength and ability to withstand the passage of centuries. In the Americas, as in other parts of the ancient world, these stone edifices are comprised of monolithic blocks weighing upwards of hundreds of tons each. Unsurprisingly, these structures have persisted into the modern period to become silent testaments to lost civilizations. In fact, it is difficult to hear mention of the Mayans or Aztecs without summoning to mind the familiar stepped pyramid shape, just as one does when the ancient Egyptian civilization is referenced. Indeed, the pre-Columbian pyramid looms large in the imagination of America's past and is among the iconography often adopted by Latinos in the United States to signal pride and identity—a visual connection to the mythical Aztlán. In other terms, the pre-Columbian pyramid such as the iconic Pyramid of Kukulcan, as a symbol, unambiguously hearkens back to the indigeneity of Latinos in the Americas by authorizing and legitimating their presence in a nation that has existed a little more than two hundred years—relatively puny when one considers the Pyramid of Kukulcan was nearly a thousand years old when the Founding Fathers signed the Declaration of Independence.

Understandably, the familiar Mesoamerican pyramid is, quite literally, the last image one expects to find at the end of Robert Rodriguez's B-flick homage to exploitation cinema, *Planet Terror* (2007). After nearly ninety minutes of government military conspiracies, zombie terror, and exploitation cinematic gore, the ancient Mayan ruins of Tulum, flanked by stunningly beautiful beaches, appear on-screen as the survivors make it their place of defense. Rodriguez's use of the Tulum, Mexico, site dynamically alters the sensibility of the film, complicating the audience's sense of Latinidad[1] by contributing to his withholding stereotypical depictions of Latinos and Latino/a culture. Instead, Rodriguez creates a cinematic storyworld where issues of Latinidad seemingly fall to quiescence in favor of the more familiar tropes of the zombie B-flick that appear to be the overt impetus for his *Grindhouse* collaboration with fellow director Quentin Tarantino. The inclusion of the final migration to Tulum scene compels the audience to reevaluate the film entirely and calls into question Rodriguez's subversive use of Latino identity markers.

In this chapter, I argue that Rodriguez uses the B-flick aesthetic to suggest a way out of stale, cookie-cutter depictions of Latinidad in cinema. Just as he has done in the majority of his films, Rodriguez embraces a method of storytelling and cinema direction/production that always seeks to engage Latinidad in unexpected ways as opposed to the stereotype—often inverting stereotypes on their heads—resulting in his own brand of the Latino aesthetic, what I call "post-post-Latinidad." As an example of this, Rodriguez uses the zombie narrative as a means of creating an innovative commentary on the troubled issue of illegal immigration. As a Texas-based filmmaker, Rodriguez often overtly deals with issues of immigration and Latinidad in the United States within his films such as *Machete*. Additionally, Rodriguez typically appropriates many genres—especially the speculative genres—as vehicles for his films. His films often intertextually overlap in interesting ways, creating intriguing inroads for thematics that connect his seemingly disparate films. Ultimately, Rodriguez uses the zombie genre to comment satirically on real life-or-death situations and material realities that compel people to cross human-made borders at all. Rodriguez, I maintain, makes this most stringent commentary in his film *Planet Terror*.

Machete and Rodriguez Intertextploitation

Though *Planet Terror* presents itself as a zombie B-flick, Rodriguez infuses this film (as with many of his films) with Latino actors and markers of Latinidad in a subversive way. Rodriguez himself, in an interview with Charles Ramírez Berg, talks about his desire to avoid overt markers of Latinidad in his films:

CRB: So in your case, you'll be true to your experience, and if you're true to your experience, your ethnicity will come out.

RR: Yeah, it's going to come out naturally. Rather than forcing it. I think that one of the problems is that when Latin filmmakers get that chance to make a film, they try to do too much, and make up for all the movies that were never made before. And then it becomes too preachy. You can be much more subversive, you can be much more sly than that, and get everything you want in there. If you're just conscientious about it and try to trick people by getting them to watch something entertaining and show them something else at the same time. Slip it in the genre. (Ramírez Berg, *Latino Images* 255)

Here, Rodriguez admits to "slipping" things into his films that unambiguously invite commentary on certain issues of ethnicity—in this case, Latinidad. For example, *Planet Terror* is preceded by a "fake" trailer for the film *Machete*, and though Rodriguez's film that bears that name would not be made for another three years, the trailer provides an important lens for viewing *Planet Terror* as a commentary on immigration, as well as for coming to terms with the final scene at the Mayan ruins of Tulum. In fact, it is useful to think of the *Machete* trailer as the opening scene for *Planet Terror*. While the Machete character is himself based on any number of 1970s vigilante figures—specifically those played by Charles Bronson in films such as *Death Wish* and *Mr. Majestyk*—it is what Jeff Fahey's character Michael Booth says to Machete that is salient here, for it informs part of my analysis: "As you may know, illegal aliens such as yourself are being forced out of our country at an alarming rate. For the good of both our people, our new senator must die." The issues of "aliens" and "being forced out of our country" are foregrounded in both *Machete* and *Planet Terror*, and as the *Machete* trailer serves as a sort of introduction for *Planet Terror*, we can view the film as a commentary on the politics of immigration without overtly being about immigration.

Most important of all is how Rodriguez manages to make smart commentary on salient Latino issues while staying away from typical, heavy-handed engagements with Latinidad. That is not to say that narratives (both in film and in print) that deal with obvious tokens of Latinidad cannot be well rendered. Chris Weitz's 2011 film *A Better Life* received high critical acclaim, dealing unambiguously with the Mexican immigrant trope. Demián Bichir's character does work as a gardener—a stock and stereotypical Chicano character to be sure. Similarly, in Héctor Tobar's well-received 2011 novel *The Barbarian Nurseries*, Latinidad is practically everywhere: in the ancestry of its characters, in the city in which it is set (Los Angeles), in the hired help (another gardener and a maid), and so on. These two recent examples of how Latinidad is used in the design of their narratives work to a large extent because they reframe signs and icons that have come to be expected of and associated with Latinos in the United States rather than reuse such stereotypical material in the lazy, shorthand fashion that is often seen whenever Latinos are invoked in media and advertising. We have seen the fruition of rich and complex representations of Latinos signaled in Ramírez Berg's work cited above as well as Chon A. Noriega and Ana M. López's edited collection *The Ethnic Eye: Latino Media Arts* (1996). As Noriega and López state in their introduction:

[H]ow do we acknowledge the desire of many of the media artists themselves to occupy those generic registers usually precluded by a body identification—that is, the default arenas of nation, medium, and mode within which all media artists operate? There are, after all, filmmakers and *Latino* filmmakers, just as there are women video artists and *Latina* women video artists, and gay and lesbian documentary filmmakers and *Latino* gay and lesbian documentary filmmakers. In each instance, these distinctions have practical consequences, determining how and to what extent the *Latino* media artist enters into competition for festivals, grants, fellowships, and so on. (x)

In the intervening years since Noriega and López's collection, there has been an explosion of Latinos in media that has continued to complicate this issue of how Latinidad is depicted and used in media, and particularly, narrative fiction and film.

But Rodriguez is no stranger to rearticulating and repositioning stereotypical material. He has done so in films such as *Desperado* and *Machete*. Yet more interesting is when he creates a film that eschews overt markers of Latinidad and instead uses a handful of decisive signs of Latinidad in specific moments in his cinematic storyworlds. By withholding such markers of so-called Latino identity in a film about, say, zombies, Rodriguez presents his audience with an unexpected reframing of Latino issues, leading viewers to reconsider such issues in a new light. And one of Rodriguez's methods of achieving this effect is to have elements from his cinematic storyworlds overlap upon one another, so that there is a cumulative intertextual effect when viewing his films—or in the case of Rodriguez, what I call "intertextploitation."

Exploitation films are a rich tradition in both American and European cinema, as they characteristically unify genre with low-budget aesthetics. These films rely on or exploit particular kinds of subject matter, such as violence, in an effort to garner an audience. They follow specific tropes and formulas that often meet with audience expectation and approval.

Slasher films, biker films, sexploitation films, and blaxploitation films are all types of exploitation films. Both zombie films and blaxploitation films dominated 1970s exploitation cinema, as Glenn Kay notes. In *Zombie Movies: The Ultimate Guide*, Kay writes,

> For instance, the decade saw the emergence of the black exploitation, or blaxploitation, film, which tackled such issues as racism and urban crime with uncommon directness—if not subtlety. The blaxploitation movement began with the modestly budgeted smash hit *Shaft* (1971). It featured Richard Roundtree as an outspoken (and quite witty) black detective who fights the white Mafia and other forces suppressing his urban community. It wasn't long before the formula was mixed with popular horror elements in films such as *Blacula* (1972), *Blackenstein* (1973), and *Scream Blacula Scream* (1973). Zombie blaxploitation efforts quickly followed. (59)

Thus, blaxploitation films, while being steeped in low-budget aesthetics and production values, also took sociopolitical issues head on and without apology.

But Rodriguez does not merely produce an homage to exploitation cinema in *Planet Terror*. Rather than exploit the genre or specific issues as was done in the past, he exploits *himself*. That is to say, the intertextploitation I identify occurs at the level of filmic aesthetic (i.e., low budget) as well as Rodriguez's own body of films, as well as those of Quentin Tarantino (and Tarantino himself!). Actors, characters, props, and so on Rodriguez has used in earlier films also make appearances in *Planet Terror* and work to extend and enrich the storyworld beyond the bounds of the film proper, rewarding a constant viewer of Rodriguez's films. Moreover, though Tarantino revels in a similar world-bridging activity in his many films (think of the Vega brothers played by Michael Madsen and John Travolta in *Reservoir Dogs* [1992] and *Pulp Fiction* [1994], respectively), he does not incorporate a sociopolitical ingredient to the extent Rodriguez does, the exception to this being Tarantino's much-ballyhooed film of 2012, *Django Unchained*. So, not only does Rodriguez's level of intertextuality work horizontally across genres, he also works vertically within his own oeuvre.

Generally speaking, the heightened intertextuality of Rodriguez's films creates a type of "insider knowledge" that cues certain audiences for a richer experience—those viewers who, for instance, are familiar with blaxploitation films, zombie movies, or immigrant narratives. In effect, Rodriguez relies on this prior experience the audience may have with these inter-texts by often subverting audience expectations or re-presenting them in a new way. For example, *Machete* makes use of the trope of the illegal bor-der crosser who only wishes to unobtrusively make a living wage in the United States. Cary Fukunaga's *Sin Nombre* (2009) and Weitz's *A Better Life* are examples of exactly this type of immigrant narrative. Rodri-guez, on the other hand, deviates from this narrative by having a Charles Bronson-type vigilante who poses as a day laborer but is actually a Mexi-can *federale* code-named "Machete." *Machete* also works with audience ex-pectations of blaxploitation films, as Rodriguez creates his Latino version of such films. Rodriguez, and Tarantino as well, are both very mindful of the intertexts they invoke and understand how valuable audience famil-iarity and experience with these intertexts can be for their own films.

In addition, Rodriguez uses some of the same actors in both films, as well as similar set pieces—such as the sexy-woman-with-huge-gun figure, the quiet-outsider protagonist, the actor Jeff Fahey, and so on. Though the storyworld of *Machete* appears not to be that of *Planet Terror*, there is a transworld feel about them both, as if they exist in the same universe. Brian McHale describes this phenomenon of "transworld identity" in *Postmod-ernist Fiction*, where characters that belong to "different fictional worlds" are brought together, resulting in an "intertextual boundary-violation" (17).[2] For viewers familiar with Rodriguez's oeuvre, these intertextual mo-ments resonate in significant ways. The result is that many of Rodriguez's films seem to overlap, ontologically speaking. One cannot help but see the antagonism between respective groups in both films. Indeed, in *Machete*, Senator John McLaughlin (played by Robert De Niro) calls the immigrants "terrorists," a word that clearly relates to a film with the title *Planet Terror*.

In *Planet Terror*, the zombies are a product of governmental experi-mentation and scientific hubris, and the film accordingly owes a huge debt to the zombie and science fiction genres and relies heavily on intertexts such as Dan O'Bannon's *The Return of the Living Dead* (1985). Conversely, the "illegals" in *Machete* ultimately rise up in revolution to become an as-similating, zombie-like force in their own right. Churning these waves of revolution is Machete—a Bronson-esque badass who turns out to be a Minuteman's worst nightmare. Rodriguez's intertexts even extend be-yond fiction. Audiences aware of the so-called "Minuteman Project," whose members take it upon themselves to patrol the U.S.-Mexico bor-der, will see it reflected in a scene from *Machete* where a member of a fictional version of the Minutemen shoots and kills a family of border-crossers, one of whom is a pregnant woman. Audience familiarity with these intertexts allows Rodriguez access to an already activated emotional response to this issue as well as providing him with a larger canvas upon which to detail his satirical take on immigration. *Planet Terror* rides high on the wave of intertextploitation.

Recasting the Zombie Narrative

Rodriguez's approach to immigration in *Planet Terror* can be contextualized by reviewing a few conventions of the zombie film genre. In a typical zombie narrative, the viewer is carefully guided to empathize with those characters that struggle to survive, even those characters that may be reprehensible or downright unlikable. In fact, this artificial social dynamic is partly responsible for the dramatic tension in zombie films. In George A. Romero's *Night of the Living Dead*, a black man and a white woman must come together in their desperate attempt to survive. To have a black man and a white woman rely on one another in a film released in 1968 was certainly controversial for contemporary audiences. Even in more recent zombie narratives—such as the AMC series *The Walking Dead*—there is still a tradition of bringing survivors from disparate social groups together so that they must depend on one another.

In season one of the AMC show, there is a white supremacist and an African American among the group of survivors. Tension arises almost immediately when the two must work as a unit. Here, despite the disdain any sensible viewer has towards the white supremacist, there is a moment when the character finds himself alone, handcuffed to a pipe on a rooftop. He may be a dislikable character, but he is still human. Thus, the creators of *The Walking Dead* play with the tension the audience feels in this scene. Zombies are the built-in antagonists, but in this scene audiences are torn. As zombies are generally blank slates with no affect, audiences may empathize with a human character, even if he is despicable.[3] Because of the ubiquity of the zombie genre in popular culture, there is already a firmly established identification that audiences have with nonzombie characters. In fact, this willingness to identify with a character creates tension within an audience, just as it does amongst the characters that are united of purpose but may not trust one another. But more importantly, as Gerry Canavan notes,

> Zombie apocalypses, like imperialistic narratives of alien invasion, repackage the violence of colonial race war in a form that is ideologically

safer. Zombie films depict total, unrestrained violence against absolute Others whose very existence is seen as anathema to our own, Others who are in essence living death. (439)

In essence, zombies function as a near-automatic Other that cannot be dealt with reasonably. As a result, members of widely divergent social groups must coalesce around a common purpose, even when those group members would otherwise avoid one another.

Thus, as a standard, we often identify with the protagonist of the zombie narrative while seeing the zombie as Other. Consequently, audiences generally want the protagonists to survive the zombie apocalypse, and the struggle for survival is what drives the narrative progression. In zombie films we crave homeostasis of the storyworld despite knowing it will be denied; zombie narratives function like a Pandora's Box, with no return to the world as it was before the box was opened.[4] There are typically two reasons for this characteristic of a zombie film: either there are just too many zombies to contend with and they overwhelm the world, or the thing that generated the zombies in the first place (say, top-secret biochemical agents) is still out there to begin the zombie apocalypse anew.

Rodriguez makes use of these prototypical elements of zombie narratives and weds them to another genre of American cinema, the exploitation B-flick of the 1960s and 1970s. But *Planet Terror* takes a step beyond simply being a "knockoff" or homage to this brand of gratuitous violence and schlock by carefully bringing together contesting aesthetics and expectations of audience. Such mixed forms unite, for example, horror and humor, which results in the film's being somewhat uncategorizable. For instance, O'Bannon's *The Return of the Living Dead* is a clear progenitor to *Planet Terror*. In O'Bannon's film, a military canister is opened, releasing a gas that is capable of reanimating corpses. And like *Planet Terror*, *The Return of the Living Dead* is steeped in dark humor and slapstick comedy. Likewise, both films were panned by most critics and performed poorly at the box office. This mix of genres and cinematic traditions, however, may be related to the cold reception by moviegoers and critics, though both films have a healthy cult following.

It seems that *Planet Terror* had an onerous task from its inception. On the one hand Rodriguez seemed to be doing nothing more than imitating a type of film rather than doing something creative within that tradition; it is often the case that films or literature "in the style of" bygone directors or authors are typically disparaged because they often do nothing more than simulate something already created. On the other hand, Rodriguez, like O'Bannon and others, challenged audiences to recognize the creative outcome of bringing together a multiplicity of genres and styles in *Planet Terror*. Thus, Rodriguez's film seemed like a cheap imitation or a strange mash-up of discrete cinematic traditions.

Mixed Forms

Planet Terror falls partially in the horror genre, but it also makes strong use of dark comedy throughout the film. This of course follows a rich tradition in film and literature of blending what seem to be antipodal emotions: amusement and horror.[5] Noël Carroll encapsulates the counterintuitive pairing of horror and humor this way:

> There is some intimate relation of affinity between horror and humor. . . . it appears that these two mental states—being horrified and being comically amused—could not be more different. Horror, in some sense, oppresses; comedy liberates. Horror turns the screw, comedy releases it. Comedy elates; horror stimulates depression, paranoia, and dread. (146–147)

Rodriguez's film revels in its gore, just as the exploitation films of the 1970s were apt to do. One brief example from the film will serve to illustrate the point.

Dr. Dakota Block (Marley Shelton) has been discovered in a lesbian affair by her husband, Dr. William Block (Josh Brolin). He is enraged and menaces her with a set of hypodermic needles, aping Dakota's own routine for administering a series of three color-coded, anesthetizing shots. But this time Dakota is at the other end of her own needles, and she puts her hands up to protect her face. Her husband jabs the needles into her hands, anesthetizing them in the process. Just at the moment when the audience is led to believe William will murder Dakota, the scene is interrupted by a nurse who breaks into the small room to report the hospital is under siege. This scene simultaneously relies on the apprehension that William may murder Dakota at any moment, but also the slapstick absurdity of having one's hands completely numbed. Later, as Dakota flees the hospital as it is overrun by the undead, her attempts to open her car door with her numbed hands are farcical. The humor of the scene, however, is immediately undone when Dakota slips her hand into the door handle and subsequently slips to the ground, gruesomely breaking her

wrist in the process. Despite such repeated juxtapositions of slapstick humor and exploitative horror, no one will mistake *Planet Terror* for a comedy. It is, above all else, an homage to splatter films that occasionally uses
outrageous comedic situations.

"Horror films," as Fred Botting notes,

> deal primarily in the production of extreme affects, affects evoked by
> taboos, shocks, suspense, and violence, by the promise and delivery of
> blood and gore, by repulsive eviscerations, decapitations, and destruc-
> tions of bodies on screen and calibrated through an array of special and
> technical effects, to assault the eyes and sensibilities of spectators before
> the screen. (180)

This idea of "extreme affects" is manifest in Rodriguez's willingness to
depict the horrific with slapstick humor. Thus, by using the zombie narrative within the horror genre, coupled with gritty humor, Rodriguez has
selected the perfect filmic combination to engage his audience's emotions,
a significant point that has specific consequences as it relates to larger
issues of immigration and Latinidad in the United States in *Planet Terror*,
as I argue in this chapter.

The juxtaposition of a zombie apocalypse with the issue of illegal immigration seems even more unlikely than the juxtaposition of humor and
horror. In fact, however, the idea of the zombie and the illegal immigrant
as being linked is one that has been explored before, such as when Jon
Stratton maintains that

> excluded from the rights and privileges of the modern state, those dis-
> placed people are positioned legally as bare life; and that in this legal
> limbo, these people can be treated in a way that enables them to be-
> come associated with a condition mythically exemplified in the zombie.
> The consequence is that not only can the zombie texts of films and other
> media be read as reproducing this connection, drawing on present-day
> anxieties to increase the terror produced by these texts, but displaced
> people are characterized using the same terminology that describes the
> threat that zombies generate in zombie apocalypse texts. (267)

Yet in *Planet Terror*, the zombies are not simply metonyms for illegal immigrants. Rather, Rodriguez ingeniously subverts the archetypical zombie trope of defending a small space by having his survivor group—a
group the audience is cued to identify with—leave their nation by cross-

ing a border because their lives depend on it. In essence, it allows the audience to simulate crossing a border in order to actuate a survival plan. Ultimately, despite its trappings of the B-flick, *Planet Terror* is actually a stringent commentary on the nature of being Latino in the United States.

Zombie Nationalism

In choosing a genre made prominent by Romero, Rodriguez understands the political valences available to him in the genre's ability to reflect difficult contemporary issues such as racism, capitalism, consumerism, unabated military power, and immigration. For example, Botting notes that

> George Romero's deployment of the zombie in his politically calibrated series of movies spanning five decades remains attuned to the shock effects of mass culture and media. His first, *Night of the Living Dead*, offers a zombie reading of a United States negotiating the Vietnam War, the Civil Rights movement, and the Space Race potlatch against Communism. (183)

To be sure, Rodriguez establishes the idea of "alien" bodies being forced out of the country before the beginning of *Planet Terror* proper via the *Machete* trailer. When considering the final scene of the film, however, the idea of being forced out of the country takes on a new meaning. I will come to the final scene momentarily. But before I do, I would like to introduce one more link between the two films.

Each film takes place in Texas: a border state with a high-profile governor, a rebellious spirit, and a frontier attitude toward the challenges it faces. Texas is a centerpiece in discussions of illegal immigration, the driving force both in *Machete* and in *Planet Terror*, which examine the possibility that some people could find life so intolerable at home that they would have no choice but to leave the country of their birth. Putting it differently, *Planet Terror* asks: what could force a group of Texans—whose pride is rooted in their history of independence and the state's onetime status as an independent republic (represented in the state's flag as a "Lone Star")—to cross their own southern border into the safety of Mexico? If we view Rodriguez's film through the lens of immigration and the question of illegality, we see that *Planet Terror* is an intriguing commentary on one of the most volatile issues of our time.

Indeed, Rodriguez uses the trope of illegal immigration and turns it on its head in the guise of a zombie narrative. Issues of Latino immigration and forces of assimilation creatively play out in *Planet Terror*. While on the surface the film plays as a B-genre flick, it actually textures the tensions that arise when two communities—"alien" and human—come together. In *Planet Terror* the proliferating "alien," or zombie, group—the result of military science gone horribly wrong—causes panic and fear among the small-town inhabitants, a fear driven by the "alien" culture. In this reversal of the assimilation narrative that was so popular in the early twentieth century—one where the immigrant works through hardship to become a success in a new land and ultimately assimilates by marrying a local girl and raising a family—Rodriguez models a *fear* of assimilation into the alien culture through specific aural and visual devices to trigger the audience's emotive—even empathetic—response to the townsfolk. This is a long-established convention of horror films generally, and zombie films specifically. The audience, despite racial, cultural, political, national, or linguistic differences with specific characters, will consistently gravitate to the nonzombie group. (There have as yet been few easy-to-identify-with zombie characters or first-person zombie narratives.) Rodriguez uses this convention to encourage audiences to align themselves with the non-zombie group in his film, which has significant ramifications given the immigration subtext of *Planet Terror*.

Rodriguez later reverses the assimilatory forces in *Machete*, where the immigrant community rises up to become the dominant group, forcing the Anglo-as-Other to assimilate. Though *Machete* is not the primary focus of this chapter, it does bear some mention in this examination of *Planet Terror* as a satirical comment on current policy on immigration. It is important to note that Rodriguez deploys a heightened sense of what I call "Rodriguez-intertextuality" (the thick cross-referencing between his films) that itself creates an assimilatory flow from audience out-group to a Rodriguez-intertextual in-group—a flow that he rewards in the experience of watching his films cumulatively. The net effect is that Rodriguez's creative couching of the so-called "Latino question" at the level of form and content in *Planet Terror* urges viewers to reframe the current political debate on immigration. More importantly, Rodriguez reframes audience understanding not only of immigration, but of Latinidad—and how Latinos are used and portrayed in film. Rather than make these important issues the centerpiece of *Planet Terror* (as he does in *Machete*), Rodriguez concentrates on the fluid nature of relationships in small social groups where hierarchies of identity come to the fore.

Identity in *Planet Terror*

Whether or not a cast of characters in a zombie narrative will survive depends on how well they can function as a unit. This is why an already-established group—a military unit, for example—never forms the entire cast of a zombie film; there must be doubt that the group will continue to cohere through the various challenges posed by the zombies. Enrique García's chapter "*Planet Terror* Redux: Miscegenation and Family Apocalypse" in this collection describes the group cohesion in *Planet Terror* as a family structure, arguing persuasively that

> the film's contribution to the zombie genre is in that it portrays the collapse and rebirth of the American family as occurring through racial miscegenation outside traditional social structures, an idea suggested in other zombie films but never explicitly visualized for the screen.

My attention, however, lies in the fluid nature of identities within the newly formed group in the face of the zombie outbreak.

Yet while differences are always present in an in-group—enabling the narrative to explore group dynamics against a common enemy—identity categories are prioritized depending on social situations. Patrick Colm Hogan discusses identity hierarchies in *Understanding Nationalism* in terms of five parameters. The parameter mentioned by Hogan that is most applicable to my analysis is that of "opposability," defined as "(1) polarization or near polarization of in-group and out-group and (2) categorial unification of the in-group, and to a lesser extent, categorial unification of the out-group" (80). In short, opposability is another way of thinking about how easily groups are able to adopt an "us versus them" view from the in-group. It is akin to concentrating actions and efforts against a common enemy.

In *Planet Terror*, the range of socioeconomic strata represented among the survivors takes precedence over the cohesion of the group in the face of the zombie assault, which heightens the tension between the survivors. Rodriguez uses this commonplace of the zombie genre to great comedic effect. Protagonists Cherry Darling and El Wray (Freddy Rodríguez), having once walked out on one another, are thrust together because of the zombie event. Dr. Dakota Block, forced to seek help from her estranged father, is only allowed to enter his house after he disgustedly concludes that he has no choice. Sheriff Hague (Michael Biehn) and J. T. (Jeff

Fahey), brothers whose tense relationship is strained by J. T.'s refusal to reveal his secret techniques for cooking award-winning barbeque, are united in their fight against the zombie horde. The rupture in their relationship is healed only when both are dying from gunshot wounds, and, as an act of brotherly love and kindness, J. T. begins to explain his cooking process, which an eager Sheriff Hague jots in his memo pad.

Two relationships in the film in particular demonstrate how the "us" versus "them" binary present within the social dynamic of zombie narratives functions. (For a more general discussion of the us/them dichotomy with Latino representations, see Ramírez Berg's *Latino Images in Film*.) Though the specifics are never actually revealed (Rodriguez keeps many plot points hidden in *Planet Terror*), there is a backstory that has created distrust between Sheriff Hague and El Wray. This is exactly the type of moment when a racial or ethnic prejudice would manifest in many narratives. However, despite this expectation, Sheriff Hague has *other* reasons to distrust El Wray—reasons that don't have anything to do with his Latinidad. When the two characters encounter each other for the first time in the film (though it is not the first time they have met), Hague cannot bring himself to trust El Wray. His determination to keep El Wray from having a gun is a running gag for most of the film. Once Hague learns El Wray's true identity as a significant military or law enforcement agent (a moment that is literally cut out of the film via a deliberately "missing reel"), Hague tells the rest of the group concerning El Wray: "Give him the guns. Give him all the guns." Despite all prior differences, Sheriff Hague finally understands that he and El Wray are members of the same group. But more significant is the fact that Rodriguez does not fall for the easy lawman versus ethnic other trope so common in American cinema. El Wray's Latinidad is evident, and yet it isn't.

On the other hand, there are William and Dakota Block. Married with problems (which lead to his murder attempt), their relationship seems doomed when Tammy is brought into the Emergency Room, dead as a result of a zombie attack: "It's a no-brainer," a nurse jokes as Tammy is revealed to be missing her brain. William, now understanding the betrayal of his adulterous wife, confronts her with murderous intent. As their relationship seems irreparable, it fits the zombie-film trope to have one of them become one of the undead, and there is little surprise when William "dies" at the hands of his own father-in-law and becomes a zombified Other. So, while members of the nonzombie group can ultimately overcome other important differences, identity categories that unite members of the group are rendered meaningless when zombification occurs due to opposability.

In fact, *Planet Terror* uses a Russian doll structuring of identity—smaller identity categories located within larger ones. Each of the major characters carries on in a way that has isolated them from their most salient group. Cherry is a go-go dancer who longs to be a stand-up comedian; Dr. Dakota Block is married to a man but longs to be with her lover, Tammy; El Wray, apparently a retired member of a law enforcement or military organization, is isolated and treated as an ex-convict for most of the film. Each of these characters, through the imposition of the zombie force, must cohere with the others to form a new in-group. As the characters come together, Rodriguez structures the film so as to allow audience movement into the new in-group along with the characters. The result is affinity for, and identification with, these disparate on-screen personalities. The audience is then aligned to identify with the same goals as the group on-screen. Beyond simply surviving to see the next day, the superordinate goal of the survivors in *Planet Terror* is voiced by El Wray to Cherry Darling: to move from Texas (the center of the zombie outbreak) to Mexico, with, as he says, "the ocean at your back" and thus in a defensible position. The film's final scene shows the group, grown larger as they find others seeking safety in numbers, on a Mexican coastline with the easily identifiable, iconic pre-Columbian pyramids and ruins of Tulum.

This final scene of migration is perhaps the most striking moment in the entire film. One way of thinking about its value and contribution to *Planet Terror* is to imagine the film without the survivors at Tulum. Narrative closure is still achievable without the final scene if Rodriguez had chosen to depict the survivors leaving Texas. The characters have survived the night (generally the ultimate short-term goal of a zombie film), and thus the fact that they have made it to see another sunrise is closure enough for the type of film Rodriguez has crafted—*if* his aim is to create a B-flick zombie film.

Clearly, though, Rodriguez does not simply want the survivors of the zombie outbreak just to make it to the next day. Instead, he caps his film with unambiguous markers of Latino identity. For example, as Cherry Darling leads her fellow survivors into Mexico, she is a reimagined and irreverent *Virgen de Guadalupe*, a powerful madonna for her people. Indeed, one notes the ironic humor in her name: "cherry" euphemistically connotes "virginity." Though the women in *Planet Terror* are often used as evidence of misogyny in the film, it is not insignificant that not only do both Cherry Darling and Dakota Block survive the zombie outbreak, they become leaders among the survivors.

However, it is the Mayan ruins of Tulum that serve as the most iconic aspect of *Planet Terror*'s ending. Again, we turn to El Wray's idea of traveling south to Mexico as a means of self-preservation. El Wray, the ambiguously identified Latino and tragic hero that he is, articulates the plan in the first place, though he will never see his plan come to fruition. Of all of the places of refuge, his instinct leads him to the ancestral home of many Latinos, signified by the monolithic structures at Tulum. In practical terms, Tulum historically served as a military outpost positioned against the Pacific Ocean. Not only does Tulum signal a place of refuge for *Planet Terror*'s "immigrant" characters, it is a symbolic return to the Mesoamerican roots of many Latinos in the United States.

This outcome illustrates the different tack Rodriguez takes in concluding his zombie narrative. Stratton has theorized how Romero's pioneering zombie films explore their connections to illegal immigration:

> The trope of a group of humans defending a space from threatening zombies has become a common theme in zombie apocalypse texts, and it is now even more open to be read in terms of the threat considered to be posed by illegal immigrants than in Romero's first film. In Romero's fourth zombie film *Land of the Dead*, released in 2005, the parallel between the zombie siege of Pittsburgh and the fear over illegal entry to the USA across the Mexican border is easily made. (274)

In his final scene in *Planet Terror*, however, Rodriguez has his survivor group migrate across a border to defend a position in Mexico, making any American-made zombies the trespassers of a new promised land. Indeed, this scene at Tulum complements the fake *Machete* trailer at the beginning, creating a significant frame for viewing *Planet Terror*. Rodriguez has satirized the fear of an alien presence manifested as an easily identifiable zombie Other—a group that has the ability to elide differences among groups who would otherwise not be members of the same social groups. It is a strong critique of nationalism that depicts a solution that rests in completely eradicating the other group: zombies and human Others alike are purged from the landscape.

What ultimately makes the final scene so powerful is the very fact that the survivors must move south into Mexico. Here Rodriguez takes a problematic issue for both nations and recasts it as the solution of his film. In order to survive, the group must cross into Mexico, as an untold number of Mexicans must, in reality, brave the crossing of the border northward as they seek a better life with the prospects of a future worth having. These realities often go unnoticed in prominent discussions of immigration reform because it is difficult for many U.S. citizens to empathize with Mexicans who cross the border, since the United States does not have a history of its citizens wishing to flee to another nation.[6] In fact, the opposite is true; the United States tends to be a nation of possibility for many of the world's citizens. Those who cross the border into the United States often hide themselves in an effort to be unobtrusive, and so quite often their story may be known in trusted intimate social groups while remaining untold outside their communities for fear of reprisals, and thus remain unknown. Rodriguez accomplishes this feat by bringing together familiar popular cinematic genres and infusing them with markers of Latinidad. Thus, the core of *Planet Terror* is not just a story about zombie proliferation. It is also a commentary on the struggle of Latinos who, though culturally distinct from other groups in the United States, share many of the same hopes, aspirations, dreams, and hardships as everyone else.

In *Planet Terror*, Rodriguez depicts how U.S. citizens—even famously proud Texans—might wish to flee across their own nation's expansive borders. And while *Planet Terror* is a work of fiction, it is rooted in a plausible reality as all fiction is (otherwise we would not recognize it). We have seen the mass of people who fled during the devastation caused by Hurricane Katrina and the failed human-made levees in New Orleans. In those moments of desperation, rules and regulations instituted by human-made committees often seem silly and superfluous. We recognize the human instinct for self-preservation when unimaginable decisions must be made. There is a level of empathy that is inculcated when watching those moments, even many years after the fact.

Though Rodriguez uses the trappings of a B-movie in *Planet Terror*, the social factors operating in the film are no different than those we encounter in everyday life. Sometimes disasters happen. Sometimes we are forced to leave our homes, our native lands, in search of safety or refuge. However, just as a disparate but cohesive band is able to look past individual differences for the common good, Rodriguez's film is an instructive commentary on how U.S. citizens might show empathy towards their southern neighbors. Policies that respect the common ground among groups rather than simple characterizations that render people as Other are warranted even in difficult situations. Moreover, Rodriguez manages to create his cinematic storyworld while staying away from conventional representations of Latinos in films. In effect, he is signaling a post-post-

Latinidad in which markers of Latino identity are subtle and deployed strategically throughout the film's design as a significant element rather than for the benefit of simplistic coloring.

Rodriguez's method is far from perfect, but his emphasis on identity negotiation among contesting groups—from *Machete* to *The Faculty*, and in both *Planet Terror* and *From Dusk till Dawn*—is worth noting. These films exemplify Viktor Shklovsky's concept of *ostranenie*—what he describes as "to make a stone feel stony" (6). Rodriguez expertly defamiliarizes the ways in which social groups can be united in the face of terror despite differing identities. By including characters who defy our expectation of particular groups such as El Wray, the Latino ne'er-do-well who is actually a high-ranking military agent, or Cherry Darling, the go-go dancer who ultimately has the courage to lead her people to safe haven as a militant mother figure, he opens the door for audiences who may not have the cultural or experiential capital to identify with an out-group. The fact that these are works of fiction, conjurations on celluloid or digital media, does not preclude the fact that the emotions an audience experiences are real. Rodriguez presents viewers with the possibility of transferring a similar empathetic response for real people—people they know little to nothing about—to real human beings who otherwise might only register as statistics on a CNN ticker at the bottom of their television set. Ultimately, such an inference suggests the power of narrative fiction and the human capacity for reconstructing fictional worlds that move us as impressively as events in the real world. It evokes emotions that linger long after we have left the cinema—emotions that may leave us, and our minds, changed.

Notes

1. The term "Latinidad" is a difficult and slippery concept. Laura P. Alonso Gallo calls it an "unstable concept, much like that of postmodern identity. . . . Critics and intellectuals use the term *Latinidad* acknowledging the heterogeneous nature of the Hispanic group in the United States as well as the different degrees found in their process of transculturation" (242). Simply put, Latinidad indicates the quality of being Latino, or Latino-ness. It is an imperfect term, one that suggests an essentialist take on Latinos in the United States. However, the term itself is a marker for the problems associated with stereotyping and representation of Latinos in literature and film, which is why I am highlighting it in my chapter.

2. McHale credits Umberto Eco with coining the term "transworld identity" (35).

3. This may hold true with audiences until a threshold is breached where the character seems to deserve his end at the hands of the undead. But my point here is to suggest that in the survivor–zombie dyad, audiences tend to root for the survivor until led by the author or director to do otherwise.

4. It is interesting that in many zombie narratives, whatever caused the zombie outbreak is rarely reversed or undone. Instead, the aim seems to be survival. One exception to this is Robert Matheson's *I Am Legend*, whose protagonist works frantically to find a scientific cure for the vampiric outbreak.

5. For a brief but enriching recapitulation of this horror/humor dichotomy in film and literature, see Carroll ("Horror and Humor").

6. One notable exception would be those individuals that fled the U.S. to avoid conscription during the Vietnam War.

CHAPTER 7

Planet Terror Redux:
Miscegenation and Family Apocalypse

ENRIQUE GARCÍA

Planet Terror was released in 2007, along with Quentin Tarantino's *Death Proof*, as part of a double-feature bill called *Grindhouse*—a term used to describe theaters showing exploitation films. This experiment, sponsored by Hollywood mogul Harvey Weinstein under the Weinstein Company studio, had good critical reception and was embraced by film aficionados; however, it was a complete failure at the American box office. It made $25 million in the United States out of a budget of $53 million, and the project recouped its budget only after the two films were split for their international and home video release. *Grindhouse* is still beloved in certain film circles that appreciate the filmmakers' homage to exploitation movies from the 1960s and 1970s, even though a traditional audience may find the final product too extravagant, self-reflexive, or brash for its taste.

When I teach my "Hispanic Film" survey class at Middlebury College, my choice to end the semester with Rodriguez's *Planet Terror* as a representation of U.S. Latino cinema is very divisive among the students. (I use the term "Hispanic" not in an old-school sense of seeking to ideologically aspire to an *Hispania* or *Spanish* sensibility, but to capture the selection of films taught—films from Spain, the United States, Mexico, and Cuba, among other countries.) Many love the fact that they are watching a fun and transgressive genre film that avoids the didactic messages of the academic Latino film canon. On the other hand, many others complain that the film is not "Latin enough," and are disturbed by the violence and by Rodriguez's sexualized portrayal of women that they perceive as misogynist. In many ways the students were reacting to what Christopher González identifies in his chapter in this collection as a "post-post-Latinidad." During my tenure at Middlebury College, I had students thanking me for introducing them to such a great film, and others writing long e-mails to me to explain why they were greatly offended by Rodriguez's film.

In this article, I discuss why *Planet Terror* can arouse such extreme feelings among its viewers, how it fits into the zombie genre in its gender, ethnic, and political dimensions, and why it is an important work for a Latino filmmaker who has constantly defied both the cinematic establishment and the generalizations about Latino ethnic cinema while being financially successful. I argue that the film's contribution to the zombie genre is in that it portrays the collapse and rebirth of the American family as occurring through racial miscegenation outside traditional social structures, an idea suggested in other zombie films but never explicitly visualized for the screen. Here I share a like mind with Christopher González, who is also interested in decoding the film's gesture toward a new inclusivity. I add to this a focus on sexuality, explaining how zombie genre films tend to be constructed with melodramatic devices that question the role of family as a mediator of sexuality. I enrich this position by formulating the rather controversial argument that as a sociotheoretical construction, miscegenation has been embraced by and promoted in Mexican/Latino culture. I demonstrate how it is presented in *Planet Terror* with the irony and wit that make Robert Rodriguez a special filmmaker.

Exploiting the World: Rodriguez's Ethnic Action Heroes and Stereotyping

Robert Rodriguez and Quentin Tarantino are friends and part of a group of filmmakers (such as Kevin Smith and Rob Zombie), who, under the guiding hand of Hollywood mogul Harvey Weinstein, have already made several neo-exploitation films within what I call their "Grindhouse new wave." Some examples are Rodriguez's *Sin City* (codirected with Frank Miller, and with contributions from Quentin Tarantino, 2005) and his *Mariachi* trilogy, as well as practically all of Tarantino's cinematic oeuvre. This type of film is always debatable in terms of political correctness due to the ambiguities of postmodern irony and how images are presented by the filmmakers and interpreted by the audience. In Rodriguez's case, most of his R-rated films abound in Latino stereotypes that used to appear in mainstream Hollywood and American culture in general, such as the "bandito," "the half-breed harlot," and the "dark lady," which prominent Latino scholar Charles Ramírez Berg ("Stereotyping") singled out as some of the main problematic Hispanic constructions in the American media. Interestingly, Ramírez Berg himself presents Rodriguez in a positive manner in his book *Latino Images in Film: Stereotypes, Subversion, and Resistance* because the director's *El Mariachi* "calls into question dominant notions of masculinity, heroism, the U.S.-Mexico border, and finally cinema" (239). In his chapter about Rodriguez, Ramírez Berg specifically points out that beneath the action movie and genre archetypes found in the film, there is a social narrative that criticizes the drug trade and the American exploitation of the Mexican border towns (237), while also creating an atypical action hero, whose behavior is outside both American and Mexican parameters of masculinity/machismo (236). In addition, Ramírez Berg points out that the low-budget style of the film in itself is transgressive because it shows an aesthetic outside of the "system" that does rely on big-budget spending (238). Still, *Planet Terror* was made at a different stage in Rodriguez's career, which later included higher budgets (but low for the typical Hollywood action film) and an association with Hollywood moguls such as Harvey Weinstein and Hollywood actors such as Bruce Willis. (See also the important interrogation of masculine ideals in the work of Richard T. Rodriguez, specifically his *Next of Kin: The Family in Chicano/a Cultural Politics*.)

Ramírez Berg considers Rodriguez's *Mariachi* to be a transgressive ethnic narrative. This observation can be linked to how some blaxploitation films in the 1960s and 1970s are currently perceived. While driven by silly plots abounding in fantasies and stereotypes about African American society, these films were important in countering white hegemony and in providing visibility for a minority group that was suffering from lack of representation in the American national media. Rodriguez's films can be very divisive because he continues to rely on stereotypes. However, the content of his films can also be interpreted as subversive because he creates Latino heroes who can be disseminated into the American mainstream. Just the fact that his characters are well liked and admired is a triumph for a Latino ethnic culture that historically has been held back in Hollywood. In *Planet Terror*, the Latino hero El Wray is a sensitive yet "badass" action hero who can be admired by anyone from around the world.

Rodriguez has directed exploitative films, but he has also done positive mainstream representations, such as the *Spy Kids* series, where Hispanic characters are intelligent, have access to technology, and also are accessible to American mainstream audiences. When I was teaching *Planet Terror*, many of my students who had issues with the film were surprised that Rodriguez had directed the *Spy Kids* series, because they had consumed these works as safe diverse family entertainment that they did not find offensive in any way. *Spy Kids* offers a "safe" version of ethnic representation, in which the system does not change, and the assimilation of ethnic minority into the mainstream is easier to digest as a concept.

One of the reasons *Planet Terror* may be perceived as a shallow aesthetic exercise is related to how the *Grindhouse* project was and still is sold to audiences. In many of their interviews, Tarantino and Rodriguez emphasize their aesthetic homage to exploitation films. The filmmakers claim they wanted to re-create the cheap and imperfect visuals that were the result of the low budgets of the features they enjoyed in their youth and continue to consume. Both tend to overexplain aesthetic choices such as the parody of B-movie acting, the music, the lesbian overtones, the artificial problematic frame rate, the jumpy editing, and the fictional missing reels that make *Planet Terror* and Tarantino's *Death Proof* resemble Grindhouse features. In *Grindhouse*'s official tie-in promotional book, *Grindhouse: The Sleaze-Filled Saga of an Exploitation Double Feature*, both directors talk at length about how they are visually reproducing the cinematic past. However, they never mention the fact that they are also updating these features in terms of gender, race, and other controversial issues. Rodriguez's commentary in the home video release mostly focuses on how he filmed the movie but does not provide too many details about the meaning of the film. In fact, he gives the impression that the film was improvised, and that the screenplay took shape according to how much he liked certain actors. Still, I believe that the film reproduces the visual absurdity of past exploitation films but has a political irony that should be the main focus of analysis, and that makes it one of Rodriguez's best works.

In the following segment I will explore the construction of minority heroes in two earlier and very influential zombie films, *Night of the Living Dead* and *28 Days Later*. In these two films, the heroes are perceived as an "other" because of visible racial features, and not necessarily because of distinct ethnic belonging, like Rodriguez's hero of Latino descent. My goal in this segment is to explain how the earlier characters' limited otherness was used for political purposes, and how Rodriguez in turn relies on the already established representational framework to make a political film that updates issues of ethnic representation and tackles concerns related to post-9/11 American society.

Zombie Films: Collapse of the Family Structure, and Minority Action Heroes

One of the most important contributions of the zombie genre is that it introduced two charismatic and popular minority action heroes who are still relevant in contemporary popular culture because of their social significance. Latino film director George Romero's *Night of the Living Dead* (1968) featured the character of Ben Huss, an African American hero who is the leading man in the picture, as well as the most attractive and sympathetic character. This was specifically groundbreaking in the 1960s, as this film was released at the height of the Civil Rights struggle and close to the date when Martin Luther King was assassinated. More recently, British director Danny Boyle's zombie apocalypse, *28 Days Later* (2002), included the character of Selena, who was also an interesting black action heroine. Her importance lies in the fact that she was a sympathetic minority character defiant of the system in a post-9/11 British society, and a key figure in representing a new multicultural British family unit, an idea that is very relevant for European audiences at this time. Both characters were essential in their function as counterpoints to the dissolution of the white family structure in both the American and British zombie apocalypses that mirrored troubled times respectively in different decades.

Throughout the twentieth century, the family structure has been a controversial subject among progressive thinkers because it represents the basic social unit of the dominant economic and national culture. These social debates led to the creation of films such as *All That Heaven Allows* (1955), *Giant* (1956), and *Rebel Without a Cause* (1955), which visualized and criticized traditional family structures. A number of film scholars, such as John Mercer and Martin Shingler, have studied this phenomenon and consider these themes the essential narrative frame for what is currently known in Film Studies as melodrama. As a result, various studies have been undertaken of the oeuvre of directors such as Douglas Sirk, Rainer Werner Fassbinder, Pedro Almodóvar, and other filmmakers who are known for focusing on the dysfunctional idea of the traditional family. However, the cinematic family struggles that define the modern idea of melodrama have also found their way into bizarre genres such as mainstream zombie narratives, ever since George Romero's *Night of the Living Dead*, which established the use of ghoulish metaphors to represent the collapse of civilization and the family structure.

Night of the Living Dead has an interesting depiction of the collapse of the American family, as it portrays Ben as an attractive character due to his nonbelonging to the "white" family nucleus, which allows him to survive the night until, ironically, he is killed by policemen and rednecks who mistake him for a zombie. The other white families are portrayed as "unprepared" for the zombie apocalypse, in that their loyalty to their relatives only leads to their destruction at the hands of the infected attackers. The character of Barbra is upset throughout the entire film because she does not know the fate of her bully of a brother. Ultimately, the brother and other zombies kill her in the final segment of the film. The young couple, Tom and Judy, die in an explosion that occurs while they are trying to refuel a truck (and Judy is partially to blame for the failure of this task), and the older married couple of Harry and Helen is murdered and eaten by their zombie daughter Karen. At the end, the irony is that what destroys Ben is not the white family institution to which he fortunately does not belong, but rather the white authority system or government, which is what oppresses him as a member of a minority ethnic group.

In *28 Days Later*, the character of Selena is portrayed at the beginning in a similar way to Ben in *Night*. Unlike the characters of Jim and Hannah, who have attachments to their white parents and are almost destroyed by them, Selena is detached from any type of family. The film makes this point by having her suddenly kill her initial white partner, Mark, when he is bitten by an infected man, which shocks Jim as well as the audience. The difference between *Night* and *28 Days* is that in Boyle's film, the authority figures (represented by a rogue British soldier squad) are also a threat to the Caucasian characters, a topical concept in post-9/11 society. In *Night*, the white family members, the African American hero, and the zombies all die, but the traditional American authorities remain in power, which represented the fatalism of the struggle in 1968. *28 Days* has a more positive ending because Selena, Jim, and Hannah survive, defeating the soldiers/authority (with the help of a black zombie), and a new interracial British family is born at the end of the film that is devoid of any biological connections. (For more details on the representation of family in *28 Days*, please see James Rose's *Beyond Hammer*.)

What is interesting about Ben and Selena is that their outsider status or otherness may be initially perceived by the audience to be the result of their race (difference in terms of physical features), but not because the actors perform in any way an African American or Afro-British ethnic behavior. According to critic Ben Hervey, Ben's character (42) is clean-cut, he does not speak African American ethnic dialects, and his race is not addressed at any point in the movie. No background is provided about the character in the film, including elements such as social class, education, or profession.

In fact, an Anglo actor could have played the character and the plot would have remained the same. However, Ben's race remains key to avoiding any empathy with the foolish white characters, and to defying the authority of Harry, the older Caucasian character, who is trying to impose his will onto the others in the film. I think the irony of the ending of the film would have also been shocking if Ben would have been played by a white actor; however, linking his death visually to the representation of a lynching made the movie more political and not just good B-movie entertainment.

The character of Selena in *28 Days* is portrayed as violent at the beginning of the film, and one wonders if her blackness was key in making the audience accept a female character who would dispatch people in such a violent and detached manner. As the story progresses, Selena softens up as a character, and at some point she reveals that she was a chemist, therefore implying attributes of education and middle-class status. She does not speak with an accent or have ethnic markers from Jamaica or Africa, which is very similar to Ben's original portrayal. Still, having had a profession makes her more attractive for inclusion into the new multicultural British family that the film promotes.

In Rodriguez's *Planet Terror*, the ethnic hero is the mysterious El Wray, whose background remains unclear throughout the entire film. As opposed to Ben and Selena, who are perceived as "others" because of race and not because of ethnic culture, El Wray is constructed mostly as an outcast or youth rebel through his costume, leather jacket, and tough-guy persona. His links to his Latino ethnic background are more obscured than with other Rodriguez heroes of Hispanic descent; however, there are a few hints that the audience has to recognize. First, his name (El Wray) appears to be an Anglophone name, but phonetically it sounds like *El rey*, which translates to English as "The King." The phrase *El rey* has been used several times by Rodriguez in his other works, including the name of the Mexican town where the vampires are located in *From Dusk till Dawn*. It is also the name of Rodriguez's Comcast-commissioned TV network that has begun to produce media by and about Latinos in 2014, such as his TV adaptation of *From Dusk till Dawn* that premiered in March 2014. Second, El Wray constantly refers to his love interest, Cherry Darling, as *Palomita* (Little Dove), one of the few Spanish words he uses throughout the film but a definitive ethnic marker. Third, he is constantly harassed by local sheriff Hague—a synecdoche of sorts that stands in for southern border police persecution of Latino people as a whole. Fourth, his improvised plan to save the survivors is to immigrate to Mexico and "put their backs to the ocean." The survivors at the end achieve this goal, finding refuge next to a Mexican pre-Columbian pyramid in order to survive the American apocalypse. No less importantly, Freddy Rodriguez, an actor of Puerto Rican descent, plays El Wray. He is known for playing Latino characters, specifically the Puerto Rican mortician in *Six Feet Under*, but phenotypically he could pass as any number of dark ethnic (Greek or Italian, for instance) Americans. These cultural constructions may be enough to define him as a Latino character, yet every time I teach the film I have to explain to the students that El Wray is of Hispanic descent because the character never self-identifies as Hispanic in the film.

Planet Terror was produced at a very controversial time, when some of the 9/11 jingoism had begun to be dismissed in the face of the economic meltdown and the conflicts in Iraq and Afghanistan. The main antagonists are the military squad under the command of Lt. Muldoon (played by Bruce Willis) who have unleashed the zombie virus plague on American soil with the intention of finding a cure. Contrary to the mad British soldiers in *28 Days* who want to rebuild British society, these American soldiers have fallen from grace after getting infected with a virus while trying to kill Osama bin Laden. They are evil antagonists but also victims with tragic overtones, therefore providing a rare nuance that barely appears in the genre (including *Night* and *28 Days*) where authority is simply dismissed as destructive.

There are several elements in *Planet Terror* that make it different from *Night* and *28 Days* in relation to their minority heroes' relationship with the system. First, El Wray has a different relationship with state and federal authorities. The sheriff, representing local state authority, constantly harasses him. Yet, the antagonist soldier Lt. Muldoon (a synecdoche of sorts that stands in for a militarized nation as a whole) admires El Wray. Muldoon is the most powerful villain in the film, and his platoon stands for American military might. In the final part of the film, it is revealed that El Wray is some type of American super-soldier, which transforms him from an ethnic outcast to a national hero fighting the degeneration of the United States into a monstrous society. Towards the middle of the film, the sheriff acknowledges this when he tells El Wray: "If only I knew who you were." This particular ability to be perceived as both the fringe of society and part of the system makes him a different type of hero than the ones previously discussed. Along with the Middle Eastern scientist Abby, he kills Bruce Willis's corrupted character and former hero Lt. Muldoon, but not before thanking him and recognizing his duty for supposedly killing American nemesis Osama bin Laden; of course, with prescient irony this alludes to an event that had yet to take place given that it was released before Bin Laden had been killed. In the film it plays as a joke on American jingoism. This particular scene shows that he is patriotic even though he is eliminating one of his own. He does not have an issue with the state, but rather with its corruption.

Another aspect in which El Wray differs from previous ethnic heroes is in that he sees himself as part of a Texan community rather than as belonging to the Mexican American ethnic group. Contrary to Ben, who is not able to work well with the Caucasian survivors in *Night*, and Selena, who only becomes a team player toward the end in *28 Days*, El Wray unites the different social classes in Texas to form a survivor group that will resist the excesses of the American military. In his group he has Caucasian outcasts like stripper Cherry Darling, barbecue master J. T. Hague (brother of Sheriff Hague), lesbian and battered-wife Dr. Dakota Block, her deputy father, and others that represent a Texas collective rather than the plight of an ethnic group. This bonding is visualized particularly well with something irreverent such as El Wray's enjoyment of J. T. Hague's secret Texas Barbecue recipe. One of the main subplots of the film is that J. T. does not trust his sheriff brother with the recipe (providing melodramatic tension), which is why he only gives it to him when his brother stops being a member of state authority and sacrifices his life so that the group of survivors can escape. Still, I contend that the main difference from other ethnic characters is in how El Wray and Cherry's miscegenation produces a new reality, which, compared to the melodramatic relationship of the white Block family, is limited neither by race, nor by law, nor by the territorial space of nation states and their societal structures.

Planet Terror: Class Melodrama and Foucault's Sexuality

Michel Foucault's *History of Sexuality, Volume 1* is one of the most important philosophical works that analyzes the role of sexuality in the modern world. The reason his work was fascinating to intellectuals was its argument that our perception of sexuality had been constructed by a social system that, contrary to popular belief, was not looking to eradicate but rather to support and use sexuality for its own purposes. Foucault writes:

> The family, in its contemporary form, must not be understood as a social, economic, and political structure of alliance that excludes or at least restrains sexuality, that diminishes it as much as possible, preserving only

its useful functions. On the contrary, its role is to anchor sexuality and provide it with a permanent support. (Chapter 3: "Domain" n. pag.)

Foucault further expands his discussion about how the bourgeoisie originally submitted itself to this social reality and the deployment of sexuality. He also discusses how the proletariat, or working force, was eventually assimilated into this commodification of sexuality. Foucault writes: "we must say that there is a bourgeois sexuality, and that there are class sexualities. Or rather, that sexuality is originally, historically bourgeois, and that, in its successive shifts, and transpositions, it induces specific class effects" (Chapter 4: "Periodization," n. pag.). This is important to understand because *Planet Terror*'s melodrama involves two couples from different social classes whose sexuality is depicted in a similar yet distinct fashion.

The first, traditional, couple is represented by the Block family, which consists of Drs. William and Dakota Block and their son, Tony. Dakota is one of the heroines of the film, and her introduction is a gloomy one, not because of a zombie attack, but rather because of her domestic situation. She has to take care of her young son, work a night shift at the hospital with her unappealing husband (played by Josh Brolin), and keep silent about her lesbian affair. On paper, they are the perfect middle-class family, yet, while Dakota has good social status, she is unhappy with her middle-class achievements. On the other hand, the working-class love story is represented by El Wray and Cherry Darling's romance. El Wray works as a tow-truck driver, and he is perceived as someone outside of the system, while Cherry Darling is a stripper who initially wanted to be a doctor and now dreams of being a comedian. It is gradually revealed that after a seemingly very passionate relationship, Cherry abandoned El Wray because he would not commit to marriage. Both characters thus avoided entering what Foucault dubs the "bourgeois deployment of sexuality."

However, based on Foucault's writing, one could argue that Cherry's sexuality is, at least at the beginning of the film, also part of the system because she is using it to acquire capital and to perform for customers in an employment that channels the customers'/workers' sexual desires. This is well represented in one of the earlier scenes of the movie. Cherry's strip club manager yells at two strippers who are kissing each other in private, since they need to do it in front of paying customers, and it is the manager's job to redirect their sexuality by channeling it towards the accumulation of wealth.

The film features a lot of violence against Dakota and Cherry, which is why viewers (including my students) sometimes assume the film is misogynist. Throughout the film all types of masculine figures harass Cherry. She is yelled at by her manager, she is almost run over by soldier trucks, her leg is eaten by male zombies, and she is almost raped by a couple of infected soldiers at the end. Dakota has a different experience but it is equally violent: her lesbian lover is devoured by the zombies, her husband attacks her physically with her own anesthetic syringes, she breaks her hand, she sees her son die, and she is also almost raped by the soldiers at the end of the film. All of this violence and sexuality in the film is homage to Grindhouse movies, specifically to what the documentary *American Grindhouse* (Elijah Drenner, 2010) describes as a subgenre called "the roughies." The documentary implies that because of the censorship against showing sex on the screen, sometimes these B-movies would emphasize violence against women as a substitute for sexuality. However, Rodriguez's violence against women serves a purpose because it is used to establish how they are not in control of their bodies and how the American apocalypse serves as a way of collapsing the social structures that encourage but control their sexuality.

Some of the scenes that may be seen as controversial are related to El Wray's harsh physical treatment of Cherry after she loses a leg to a zombie. These parts of the movie can be uncomfortable for the audience (El Wray's rough love would not be well received in today's cinema). For example, he rushes to save Cherry from the hospital, but when she complains that she cannot walk, he violently sticks a piece of wood into her wound to create a stump that will allow her to move. He does not help her to get inside his truck, and she has to run alongside comically until she is able to jump into it. As the film continues, and she has a very erotic sex scene with El Wray, she becomes a stronger physical figure, and one of the bravest characters in the film. Finally, El Wray sticks a machine gun to her leg wound that transforms her into a lethal weapon. As they escape the army base in the last segment of the film, El Wray tells her, "Cherry Darling, it's all you." She then proceeds to wipe out the soldiers in a transcendental scene that finalizes her transformation from victim to warrior. I personally find this evolution to be progressive for the zombie genre, which tends to be misogynist in general. Outside of generic conventions and history, however, one may also argue that the masculinization of the female body, including its sexualization and weapon fetishism, is little more than a reflection of male fantasies.

The other female protagonist in the film, Dakota Block, is liberated in several forms. Although her lesbian lover is murdered, Dakota's lesbian sexual desire does not subside in the face of apocalypse, as depicted in the scene in which she is holding onto Cherry Darling's waist while they are riding a bike together, and the audience is aware that she is taking the opportunity to grope Cherry. Throughout the film, she also loses her son (who accidentally shoots himself) and her husband, who is killed by Dakota's father. She is also freed from her profession and, instead of using anesthesia for medical purposes, she uses her syringes to transform into a cool warrior.

Cherry also transforms herself by becoming a warrior instead of a stripper, by using her dance moves to fight as a heroine against the system, rather than to cater to paying customers. She finds true love with El Wray, but Rodriguez disposes of him (like he does of Dakota's lesbian lover) before their relationship can become entangled in the power relations associated with the family structure. Cherry and El Wray's love is pure because it cannot be corrupted by marital status. Both female characters' emotional and physical suffering throughout the film then becomes empowering because it is obvious that it is the product of an androcentric society that will collapse with the advance of the zombie apocalypse. The new society that will rise will empower women, men, and workers and will be made different by the working-class miscegenation promoted by Rodriguez in the film.

At the end of the film a new family structure emerges as Cherry gives birth to El Wray's daughter. In the next segment I will explore how miscegenation plays a role in the rebirth of Rodriguez's new society, and why that is important for a Latino filmmaker even if the ending of the film has some ironic overtones.

Mestizaje Saves the World?

Since colonial times, miscegenation has been perceived as the end of Eurocentric imperial civilization. French colonialist Arthur de Gobineau, one of the main proponents of racial demography, saw miscegenation as an apocalyptic concept:

> If mixtures of blood are, to a certain extent, beneficial to the mass of mankind, if they raise and ennoble it, this is merely at the expense of mankind itself, which is stunted, abased, enervated, and humiliated in the persons of its noblest sons. (210)

However, in regions such as Latin America, nationalist discourse has promoted the idea of interracial coupling as a way of providing an alternative that unifies a nation-state of multi-plural voices and allows it to form its own identity away from Eurocentric powers. In fact, many of the great Latin American essayists have promoted the concept in their written works, including luminaries such as Cuban Fernando Ortiz, Uruguayan Angel Rama, Argentinean Néstor García Canclini, Mexican José Vasconcelos, and others. Many of these writers positioned themselves in favor of cultural hybridity as a means of understanding Latin American culture and were vehemently opposed to twentieth-century social perceptions that embraced the idea of racial homogeneity as a key element in the formation of productive and civilized nation-states. In Mexican culture, the best-known example of scholarly writing about miscegenation is José Vasconcelos's conceptualization of the *raza cósmica*, which glorifies Latin American miscegenation/*mestizaje*/hybridity in opposition to the racial homogeneity found in the United States at the time (the 1920s). Many of the precepts he developed were promoted in Mexico after the Mexican revolution, and the concept of the *raza cósmica* has become a significant part of the state's nationalist ideology.

While many of these ideas of hybridity have been incorporated into Latin American nation-state projects, modern scholars in postcolonial theory and Latin American Studies have challenged such conceptions and state practices of hybridity. In the United States, postcolonial theorists such as Gayatri Spivak have criticized or questioned the limited role of the subaltern in the construction of postcolonial nationalism. In her article, "Can the Subaltern Speak?" Spivak specifically examines the ways in which local elites, under the guise of anti-imperial nationalism, still maintain imperial power structures in order to control the masses, and how they fail to provide a voice for the underrepresented. These views are reflected in the work of certain Latin American thinkers who write about the integration of the ethnic other into the nationalist Latin American discourse and its perception by Hispanic elites. For example, British scholar John Kraniauskas writes, in his important article "Hybridity in a Transnational Frame: Latin Americanist and Postcolonialist Perspectives on Cultural Studies," that

> the key to Latin American modernity contained in García Canclini's outline of its modernisms is not to be found only in such transculturation, but rather in the ways it feeds into "the way in which elites take charge of the intersections of different historical realities." (751)

Another important scholar, Peruvian Antonio Cornejo Polar, although appreciative of García Canclini's writing, also criticizes the latter's ideas about hybridity as too celebratory because of their focus on specific strata of Latin American societies (761).

A unique take on the debate is offered by writer/performer/academic Gloria Anzaldúa, who positions herself outside of traditional masculine and nationalist discourse. In her landmark book *Borderlands/La Frontera: The New Mestiza*, she writes:

> As a *mestiza* I have no country, my homeland cast me out; yet all countries are mine because I am every woman's sister or potential lover. (As a lesbian I have no race, my own people disclaim me; but I am all races because there is the queer of me in all races.) I am cultureless because, as a feminist, I challenge the collective cultural/religious male-derived beliefs of Indo-Hispanics and Anglos; yet I am cultured because I am participating in the creation of yet another culture, a new story to explain the world and our participation in it, a new value system with images and symbols that connect us to each other and to the planet. (2214)

Anzaldúa specifically quotes Vasconcelos's cosmic race as a point of inspiration (2211) but calls attention to the fact that she belongs to a racial and gender subaltern from both a Mexican and an American perspective. She urges the reader to avoid the binaries created by the nation-states of Mexico and the United States and to create a new culture that will take advantage of cross-culturalism. It is interesting that she supports Vasconcelos's vision but does not see Mexican nationalist culture as a good representation of the beauty of the idea. (See also Rafael Pérez-Torres's *Mestizaje: Critical Uses of Race in Chicano Culture*, where he uses the concept of *mestizaje* to establish a foundational theory of Chicano identity and experience as expressed in literature, music, and the arts generally.)

In the 1950s United States, American blockbuster films like *Giant* and TV shows like *I Love Lucy* attempted to provide audiences with a positive portrayal of the mixture of races in order to show that American culture could improve through miscegenation. However, these narratives were still limited to bourgeois ideals of marriage that somehow fit the system. In *Giant*, the miscegenation in the Benedict family gives Mexican Americans access to American culture, yet class and economic structures remain unchanged. In *I Love Lucy*, Lucy's son, Ricky, is portrayed as better than his parents because of his bi-ethnic heritage, which allows him to function in both Cuba and the United States. Still, Lucy herself never improves as a woman and remains a housewife during the entire series. More importantly, successful miscegenation is linked to an upper-middle-class status that would allow the interracial spouses to function well within the established economic system.

Miscegenation in *Planet Terror* is transgressive, since the fusion of races in the film occurs between working-class characters (one Latino tow-truck driver and one Caucasian stripper) who eventually become the main authority figures among the survivors in the face of the apocalypse. The concept of miscegenation is clearly established in the film between El Wray and Cherry, and it is important especially because it is established in direct opposition to Dakota's all-white family. Dakota's son (ironically portrayed by Rodriguez's son) has to die in the film because he represents the unhappy and traditional family structure that had shackled her sexuality. Even though the boy's death in the film is tragic, and Dakota mourns him, it is clear since the beginning that he supports his father rather than his mother (he consistently doubts his mother's integrity). In addition, he is uncooperative throughout the entire film, to the point that his accidental death is a relief to the audience. At the end, Dakota acquires a genuine (her own) purpose once she has shed the roles of mother, wife, and professional. In contrast, El Wray and Cherry's daughter is conceived not through marriage and the law but rather through outlaw passion in the midst of societal apocalypse, which situates the child outside of the framework of society.

Planet Terror is a film about the collapse of the American institution but also about the collapse of masculinity, an interesting statement by Rodriguez, who has created a great Latino hero (El Wray) but has also empowered the female body, including both heterosexual (Cherry) and queer (Dakota) heroines. The positive masculine figures in the film, El Wray and Earl McGraw, function as male mentors for Cherry and Dakota, respectively. They teach the women how to survive in a man's world; however, they are unfit for the gynocentric utopia presented at the end of the film. Although one could see male survivors in the group evacuation to Mexico, it is visually suggested that the women are in power, as they hold weapons and lead the others. Some could argue that this ending is a male fantasy or that it represents a harem ideal of sexualized women, but the fact remains that it presents the bicultural death of traditional masculinity in relation to an apocalypse brought about by the wars in Iraq and Afghanistan. More importantly, this resolution has a certain social relevance, as today's most destructive structures of power are androcentric.

The film's relevance in terms of ethnic culture stems from the fact that

El Wray, as a member of an ethnic minority, does not limit himself to the vanishing nation-state where he resides. He knows there is an alternative in Mexico, which distinguishes him from John and Selena in *Night* and *28 Days Later*. John's and Selena's roles as ethnic figures are not linked to a space outside of the nation-state in which they reside, and thus there is no alternative to the characters' respective oppressive home nation-states. In *Planet Terror*, however, the survivors eventually move to Mexico, next to a pre-Columbian pyramid. Christopher Gonzalez's chapter "Intertext-ploitation and Post-Post-Latinidad in *Planet Terror*" in this collection sees the pyramids as "a place of refuge for *Planet Terror*'s 'immigrant' characters, . . . a symbolic return to the Mesoamerican roots of many Latinos in the United States." I would like to specify, however, that, while this ending could be interpreted as Mexican American nostalgia for the glories of a pre-Columbian indigenous past, it in fact provides an ironic separation of the characters from the equally corrupt Mexican nation-state that has been spoiled by colonialism and capitalism. That is why the women in the film are able to create a new utopia after the collapse of the American empire that can transcend the Mexican vs. American binaries mentioned by Anzaldúa.

In this chapter, I analyzed Rodriguez's *Planet Terror* as a film that offers much more than simply a re-creation of the aesthetic pleasures of Grindhouse cinema. I linked its politics to the transgressive aspects of the zombie genre and explained how Rodriguez's depiction of female sexuality not only exploits the female body but parodies many of the precepts that Foucault criticized about sexuality under the grasp of modern capitalist society. I also explained how Rodriguez's zombie apocalypse achieves utopia by means of miscegenation, and by collapsing the structures of society that oppress the different members of the Texan community, including but not limited to the Latino hero of the film. I find *Planet Terror* to be Rodriguez's most interesting film, because, through a zombie metaphor, the filmmaker is able to deconstruct both Latino and American masculinity. In the end, to use Christopher González's term, the film clears the space for the inhabiting of a "post-post-Latinidad." In the end, the fall of civilization in his film brings a new utopia outside of traditional gender, ethnic, and nation-state parameters that can be situated in its historical context as a reaction to the events of the wars in Iraq and Afghanistan.

CHAPTER 8

The Border Crossed Us:
Machete and the Latino Threat Narrative

ZACHARY INGLE

As several of the scholars in this collection have already mentioned, with
the release in 2007 of their three-hour homage to 1970s-era exploitation
films *Grindhouse*, Robert Rodriguez and Quentin Tarantino treated audiences to a faux, exploitation-styled trailer for *Machete*. This trailer, also
directed by Rodriguez and starring character actor Danny Trejo as the
titular figure, told of an ex-Mexican *federale* (or, *federal*, the correct singular form of *federales*) who struggles to find work as a day laborer in Texas.
Hired to perform an assassination on an anti-immigration senator, he is
in turn double-crossed and is himself shot. Machete then seeks revenge on
those who conned him. The two-and-a-half-minute trailer played up Machete's Mexican background, as the film had much in common with the
blaxploitation (anti-)heroes of the 1970s. Indeed, while this was one of
four faux trailers in the film, the *Machete* trailer became the most popular.
The tease of a "Mexploitation" film catapulted Machete as a new Latino
icon. Soon *Machete* memorabilia (posters, lobby cards, etc.) would be sold
in stores catering to younger demographics (e.g., the nationwide chain
Hot Topic), even though no plans yet existed to make the trailer into a
feature film! Over three years later, the full-length *Machete* was released.
The significance of this nascent film did not go unnoticed within academia
either; published just weeks before the film's release, Robert G. Weiner
and John Cline's edited collection, *Cinema Inferno: Celluloid Explosions
from the Cultural Margins*, featured Machete on its cover. In this chapter,
I will introduce the film *Machete*, discuss it in light of the "Latino Threat
Narrative," and, finally, examine some of the major themes in the film (immigration, social networks, stereotypes, the drug trade, and labor) vis-à-
vis the Latino Threat Narrative, as well as media portrayals of Latinos.

Machete was intended as a "Mexploitation" answer to the blaxploitation film cycle of the 1970s, such as *Shaft* (1971), *Super Fly* (1972), *Coffy* (1973), and *Dolemite* (1975). Although the faux trailer's intentionally grainy aesthetic (also used for Rodriguez's *Planet Terror*, 2007) was scrapped, the film followed generic conventions of the exploitation film with its outlandish plot and excessive violence and nudity. Just in case the viewer did not realize that this was an exploitation film from the decapitations and gratuitous nudity in the opening minutes, surely the hospital escape scene makes this clear, as Machete disembowels a henchman with a skull scraper and uses his intestines as a makeshift rope to swing down to the next floor.

Mikel J. Koven identifies two major types of blaxploitation films, based on the type of hero: the "baadasssss" and "the Man." The baadasssss "work[s] in those liminal spaces between the law, between illegality and vice on the one side and harmless decadence and pleasure-seeking on the other" (17). While the baadasssss (e.g., *Super Fly*'s Priest, Coffy) "sticks it to the Man," some heroes (e.g., John Shaft) *are* the Man, "represent[ing] the struggles of black America from within the system" (76). Rodriguez's creation of Machete seems intentionally liminal; after serving as the Man (i.e., a *federal* in Mexico), he becomes a baadasssss, an outlaw within the United States, first as an illegal, then as a man hunted down. In the end he triumphs, however, with an agent of the law on his side, leaving it uncertain as to how to categorize this hero.

Rodriguez codirected *Machete* with Ethan Maniquis, who had previously served as editor for Rodriguez's films *Planet Terror* and *Shorts* (2009). Nonetheless, Rodriguez was just as involved in almost every filmmaking aspect of *Machete* as has been the case for the majority of his films. He was also credited as writer, producer, editor, sound rerecording mixer, music producer, visual effects supervisor, and visual effects executive producer. Known for composing for his films as well, Rodriguez's Latino-themed rock band, Chingon, supplied the music.

Machete achieved its notoriety primarily via its two infamous trailers: the original, faux trailer and the "Arizona" trailer. The original trailer featured the grizzled veteran character actor Danny Trejo as the action/Mexploitation hero Machete. In one notable scene, Machete is picked up at a day labor site. He explains the going rates for day laborers to this prospective employer: "$70 a day for yard work. $100 for roofing. $125 for septic . . . sewage." No ordinary employer, this mysterious man hires Machete to assassinate a state senator. Machete is double-crossed and is shot in the shoulder. They discover that he is an ex-*federal* and, as the narrator's voice-over intones, "They just fucked with the wrong Mexican!" For those not part of the subculture already aware of *Machete* through the *Grindhouse* trailer, the film's controversial "Arizona" trailer brought the film to the attention of a wider audience. A highly anticipated trailer, as it was the first to feature the new footage shot specifically for the forthcoming film, it was released on May 5, 2010. The trailer begins with Machete's "special message": "This is Machete. With a special Cinco de Mayo message. TO ARIZONA!"

That this trailer appeared less than two weeks after that state signed SB 1070, then the most stringent immigration bill in the nation, should not be overlooked. (This was before the even stricter immigrant laws enacted in Alabama and Georgia.) The bill gave the police in Arizona greater power to check for documents, expediting the process of deporting undocumented immigrants. The extreme measure taken by the Arizona legislature caused a backlash across the country, especially among Latinos, as many saw it as too reactionary and thought it could lead to racial profiling. It apparently provoked enough ire from Rodriguez and Trejo to release the "Arizona" trailer on such a celebrated holiday for Mexican Americans in the Southwest.

The "Arizona" trailer spawned numerous responses on the Internet from critics seemingly unaware of *Machete* before, including postings on discussion boards, blogs, and YouTube videos. One of the more (semi-)articulate anti-*Machete* responses found was a YouTube video entitled "Leaked Machete Script Confirms Race War Plot."[1] Syndicated radio host Alex Jones, the speaker in this ten-minute-plus video, reminds viewers of the machete's place as a symbol of Latin American uprising and connects recent violence among Latinos to the film's "Arizona" trailer. He then dismisses the film as "unspeakably evil," calling it a "Hispanic *Birth of a Nation*" (while showing posters for Nazi propaganda films, such as *Jud Suss*, 1940). Although the script looks legitimate, his claims that it positions Machete as a "race-consciousness Christ" and that the film advocates liberation theology seem unfounded, but he does make a valid point that all white characters in the film are racist villains. In his favorable *New York Times* review of *Machete*, Stephen Holden references Jones's video, but instead thinks that "a comedy showdown with the Wayans brothers would seem more likely" than for the film to initiate racial uprisings (Holden Sept. 2, 2010). Again, Holden: "For all its political button pushing, *Machete* is too preposterous to qualify as satire. The only viewers it is likely to upset are the same kind of people who once claimed that the purple Tinky Winky in *Teletubbies* promoted a gay agenda" (Holden Sept. 2, 2010).

For Holden, *Machete* contains nothing that would offend anyone, save a slim, ultraright minority, a community of a tiny fraction of the majority of Americans who, according to recent polls, want "Arizona-like" immigration laws in their states.[2]

Stephen Applebaum notes the film's controversy, as the film did become linked to anticipated race riots. It was labeled as racist and "anti-American" (160). *Machete* was supposed to launch a race war, just as *Do the Right Thing* (1989) was predicted to incite riots in yet another failed forecast. In an article for the *Huffington Post*, Alexander Zaitchik examines the controversy over the film from outlets such as Fox News correspondents and extremist conservative groups such as VDARE, the Council of Conservative Citizens, and American Border Patrol. Zaitchik concludes in his piece that the film is actually no more politically radical than other action films, in which white heroes maul Latino, Asian, or black villains or gangs ("Does Rodriguez's 'Machete' Advocate 'Race War'?," http://www.huffingtonpost.com/alexander-zaitchik/does-robert-rodriguezs-ma_b_712003.html).

So were fears of a race war unwarranted? Rarely do individual films have a discernable societal impact (a notable exception being the increased membership of the Ku Klux Klan after the release of *The Birth of a Nation*), and *Machete* was no exception. Unlike previous racially controversial films, such as *Sweet Sweetback's Baadasssss Song* (with its notorious concluding title screen stating "A BAAD ASSSSS NIGGER IS COMING BACK TO COLLECT SOME DUES"), there exists no evidence of *Machete* as being more popular among Latino audiences than among white and black audiences. It grossed less than $27 million domestically, $44 million worldwide, a disappointing tally considering the popularity of *Machete* during the film's preexistence. Still, with a budget of $10.5 million, the film managed to turn a profit. Box office success (or lack thereof) aside, this chapter will examine *Machete* and see if the film was as politically subversive as both its supporters and detractors allege.

Unlike his film, Rodriguez takes an ambiguous position toward illegal immigration, not uncommon for a later/three-plus-generation Mexican American in the Southwest. (Rodriguez is a fourth-generation Tejano.) He states,

> You're hearing a lot about immigration, which is solvable. But the corruption is the real problem in the States and that's something people don't talk about at all. . . . People talk about a border as if there's a solution of putting up a fence or something, but that just shows they don't

get it. There's no border. It becomes its own country after a while and if you and me want to get anything across the border, we can. Very easily. That's how bad it is. (Applebaum 161)

Of course, it can also be argued Rodriguez may be protecting himself from anything too controversial, as he conducts interviews such as these in order to promote his film. From these comments it should not be too surprising that Rodriguez would center his plot around the drug trade, as he apparently has given a great deal of thought to these concerns.

Perhaps a brief outline of the plot would be appropriate here. As mentioned before, *Machete* is a revenge tale of an ex-*federal* who left Mexico for Texas after a drug lord, Rogelio Torrez (played by Steven Seagal), had his wife and daughter killed, with Machete nearly killed in the process. Three years later, prominent businessman Michael Booth (Jeff Fahey) hires Machete to assassinate State Senator John McLaughlin (Robert De Niro) for $150,000, a job that Machete takes in order to donate the hit money to the "Network," which helps illegal immigrants obtain employment. As Machete positions himself for the assassination attempt, he is shot himself by a second shooter, who subsequently shoots McLaughlin in the leg. Booth had McLaughlin shot in the leg because he was low in the preliminary polls, knowing that making him a martyr would boost McLaughlin's chances for reelection. The reason that Booth is so interested in his reelection is that he works for kingpin Torrez. With McLaughlin's help, they want to construct a border wall (under the guise of immigration control) so they can actually control the drug trade, limiting it to their breaches within the wall. Although wounded, Machete recovers, and the race is on to kill Machete before he reveals the truth. Everything comes to a head in the finale, as Mexicans battle a cadre of "border vigilantes" and those associated with the drug trade. This simple plot was also the outline of the trailer, although obviously fleshed out with substantially more characters (including Torrez and the female lead characters, some of whom will be discussed below).

Rodriguez notably cast some of the major Latino actors working today. Trejo was 66 years old at the time of the film's release; not only was he an odd choice for an action hero, but the film also finally gave him his first breakout role. Machete's status as a former *federal* helps him trust Sartana, since, as Machete says, "We're both cops" (a sign that Machete is more "the Man" than "baadasssss"?).

Rodriguez also follows stereotypical media constructions in his decision to cast Michelle Rodriguez and Jessica Alba in the female leads.

Michelle Rodriguez, born in Texas and of Puerto Rican and Dominican descent, is more strongly coded as "Mexican" in the film and allies herself with the Mexicans. In *Latina/os and the Media* Angharad Valdivia comments that like Rosario Dawson, Afro-Latina Rodriguez struggles to achieve a real breakthrough (paraphrase 110–111), unlike lighter-skinned Latinas, such as Alba, who aligns herself with the law in *Machete*.

Michelle Rodriguez plays Luz, a mild-mannered operator of a taco stand, Tacos de Luz. Yet characters throughout the film also link her with the quasi-mythical revolutionary persona of Shé, a figure in both name and iconic status intended to invoke Che Guevara. Luz even refers to feeding the "workers of the world," speaking in a none-too-subtle Marxist idiom. Luz also heads the Network, which will be discussed in greater depth later in this chapter.

The multiracial Alba, whose father is Mexican American, has a somewhat lighter skin tone than Rodriguez and has a less Mexican-sounding name, perhaps factoring in Rodriguez's decision to portray her as a later-generation Mexican American who has lost her cultural identity. *Machete* may have been somewhat of a "coming out" for her, as her Latina heritage was not common knowledge. Alba has been dismissed by Latino/a bloggers such as Perez Hilton, who labeled her Jessica "Don't Call Me Latina" Alba. (See Angharad Valdivia's *Latina/os and the Media* and Isabel Molina-Guzmán's *Dangerous Curves*.) Her body includes no identifiable ethnic markers (unlike the media's portrayal of Jennifer Lopez's butt) and thus fits into Anglo ideals of beauty, yet her dark hair and eyes have made her more "ethnicized" than some blonde and/or blue-eyed Latinas, such as Cameron Diaz and Alexis Bledel. She has also embodied a racial flexibility, as seen in films such as *Honey* (2002), that actresses such as Salma Hayek and Michelle Rodriguez are less able to obtain.

Alba plays Agent Sartana Rivera of ICE (Immigration and Customs Enforcement). Sartana has been targeting Luz's taco stand, presuming it was much more than a simple taco stand, namely a center for immigration fraud and aiding in illegal entry. Mexicans scatter when Sartana—*la migra*—walks nearby. Luz asks her why she continues to buy her coffee from there. Sartana answers, "I actually like my coffee cheap and greasy." Her Mexican heritage is established in this early scene as well, as Luz asks her how does it feel "taking your brothers and sisters in?" Sartana remains optimistic about what she does, arguing, "The system still works here." In a later scene, when Luz discloses the Network's headquarters to her, Luz replies, "The system doesn't work. It's broken." Sartana's character evolves the most in the film; once a strict anti-immigrationist (as her occupation would entail), she later informs her supervisor, "There's the law and there's what's right." Part of it was a realization that she was betraying her own people: "I can't be busting people at taco stands anymore. Hell, I'm probably related to half of them." Yet Sartana also realizes that there are greater concerns in the United States than illegal immigration.

In terms of having the most appearances in a Rodriguez film, only Salma Hayek and Antonio Banderas (neither of whom appear in *Machete*) rival Cheech Marin and Danny Trejo, who have seven and nine appearances each, respectively. Marin is cast as Machete's brother Padre, another ex-*federal* turned Catholic priest. Although primarily known for the "Cheech and Chong" films, Marin also directed the political satire *Born in East L.A.* (1987), about an assimilated, later-generation Mexican American who is mistakenly deported. The film's final scene featured Mexicans running en masse towards the U.S. border, with the two immigration officers posted there powerless to stop them. Similar to Trejo, Marin tackles both Mexican and Mexican American roles in films even though both were born in California.

For its setting, *Machete* adopts a flexible geography, as the frequent shots of the Texas State Capitol building (a prominent landmark in other Rodriguez films, e.g., *Spy Kids 2*) and 512 area code place the film in Austin, yet the city's 225 miles from the Mexican border hardly fits the nearby border present throughout the film. (How is McLaughlin able to limp away from the battle and subsequently get gunned down at the border?) Yet the border is conveniently proximate when needed for a scene.

The Latino characters in *Machete* distinctly refer to themselves as "Mexican," not "Hispanic" or "Latino" or even "Chicano." Rodriguez humorously refers to this distinction in one scene, when Padre offers a Cuban cigar to Machete and simply says, "Cuban?" Machete replies, "No. Mexican," to which Padre instead opens a box full of oversized marijuana joints. I will thus refer to the characters in the film as "Mexican," an accurate term in the diegetic world of *Machete*.

The Latino Threat Narrative

The "Latino Threat Narrative," a phrase coined by Leo R. Chavez, is a Foucauldian discourse based on knowledge and power and the fear that occurs when one feels threatened by the "Other" (41). It consists of many presumptions, many of which are identified as myths by Chavez in his book *The Latino Threat: Constructing Immigrants, Citizens, and the Nation.*

He tackles such "hot-button" issues as border security, the alleged *reconquista* of the American Southwest, assimilation, language, Latina fertility, organ donation, and immigrant marches. With every issue, Chavez demonstrates how the media has exacerbated the topic, attempting to instill fear in dominant (i.e., white, established) Americans.

Chavez notes the historical antecedents to this narrative, such as the Chinese and Japanese immigration threat, the Catholic threat, and the southern and eastern European threat (paraphrase 3). Americans have often been fearful whenever immigration flow is concentrated from a dominant source, as they fear that such immigrants will not assimilate. Various immigrant groups have been targeted in different periods and regions of U.S. history, such as Irish immigrants that measured 58% of all immigrants in 1851 (Cornelius 184n7), Swedish immigrants in late-nineteenth-century Minnesota, Italian immigrants in early-twentieth-century New York, and now, Mexican immigrants (Cornelius 176) are the prime target, despite their presence for centuries in what is now the American Southwest. Just as blatant instances of racism against blacks was strongest in the states of Mississippi, Georgia, and Alabama (which had the highest concentrations of African Americans), it is in the American Southwest that anti-immigration rhetoric has been strongest (e.g., Proposition 187 in California, the recent bill in Arizona, demands for a wall along the border in Texas).

Despite these historical antecedents, Chavez notes that the Latino Threat Narrative "posits that Latinos are not like previous immigrant groups, who ultimately became part of the nation." Rather, according to Chavez, they are "unwilling or incapable of integrating. . . . They are part of an invading force from south of the border that is bent on re-conquering the land that was formerly theirs" (2). These fears are clearly evident in the vehement anti-immigration polemics captured by Dan De-Vivo and Joseph Mathew's documentary *Crossing Arizona* (2006), which concludes with the rise of the Minuteman Project in 2005. Increased fertility rates among Latino families remains another concern for those who feel threatened by Latino immigration. Much of this presumption can be attributed to anti-Catholic biases among many Americans, who connect this Catholicism with larger families. Although Mexico is still a predominantly Catholic country, many Americans are also ignorant of the fact that evangelicalism has experienced fantastic growth there as it has in much of Latin America. Furthermore, many immigrants convert to Protestantism when they arrive in the United States, particularly the later generations (Chavez paraphrase 62–63).

But perhaps the biggest fear that perpetuates the Latino Threat Narrative is that Latinos, unlike previous immigrant groups, do not assimilate. Again, Chavez provides empirical evidence that this is not the case, particularly in his tables included in the chapter "Cultural Contradictions of Citizenship and Belonging" (paraphrase 44–69). James P. Smith also notes how assimilation occurs through successive generations, particularly through increased educational attainment and higher income/wage values (paraphrase 316–317). To cite yet another study, Richard Alba determines that educational attainment among younger Mexican Americans (born 1971–1975) is much closer to white Americans than previously assumed (paraphrase 290), and Spanish-speaking in Mexican American homes is not nearly as dominant as critics, such as Samuel P. Huntington in "The Hispanic Challenge," have insisted. Furthermore, Chavez notes increased civic engagement by Latinos across generations, hardly the actions of a people attempting to reconquer the Southwest (Chavez paraphrase 63–64). The data of the last two censuses (2000 and 2010) also refute the irrational *reconquista* fear, as Latino populations in areas of the Midwest and South have experienced greater population growth than the traditional, Latino-dense areas of the Southwest.

Machete's Themes and the Latino Threat Narrative

In *Machete* the Latino Threat Narrative appears strongest in Senator McLaughlin's political campaign discourse, that is, the political commercial and speech. In the commercial, images of Mexicans climbing hills, crossing the Rio Grande, and ICE agents chasing down border trespassers inform voters of how perilous immigration problems now are. Most disturbingly, the political commercial for McLaughlin, who has "built his reputation on being a hard-liner against wetbacks," begins with mealworms and appositely closes with cockroaches to suggest the nature of this parasitic invasion, thus dehumanizing illegal immigrants. The commercial contains the following narration:

> The infestation has begun. Parasites have crossed our borders and are sickening our country, leeching off our system, destroying us from the inside. But State Senator John McLaughlin has a plan of attack. He'll fight to keep illegal immigrants out. He supports an electrified border fence. No amnesty for parasites. John McLaughlin wants to protect you from the invaders. Vote to re-elect State Senator John McLaughlin.

The words "NO IMMIGRANTS" also appear on the screen in red, white, and blue, with bullet holes. Anti-illegal immigration rhetoric thus conflates all immigration together, making no distinction among illegal aliens from Mexico, refugees from Sudan (of which there are quite a few in certain areas of Texas), or Asian immigrants. Not to mention the fact that Texas was settled heavily by German, Irish, and Czech immigrants in the decades after statehood.

With cowboy hat, black suit, and an American flag pen, McLaughlin addresses his supporters at a rally. After thanking them, his address further solidifies his political platform (as if his commercial was not obvious enough); it is worth quoting at length:

> Because we have been tested, tested by fire. Our border has been put to the test, and let me tell you, we have failed that test. The aliens, the infiltrators, the outsiders, they come right across by light of day or dark of night. They'll bleed us. They're parasites. They'll bleed us until we, as a city, a county, a state, a nation, are all bled out. But make no mistake, we are at war. Every time an illegal dances across our border, it is an act of aggression against this sovereign state, an overt act of terrorism. Everywhere I go in this glorious state, people are talking about change. I say, "Why change? This is a great state founded on the principles of liberty." I don't wanna change that. Our rightful citizens are hardworking Americans who earn their paychecks by the grit of their guts and the sweat of their brow. I don't wanna change that. Change. That's what they want. Change. Change the laws. Open the doors. Red Rover, Red Rover, let the terrorists come over. Let me tell you what change that'll bring. Sixty-eight cents. The jingle-jangle of pennies in your pocket because the scavengers, the leeches, the parasites are walking away with your money while you're left with the change.

A few attendees hold up signs depicting Uncle Sam saying, "I want YOU to speak English." Various other anti-immigration signs clutter the mise-en-scène as we scan the crowd briefly from McLaughlin's point of view, but they can be difficult to read even in freeze-frame.

McLaughlin's phrase "dance across the border" is noticeable for two reasons: one, it ignores the hardships of the millions who attempt to cross each year (most unsuccessfully); second, it again links Latin Americans with dancing, whether it is the rhumba, salsa, or the tango, a popular Hollywood stereotype of Latinas, including characters played by Carmen Miranda, Rita Hayworth, pre-"Mexican Spitfire" Lupe Velez, and Rita

Moreno. Likewise, Von Jackson (Don Johnson), who leads a group of "border vigilantes," says, "There's nothing I would like better than to see that Mexican [i.e., Machete] dance the bolero at the end of a rope."

McLaughlin also notably connects illegal immigration to terrorism. In the aftermath of September 11, 2001, fears of terrorism became an excuse for increased border patrol measures, despite the fact that no Latin Americans were involved in the 9/11 attacks. After appealing to their fears of terrorism, McLaughlin concludes his speech with the economic impact of immigrants on natural-born citizens. This recalls the massive deportation of Mexican Americans during the Great Depression, when they were blamed for astronomically high unemployment. Of course, the frequent use of "change" intentionally positions McLaughlin as a reactionary, someone not in step with President Obama's 2008 campaign buzzword. (His Texan accent and manner are also to intentionally remind us of George W. Bush.) Although McLaughlin admittedly exaggerates the anti-immigration rhetoric of certain politicians, it may not be too far off from the vitriol spewed by some conservative radio personalities, as seen in the documentary *Crossing Arizona*.

Immigration is the most identifiable theme in *Machete*. In an early scene near the border, a coyote drives a van full of hopeful migrants whom he drops off short of the border without any further assistance. This bewildered group is then confronted by Von and his border vigilantes, who film their kills of immigrants, apparently to upload on the Internet. They attack a young couple, as Von shoots a pregnant woman. McLaughlin shockingly asks, "Jesus, Von, can't you see she's with child?" Von coldly replies, "If it's born here, it gets to be a citizen. No different than you and me. . . . Somebody's got to keep watch on this great nation of ours. Otherwise, Texas will become Mexico . . . once again." The border vigilantes can be compared to a more extreme version of Jim Gilchrist and his Minuteman Project. (For more on the Minuteman Project, see Leo Chavez 132–151.)

Von's absurd observation ("Otherwise, Texas will become Mexico . . . once again") fits into one of the central tenets of the Latino Threat Narrative: that Mexicans in the U.S. Southwest hope to secede from the rest of the nation. Chavez labels this the "Quebec model," referring to the ongoing Quebecois calls for independence (paraphrase 26–36). Huntington, one of the most persistent critics of Latino immigration, claims, "Demographically, socially, and culturally, the *reconquista* of the Southwestern United States by Mexican immigrants is well underway." He also cites spurious claims that by 2080 the northern states in Mexico and the

American Southwest will form *La República del Norte* (The Republic of the North) (Huntington paraphrase 40). Multiple presidential candidate Pat Buchanan also addresses this concern in his book *The Death of the West: How Dying Populations and Immigrant Invasions Imperil Our Country and Civilization*. In a chapter actually entitled "La Reconquista," Buchanan posits the following:

> Unlike the immigrants of old . . . [m]illions of [Mexicans] have no desire to learn English or to become citizens. America is not their home, Mexico is; and they wish to remain proud Mexicans. They have come here to work. Rather than assimilate, they create Little Tijuanas in U.S. cities. . . . With their own radio and TV stations, newspapers, films, and magazines, the Mexican Americans are creating an Hispanic culture separate and apart from America's larger culture. They are becoming a nation within a nation. (qtd. Chavez 37)

Clearly, Buchanan refers to many points in the Latino Threat Narrative, including the inability and unwillingness of Mexican immigrants to assimilate or to learn English. He also apparently supports the "Quebec model" theory, stating that Latinos "are becoming a nation within a nation." Chavez rightly shoots down the notion of a Latino *reconquista* of the Aztlán. Refuting the anecdotal evidence of opponents such as Huntington, he cites data depicting how assimilationist markers such as English-language ability, educational attainment, income, intermarriage, and civic engagement all increase from first-generation Latinos through the 1.5 (those who migrated under the age of 15), second, and third-plus generations. (For more details on the markers of assimilation see the tables in Leo Chavez 52–67.)

But does *Machete* appropriate the *reconquista* theme? Arguably so. Turning from *la migra* to revolutionary figure, Agent Sartana delivers an inspiring speech that rouses the ire of the Mexicans, noting the arbitrariness of border politics: "They're just lines drawn in the sand by men who stand on your back for power and glory." Sartana concludes with the line that certainly invokes the memory of the Treaty of Guadalupe Hidalgo of 1848, when Mexico ceded present-day California, Utah, Nevada, and parts of Arizona, New Mexico, and Colorado, leaving the Mexicans in this region bewildered that they now found themselves denizens of a different country: "We didn't cross the border, the border crossed us!"

While Rodriguez insists that the film is more about corruption than immigration (Applebaum 161), the latter topic remains the more intriguing one, partly because so many action films hinge on political corruption. This is what separates *Machete* from similar films, that it actually tackles one of the hottest contemporary political topics and was fortunately released only a few months after the Arizona bill's passage.

The Network's prominent place within the narrative was not included in the original trailer. The Network helps immigrants to cross, to find jobs, and to reciprocate by eventually returning favors for others. Robert Courtney Smith's *Mexican New York: Transnational Lives of New Immigrants* details how transnational social networks operate on a smaller scale in immigration (Ticuani, Mexico, and New York City), but it sheds light on how a macroscale transnational social network might function. Luz makes daily contacts through her taco stand, but it is her warehouse that serves as the low-tech base of operations for the Network.

The Latino-targeted media are portrayed with the Exactamundo TV station. Presumably a local version of Telemundo or Univision, its viewers are depicted as kitchen employees, launderers, and hotel maids. The newscasts on the station (uncharacteristically in English) inform the audience of Machete's status and the manhunt arranged for his capture. (The turning point in the film hinges on the actions of its news anchor, when she shows the footage of Senator McLaughlin murdering the immigrant.) The Network then comes to the aid of Machete, skeptical that an illegal would have any rationale for such a terroristic act as a political assassination. After Machete is shot and almost killed in a car explosion,[3] he is taken to the hospital by people in the Network. He awakens as his body is being wheeled in, as a nurse informs him in Spanish, "Most illegals aren't given treatment at regular ERs." His nurses reveal that they and many of the physicians in the hospital are indeed part of the Network, which we are learning is much larger than just Luz's taco stand. (We have not seen the warehouse yet.)

Not all immigrants in the film are initially supportive of the Network's cause. A dishwasher seems in support of McLaughlin's platform as he pronounces in Spanish, "Yes, detain the illegals! Close the border!" The other dishwasher asks him "Didn't you cross the border?" He replies, "Well, I'm already here. Fine with me if they close it," apparently ignorant of attempts in twentieth-century American history to round up citizens along with illegal aliens, with the most egregious instances occurring during the Great Depression, but also later in the 1950s with "Operation Wetback" and Mexican repatriation. The anti-immigration dishwasher recalls the substantial Latino population supporting anti-immigration measures, or even working as *la migra*.

After Machete's failed assassination attempt, he becomes a "man with no country," another type that Luz and the Network seemingly attempt to aid. Illegal immigrants convicted of a crime are often deported to their nation of origin. Who knows what Machete would have faced as an illegal alien accused of an assassination attempt on a state senator? If something like this were to occur in real life, calls for deportation of illegals would undoubtedly increase.

The stereotypes perpetuated in *Machete* also merit discussion. Machete may be a hero, but he still has a weakness for women, tequila, and marijuana. Although Machete beds Latinas in the film (such as Luz), he also has no problem with being filmed in a sex video with Booth's (white) wife and daughter. Sure, Machete's primary motivation was arguably revenge. Still, it perpetuates a stereotype that Latino men prefer white women, although an admittedly stronger media stereotype exists concerning African American men. Moreover, it seems to arguably support Sartana and Luz as representative of the two sides of Mexican womanhood: Our Lady of Guadalupe and La Malinche ("*La Chingada*"), respectively. Machete acts like a "gentleman" when in bed beside the virginal Sartana, not taking advantage of her despite her inebriated state. Contrariwise, Luz and Machete engage in animalistic sex in Luz's bed, sex so *muy caliente* that an egg fries beneath said bed.

Here I should address Machete's relationship to machismo: "a term," Rosa Linda Fregoso notes, "that no longer requires translation, machismo conjures up Latinos as the model for the pathological transgressions of hegemonic masculine identities, thereby laying bare the tacit racism prevailing in dominant discourse as well as critical scholarly works" (30). Still, machismo dominates the discourse on Latin/a/o culture to the extent that failing to comment on it here would be an oversight. Machete seems to defy certain aspects of machismo, especially when he does not take advantage of Sartana, nor does he view the female agent as unworthy to be an ally in his mission.

One key scene saturated with stereotypes occurs when the Mexicans take to the streets. After some outfitting at an establishment called Machete's Chop Shop, lowriders bounce down the street, as some automobiles are armored in a *Mad Max*–style, battle-ready mode. These lowriders are used in the mêlée, and this may be the first film ever in which someone is crushed to death by a lowrider on hydraulics.

The stereotypes work both ways, however, as Rodriguez portrays the vigilantes as clichéd "redneck" types. When they betray McLaughlin and he decides to fight back against them, he still refers to them as "good old boys." In order to preserve his life while fighting on the Mexican side, he acquiesces to "become Mexican" by wearing the stereotypical garb of the northern Mexican peasant, replete with baja pullover hoodie sweatshirt and a shabby cowboy hat. While these items (with the help of a bullet-proof vest) save him during the battle, McLaughlin ironically dies at the border, still dressed like a Mexican.

Julio (played by Daryl Sabara of the *Spy Kids* films, who is the focus of Phillip Serrato's chapter in this collection) alludes to being adopted to explain his white phenotypic features, but he and Jorge (Gilbert Trejo, Danny's son) play stereotypical cholos. Another common stereotype, that *pochos* only use Spanish for vulgarities, is perpetuated by *Machete*. There are a few in-jokes that cater to Spanish-speaking audiences, or at least those familiar with Mexican/Spanglish slang. Spanish vulgarities (e.g., *puñeta*; *pendejo*; *cabrón*; *¡No mames guey!*) are often left untranslated, as are other Spanish words and phrases thrown into the normal English conversations.

Just as the word "nigger" and other racist terms are frequently used in blaxploitation cinema, Rodriguez's film uses derogatory language for provocative means. Many of these come from McLaughlin's mouth about Machete: "cucaracha" and "Frito Bandito"[4] (along with "burrito" in a deleted scene available on the Blu-ray DVD of *Machete*). When the battle between the border vigilantes and the Network is about to commence, the former refer to the latter as "beaneaters," an older slang term less common in Texas than the equally offensive "wetbacks." The border vigilantes train by stabbing dummies bedecked in ponchos and sombreros as they exclaim, "Kill the wetbacks!" Surprisingly, it was (white) conservative commentators that seemed to take the most offense at the racist language, fearing it would incite racial hatred.

As Booth and family gather around the dining table, what are they eating? Tacos! And salsa! This may not be a stereotype, but it supports the claims of Latino sociologists that while Americans like certain aspects of Latino culture (especially Mexican food), that does not mean that they want to live in the same neighborhoods as they do. This irony was not lost on audiences; when viewing the film with the "audience reaction track" on the DVD or Blu-ray, one of the film's most raucous laughs occurs at this moment.

While seemingly gratuitous on first viewing, the violence in *Machete* arguably even comments on the Latino Threat Narrative. One significant leitmotif involves the violation of the eye: Machete jabs a corkscrew into a villain's eye; Von shoots Shé in the eye, forcing her to later wear an eye patch; and when henchmen invade Sartana's home, she retaliates by stabbing one in the eye with her high-heeled shoe. Besides paralleling the violation of the eye that the film performs hyperdiegetically (just as the slicing of the eye in *Un Chien Andalou* [1929] functions metaphorically), the abundant scenes of eye trauma might suggest a cultural blindness, another cause for damaging stereotypes related to the Latino population.

McLaughlin wants all Mexican immigrants to go back to Mexico, but he first wants a border wall built by free labor. (Sound familiar?) The wall is apparently good for the drug trade, as a secure border limits supply, driving prices up. Torrez wants McLaughlin to build a border fence so that he can control weak spots along the fence and will not have to "compete with every *pendejo* with a 'dimebag' and a dream."

Films and television shows about the border and U.S.-Mexico relations have often centered on drugs, whether it is dramas such as *Traffic* (2000), *Blow* (2001), and the Jean-Claude Van Damme straight-to-DVD *The Shepherd: Border Patrol* (2008) or comedies like *Up in Smoke* (starring Marin, 1978). The use of drugs fits into the Latino Threat Narrative, but Rodriguez indicts the drug trade in a political fashion as early as his first feature, *El Mariachi* (1992), in which the central villain is the white drug lord named "Moco" (Spanish for "snot"). Rodriguez stated in interviews that this was intended to be a critique of the post-NAFTA (North American Free Trade Agreement) situation. (NAFTA was not yet in effect at this time, but the proposal had been in the works.) Granted, drugs might have been employed in the film primarily as a plot device, but it seems significant that Rodriguez would tackle another aspect in the critique of the Latino Threat Narrative, specifically that tighter borders will not curtail drug flow to the United States.

Machete was released Labor Day Weekend, appropriate considering the significance of unskilled labor in the film. After Machete flees Mexico, the film shifts to "THREE YEARS LATER, DAY LABOR SITE, TEXAS." Machete has apparently picked up odd jobs at this site for some time. Booth constantly refers to Machete as a "day laborer," a transitory, insignificant participant in the American economy from his perspective. When the skeptical Machete wonders why Booth wants McLaughlin killed, he explains that the state thrives on cheap labor and a hard-liner like McLaughlin handicaps his economic interests.

Machete first gets into Booth's mansion by posing as a gardener. He has no trouble gaining entry even though his "wanted" face has been ubiquitous on TV. One of Booth's bodyguards expresses his sentiment towards immigrant labor: "You know, I've been thinking. We let these people into our homes, watch our kids, park our cars, but we won't let 'em into our country. Does that make any sense to you?" This is not to suggest that this bodyguard is making a radical statement here. Indeed, this type of argument can be aligned with the soft view toward illegal immigration espoused by some conservatives, such as George W. Bush. Illegals serve an essential function in our economy, performing tasks that citizens won't.

As the Mexican community gears up for battle, texts go out across the Network, as workers leave their jobs to battle at Von's armory. Fueled by righteous immigrant indignation, construction workers, gardeners, dishwashers, and car body shop mechanics join in. Those who do not come with guns arm themselves with shovels, rakes, and other agricultural markers, aligning themselves with the hero whose very name implies an agricultural implement. Workers coded as "illegals" fight alongside *pochos*. There are noticeably no Mexican professionals who join in the fray, except for Sartana and the nurses and doctor seen earlier in the film. Despite his dismissal of the film as overtly political, Zaitchik considers this a notable scene:

> It is this battle royal that follows . . . that most angers the film's conservative critics. It is not hard to see why. It is the most provocative pro-immigrant set piece since . . . *Born in East L.A.* For 15 minutes, *Machete* indulges in no-holds barred undocumented catharsis in broad daylight: Mexican day laborers confronting and disemboweling the Anglo border vigilantes that once hunted them in the desert for sport. The Mexicans win handily and raise their machetes in victory. (paraphase 12)

According to this reading, Machete leads the new peasant revolution.

The end of *Machete* promises two sequels: *Machete Kills* and *Machete Kills Again*. Rodriguez delivered with the first film, released in 2013, which again included a trailer that bookends the film, for *Machete Kills Again . . . in Space*. *Machete Kills* is almost entirely void of *Machete*'s political elements, even if talk of "the people" and "the revolution" persists. Still, this should not undercut the original film's topicality. While right-wing fears that *Machete* would start a race war were unfounded, I do think that dismissals of the film as nothing more than silly fun do not take the film seriously either. *Machete* remains an earnestly political film, one worthy of scrutiny, particularly in how it critiques the Latino Threat Narrative.

Notes

1. Found at http://www.youtube.com/watch?v=k9tIoJBhp18. Retrieved March 13, 2014. Other YouTube videos of Jones on *Machete* include "Racist Film Machete Produced with Taxpayer Funds!" and "'Machete' Producers Lied about Racist Bloodbath Film." Interestingly enough, Jones (a filmmaker himself besides being a conservative radio personality), also based in Austin, has appeared in both *Waking Life* (2001) and *A Scanner Darkly* (2006), films by Richard Linklater, Rodriguez's friend and fellow Austin filmmaker.

2. "52% Support Arizona-Like Immigration Law in Their State," Rasmussen Reports, http://www.rasmussenreports.com/public_content/politics/current _events/immigration/52_support_arizona_like_immigration_law_in_their_state. Retrieved March 13, 2014.

3. Machete was beaten by two men disguised as police. Although not real cops, the scene still recalls the issue of police brutality and discrimination often experienced by minorities. They call Machete "poncho," while one states that they (the authorities) are going to "hang your ass like Saddam," again connecting illegal immigration to terrorism.

4. For a brief summation of the Frito Bandito controversy of the late 1960s/ early 1970s, see Angharad Valdivia's *Latina/os and the Media* and Chon A. Noriega, *Shot in America*.

CHAPTER 9

The Development of Social Minds
in the "Mexico Trilogy"

JAMES J. DONAHUE

Often visualized with flamboyant attire, large sombrero, and performing with violins, trumpets, and *guitarrón*, the mariachi band has become Hollywood's most dependable visual reference to Mexican culture. From John Landis's *¡Three Amigos!* (1986)—where three out-of-work actors are hired to reprise their roles as gunfighters/mariachi troupe in a terrorized Mexican town—to the Coen brothers' adaptation of Cormac McCarthy's *No Country for Old Men* (2007)—where Llewelyn Moss (Josh Brolin) is serenaded by mariachi after crossing the Mexican border—the mariachi has become a cross-genre signifier for American film audiences, and its presence undoubtedly represents Mexico. And although "Lucky Day," "Dusty Bottoms," and Ned Nederlander carry and use guns, the crime-fighting mariachi band in *¡Three Amigos!* is clearly a musical/dancing act, whose bumbling efforts at crime fighting make up much of the film's humor. The mariachi is an entertainer, not a gunslinger.

However, with Robert Rodriguez's "Mexico Trilogy"—*El Mariachi* (1992), *Desperado* (1995), and *Once Upon a Time in Mexico* (2003)—the mariachi is reconceived as a deadly assassin. Gone are the colorful costumes; Rodriguez's mariachi wears a neat black suit. And while the mariachi can play the guitar, early in the trilogy his instrument of entertainment is traded for instruments of violence. More than just a vehicle of vengeance, however, the character of the mariachi experiences significant growth over the course of the trilogy. Rather than simply representing Mexico for Rodriguez's audience, as the mariachi has done in Hollywood for decades, El Mariachi (or "The Man in Black," as he is also known, recalling a stock characterization in American westerns)[1] develops from a loner to an integral part of a larger social unit. In this chapter, I will explore the development of El Mariachi by means of adapting Alan Palmer's methodology from his *Social Minds in the Novel* (2010) to the study of film. Treating Palmer's typology of intermental units as a progression, I will show how El Mariachi develops from small intermental encounters to participation in increasingly larger intermental units. To be clear, I am not claiming that Rodriguez had in mind intermental development, or even a sequel—much less a trilogy—when he wrote, filmed, and edited *El Mariachi*. Rather, Palmer's taxonomy of intermental units provides a means of understanding the development of the title character in ways that connect to the trilogy's larger thematic concerns.

Social Minds in Literature and Film

Focusing strictly on an externalist perspective on the minds of characters in fiction, Palmer's study explores how social minds are constructed and operate. As Palmer defines it, *intermental thought* is "joint, group, shared, or collective, as opposed to *intramental*, or individual or private thought" (41). Where much study has been done on the representation of the inner thoughts of characters,[2] Palmer here explores the importance of social thought: "just as in real life, where much of our thinking is done in groups, much of the mental functioning that occurs in novels is done by large organizations, small groups, work colleagues, friends, families, couples, and other intermental units" (41). Although all of Palmer's major examples come from narrative fiction, he does note at the end of his study that "the sort of approach to narrative outlined in this book is well suited to graphic novels and related narrative forms" (198), including film (briefly discussing *The Godfather, Part I* and *The Usual Suspects*).

Palmer demonstrates the operation of a large intermental unit with "the Middlemarch mind," as developed in George Eliot's *Middlemarch* (1874). This is an example of a social mind shared by an entire community, as evidenced by how the narrator characterizes various opinions, customs, and how certain actions are usually done; in other words, the Middlemarch community operates in certain key ways in terms of what we might call groupthink. More importantly for the present chapter, however, is Palmer's reading of Charles Dickens's *Little Dorrit* (1857). Here, Palmer reads the means by which characters engage in intermental communication and form small intermental units. For Palmer, much of the novel's intermental communication taking place among small intermental groups is focused on the face and on issues of vision: "[a]s we do in real life, characters pick up cues about the mental functioning of others by reading facial expressions" (109). Just as important for Palmer is "the significance of the look" (113), which can involve such actions as staring at other characters or in some way paying particular attention to them.

So how exactly have filmmakers developed social minds in their narratives? In *The Godfather, Part I*, we are shown "three split-second close-ups showing the reactions of Sollozzo and two others [Don Corleone using a hand gesture to silence Sonny]. These lightning-quick shots show in an instant that all three understand perfectly what has just happened" (198). The suggestion that Palmer makes here is that we come to understand the operation of social minds in film narratives through the means by which the filmmaker films and edits shots of characters' faces. Although faces are also one means (though not the only means) of identifying intermental thought in fiction, I would posit that reading faces is the predominant means of expressing intermental thought in film, both because film is a visual medium and because film uses specific techniques that focus on the eyes/the face in certain kinds of editing for continuity. In this regard, identifying social minds in film is not unlike Lisa Zunshine's application of Theory of Mind to fiction.[3] The key notable distinction is that audiences are not taking in a variety of visual data with respect to characters in trying to understand their current mental state; rather, audiences are looking for those visual cues that suggest how two (or more) characters share a social mind, connect on a level that need not be directly articulated through characters' speech or narratorial involvement. I'd like to posit that eye-line matching—traditionally one of several means to maintain continuity in editing—is the most effective means by which filmmakers can suggest the development of a small intermental unit. As with print narratives, however, a variety of devices must be used to define the operations of large intermental units, as we will see below. Specifically, filmmakers like Robert Rodriguez can employ eye-line matching, along with well-placed close-ups, to suggest that characters are of the same mind. And in this regard, Rodriguez's Mexico Trilogy can be read as a paradigmatic example of the development of intermental units in film narratives.

El Mariachi: Loner

In *El Mariachi* (1992), we are introduced to the nameless mariachi (Carlos Gallardo), a traveling musician looking for a steady job, following in the footsteps of his father and grandfather. An initial misunderstanding—as both Azul (Reynold Martínez) and the mariachi are dressed in black and carrying guitar cases—leads the mariachi to be confused for Azul, a recently escaped killer seeking revenge against the local crime boss, Moco (Peter Marquardt). The mariachi manages to kill Moco's hitmen, after which he seeks refuge in a bar. Unfortunately for the mariachi, the bar is owned by Moco, for which reason Azul also pays the bar a visit. Azul mistakenly takes the mariachi's guitar case with him, leaving the mariachi with a case full of guns. Eventually, Azul kidnaps Dominó (Consuelo Gómez) and forces her to lead him to Moco's. The mariachi, having earlier been taken to Moco's and released, follows them there to save Dominó. Unfortunately, he arrives too late; Moco guns down both Azul and Dominó and then shoots the mariachi in his left hand, ruining his musical aspirations. As alone as when he arrived, the mariachi leaves town after killing Moco, taking with him the guitar case filled with weapons, as well as Dominó's dog and letter opener, suggesting their sentimental value.

This quick summary emphasizes the mariachi's status as a loner figure, though also suggests how he started to develop a connection with Dominó. As the first installment of the Mexico Trilogy, Rodriguez characterizes the mariachi as a solitary figure but provides the groundwork by which we can view him as participating in later intermental groups. Specifically, much of the movie emphasizes the growing relationship between the mariachi and Dominó. Not all relationships, however, constitute intermental units; this relationship certainly does not. While the audience does see how the mariachi and Dominó do come to share an attraction for one another, at no point do they share a fully developed social mind. But by analyzing the means by which Rodriguez uses mise-en-scène and continuity editing to develop their relationship, we can see how he lays the groundwork for the mariachi's later intermental development in *Desperado*. Also, the relationship between the mariachi and Dominó can be productively contrasted to the relationship between Moco and his unnamed female attendant. Not only are the mariachi and Moco visualized as opposites—they wear black and white, respectively, for instance—but their relationships with their female companions are also opposite. In short, Moco and his attendant form the kind of intermental unit that the mariachi and Dominó work toward but do not achieve.

Not only does the mariachi arrive in town alone, but he is predominantly shot in ways that emphasize his solitary nature. For instance, in the opening shot, the turtle gets more camera time and focus than he does. Similarly, in the following sequences, the mariachi only appears in the shot with other characters when their faces are not shown, such as the shoe shiner's hands and the mariachi's feet, or the mariachi's hands and the bartender's hands. Although the mariachi interacts with these other characters, they either do not communicate at all, or their communication is of little to no significance. I'd like to note here the importance of the face not just in general communication—in terms of speech as well eye contact—but also in developing intermental units in film. In other words, part of how Rodriguez identifies intermental units is by how he films faces—specifically, how individuals who comprise intermental units often share face time, as it were, in a shot. As such, the opening sequences suggest the mariachi's status as a solitary figure by specifically filming his face in isolation. Many of the mariachi's scenes are shot close up, minimizing the background and precluding other characters' ability to be visually associated with him. And while this is the predominant mode for filming many characters in *El Mariachi*, this only highlights both the intermental unit that the mariachi and Dominó begin to build, as well as the one that Moco and his attendant already form.

In addition to shooting many speaking characters in close-up when they speak, most of the conversations in the film employ shot/reverse shot, so that even when two characters enter into a conversation, they still occupy the shot as solitary figures (or, alternately, the nonspeaking character is seen from behind, so that character's face is not part of the shot). By filming most conversations—particularly those between the mariachi and Dominó—in such a fashion, Rodriguez visually suggests that the central characters are solitary: the nameless mariachi is a loner and largely unwelcome presence; Dominó has rejected the advances of Moco; Azul treats most everybody in the film as an obstacle to his vengeance. As such, conversations between two solitary individuals—between two figures who do not form intermental units—are the norm. Even those characters who share other connections—such as the mariachi's and Dominó's mutual attraction—are not filmed in such a way as to suggest their social connections (with the exception of Moco and his attendant, which I will address below).

So it is in keeping with the film's general aesthetic that the mariachi's first conversation with Dominó is filmed in shot/reverse shot. However, as they continue to speak and get to know each other, Rodriguez films their conversations differently. For instance, where the first conversation is shot so that each character occupies most of the frame, occupying the shot alone, their second conversation is shot such that the nonspeaking character is still in the frame, so that we see the speaking character over the shoulder of the other. We see instances of the mariachi's head in the frame, though his face is obscured, while Dominó speaks. Similarly, unlike in the first conversation, the mariachi reaches for and grasps Dominó's hand, their first physical contact. Although still employing shot/reverse shot, there are suggestions of extended eye contact between them. Throughout this conversation, they spend time getting to know one another—she introduces herself and we learn more about the mariachi—and the subtle changes to filming and editing suggest their growing comfort with and interest in each other.

As the mariachi and Dominó develop their relationship, we see more physical contact and more suggestions of extended eye contact, particularly in the bath and bar scenes. However, once again, at no point are the mariachi's and Dominó's faces filmed simultaneously. In the bath scene, Dominó is situated behind the mariachi, but her face is above the shot when he speaks, just as his face is below the shot when she speaks. The continued use of extreme close-ups as a means of excluding the other character from the shot allows the audience to continue to read both characters as solitary figures, even if they are developing a relationship. Over time, their physical and emotional attractions are clear to the audience—and equally clear to Moco, who is also romantically interested in Dominó—and so the audience is primed for the emotional impact of their final shot.

The mariachi does not arrive at Moco's in time to save Dominó; he arrives just after her murder. As such, she dies before she and the mariachi can complete their intermental development. This unfinished character development is hinted at when the mariachi bends down to kiss Dominó's forehead. In addition to being a touching moment charged with emotional energy in terms of the story (as it is Dominó's murder that drives the mariachi to become a force for vengeance in the sequel), this is also the only scene in the movie where both Dominó's and the mariachi's faces share a shot. The mariachi may end the movie as a solitary figure—one whose relationship with Dominó forever changed him—but I would argue that his emotional and physical connections to Dominó are best characterized as the groundwork for the formation of later intermental groups. As we will see, the mariachi picks up with Carolina largely where he left off with Dominó. As both a retelling of and a sequel to *El Mariachi*, *Desperado* assumes most of such groundwork between the mariachi and Carolina, allowing them to form an intermental unit as the next stage in the mariachi's development.

Before moving on to *Desperado*, however, I'd like to spend a moment on Moco and his attendant. Where most conversations between characters are filmed in shot/reverse shot, most of Moco's conversations are over the phone, and as such can focus on him exclusively (or move between both conversation partners) without the need to specifically exclude the other. However, during all of his conversations, he is attended to by an unnamed woman. Although she never converses with Moco, and in many cases is often filmed as background, I would like to suggest that she nonetheless does form an intermental unit with Moco. Even though she is attending Moco rather than engaging with him, they do seem to share a social mind in that she is able to attend to him without disruption.[4] That she is more than a well-trained servant is suggested by her introduction, where she is shown swimming alone in the pool, a privilege most likely denied to the estate staff (the only other character we see in the pool is Moco). Further, in contrast to the mariachi and Dominó, Moco and his attendant often share the shot, and their faces are clearly filmed simultaneously. Remembering the bath scene where Dominó held a letter opener to the mariachi's throat, we know that Rodriguez can emphasize solitary characters by use of extreme close-up, so that even characters in immediate physical proximity need not share the shot. As such, Moco and his attendant form the kind of intermental unit that the mariachi seeks to form with Dominó. In this way, Moco again serves as a foil to the mariachi. Similarly, his successful intermental relationship with his attendant puts into relief the mariachi's failed intermental development with Dominó, further emphasizing the mariachi's status as loner figure at the end of the film.

However, the mariachi does not remain a loner figure; just as his failure to form an intermental unit with Dominó sets the stage for his formation of an intermental unit with Carolina in *Desperado*, so too will we see how his participation in a small intermental unit with Carolina sets the stage for his eventual participation in a large intermental unit with the Mexican people more generally in *Once Upon a Time in Mexico*.

Desperado: Lover

Though in many ways a remake of *El Mariachi*, *Desperado* (1995) is also clearly a sequel. Reading the film as both a remake and a sequel simultaneously should help us to flesh out exactly how the mariachi figure is further developed in this movie, particularly with respect to his intermental relationship with Carolina (Salma Hayek). As a remake, *Desperado* presents another version of the revenge plot: a mariachi (Antonio Banderas) dressed in black arrives in a Mexican town, meets and falls in love with a businesswoman who has ties to the local crime boss, a figure who dresses in white; and the mariachi takes his revenge against the crime boss, after which time he leaves town. Both movies also rely on the plot device of mistaken identity (albeit in different ways).[5] As such, audiences could (and many did) watch *Desperado* without the benefit of having seen *El Mariachi* and not lose any of the continuity. However, viewing them in succession does allow for the audience to see the many points whereby *Desperado* does operate as the second act of a developing drama: in *Desperado*, the mariachi is already the gunfighter he starts to become in *El Mariachi*, and his legend has started to spread throughout the Mexican underworld.

More importantly, the mariachi begins *Desperado* not as a loner, as he both began and finished in *El Mariachi*. Whereas in the first movie the mariachi did not successfully form an intermental unit with Dominó, he does over the course of the movie form such a unit with Carolina. This is suggested through a variety of means, not the least of which is that the mariachi is very consciously presented as a figure who can form such units; in other words, the mariachi in *Desperado* is no loner. First, Buscemi (Steve Buscemi) works as a partner to the mariachi, helping to disseminate the story of the man in black. Second, the mariachi himself dreams of a night playing with his former band, a band which he did not belong to in the first movie, but which could not have been formed after the conclusion of the first movie given the damage to his hand. That the band is real is confirmed later in the movie when the mariachi calls upon them to help fight Bucho's men. So where did this band come from, and what do they reflect about the mariachi? Even though the introduction of this band poses continuity problems in reading *Desperado* as a sequel to *El Mariachi* (though none if we read the movie as a remake),[6] the band does help to establish the mariachi as a figure who can form intermental relationships with others. As such, the band—like Buscemi and Carolina—helps establish the mariachi figure's development throughout the trilogy.

That the three band members form a small intermental unit is established in the opening dream sequence. Though the mariachi himself is first presented in close-ups, much like he was introduced in *El Mariachi*, he is quickly joined by his bandmates; the title shot, in fact, includes a full-frontal view of all three band members, their faces clearly visible. If, as argued above, the mariachi and Dominó come close to forming an intermental unit at the moment when their faces share a shot, such an opening shot in *Desperado* suggests to the audience the possibility that these three characters also form such a unit. This possibility is enhanced by its being the title shot to the movie. That they communicate intermentally is demonstrated when the mariachi, with one quick look and nod of his head, suggests his intentions to break up a bar fight during their performance. Though they are not needed, the other performers follow the mariachi as backup; they will perform the same function later on.

The band reunites, as it were, to assist the mariachi in his battle with Bucho's men. As each arrives in town, distorted rock guitar plays, suggesting to the audience a showdown between two groups of "badass" characters. (Their badass nature was hinted at in the title sequence, even if the band only backed up the mariachi's actions.) The mariachi and his band reunite and share the screen in a pose reminiscent of the title shot: holding their guitar cases on either side of the mariachi, as they once held their guitars on either side of him on stage. The parallelism visually reminds the audience of their ability to work together as a band;[7] or, in Palmer's terminology, their functioning as a small intermental unit. At various points throughout the showdown, they are again able to communicate with each other with little more than a quick look and a nod of the head. Again, intermental communication is established largely by the face. Both unnamed band members die near the end of the movie—just as Dominó died near the end of *El Mariachi*—reminding the audience that the band is not the mariachi's primary intermental unit. However, the band does establish the importance of such units, particularly with respect to survival. Just as the mariachi only survives because of the intervention of his band (and their ability to think and work as one), so too does Carolina survive as a result of her ability to form the kind of intermental unit with the mariachi that Dominó did not.

Because this movie is a sequel, the knowing audience is primed to read the mariachi as a developing character. As noted above, the inclusion of his band suggests that the mariachi of *Desperado* is not the mariachi of *El Mariachi*. Further, the mariachi begins the movie with a partner, cementing the audience's reading of him as a figure participating in many social relationships, and thus not a loner. (That Buscemi dies can be read similarly to the bandmates' deaths.) As such, it should come as no surprise that the mariachi's relationship with Carolina develops much more quickly. However, this movie is as much a remake as it is a sequel, and if we read Carolina as a manifestation of Dominó, we may understand more clearly why the mariachi bonds with her so quickly.

In many ways, Carolina functions similarly to Dominó, as a quick rendering of their parallel points should make clear. First, both are played by actresses with more than a passing resemblance (Consuelo Gómez and Salma Hayek). More importantly, however, both characters are small business owners with ties to the local crime boss whom the mariachi seeks to kill. (Both crime bosses, it should be noted, are dangerous men in white suits who have a history of trying to bed the small business owner.) And although there is little similarity between a bartender and a bookstore owner, both places of business have bars. The bar is used in *Desperado* for two related functions: first, it helps to visually remind the audience of Carolina's connection to Dominó; second, and just as importantly, laying the mariachi on the bar allows Carolina to remain roughly at eye level with the mariachi. This small detail allows Rodriguez to maintain the eye-line between the actors and allows for their faces to share shots in ways that might be awkward were she tending to him on a bed.

Just as eye-line matching and extreme close-ups were used in *El Mariachi* to establish the intermental potential between the mariachi and Dominó, eye-line matching and extreme close-ups are used to establish an intermental relationship in *Desperado*. This is done largely by the absence of shot/reverse-shot filming between the mariachi and Carolina. Just as the use of shot/reverse shot helped to maintain the mariachi's separation from Dominó until the climactic scene at the end where the mariachi attends to her corpse, its notable absence in the way the mariachi and Carolina are filmed in *Desperado* suggests their almost immediate connection. Further, when Carolina attends to the mariachi's wounds on her bar, their faces often clearly share a shot whereas the mariachi and Dominó did not share such a shot until the end of *El Mariachi*. In this regard, Carolina takes over roughly where Dominó left off; Carolina is a revision of Dominó and operates in part to suggest the mariachi's overall character development, though they are still in certain ways strangers to each other. The fledgling intermental relationships that don't develop (Buscemi, remember, dies) put the mariachi's relationship with Carolina into greater relief.

The mariachi's intermental relationship with Carolina is demonstrated early on when Bucho's assassins come for them. As the assassins surround the bedroom, Carolina sings to the mariachi while holding his guitar, reminding the audience of his earlier attempts to teach her to play. This connection on the level of music primes the audience for their connection as battle partners against Bucho's assassins. (Keeping in mind, of course, the connection between music and violence that both movies have been establishing in the role of the mariachi, the various guitar cases, and the mariachi's bandmates, whose skill in fighting and small arms is never explained beyond their musical affiliation with the mariachi.) The mariachi and Carolina share a kiss—reminding the audience that their relationship has already developed beyond his relationship with Dominó—and then proceed to escape. Carolina takes to both escape and gunfighting with ease (despite no apparent background), and as they both walk away from the burning building (the scene used for the cover of the Special Edition DVD release), the audience can clearly see their shared look of determination: both holding hands as well as guns, staring at the same point in the distance, the mariachi and Carolina are shot straight on, so that the audience can note their shared attitude. This scene visually cements for the audience their connection as a small intermental unit.

In contrast to the ending of *El Mariachi*, *Desperado* ends with the suggestion of the mariachi and Carolina's continued development. The mariachi at first appears to leave town alone, though he is picked up by Carolina, and the two of them drive off into the distance. So just as *El Mariachi* ended with the mariachi as a loner figure, just beginning to form an intermental relationship, *Desperado* ends with such a relationship fully formed. As we will see in *Once Upon a Time in Mexico*, this small intermental relationship is just the first step in the mariachi's larger development.

Once Upon a Time in Mexico: National Symbol

As with *Desperado*, *Once Upon a Time in Mexico* (2003) opens at a bar, with a tale of the mariachi's exploits. And in keeping with Rodriguez's motif of reversals noted above, this time it is the bartender who tells the tale to the stranger. Belini (Cheech Marin), the bartender from the opening scene in *Desperado*, only now missing an eye, tells his story to Sheldon Sands, the sociopathic CIA agent (Johnny Depp). Just as the bar scene story in *Desperado* portrayed the mariachi as a loner figure, the bar scene in the final installment of the trilogy establishes the mariachi as one half of a pair with Carolina, with whom he had finally developed a strong intermental relationship. In the fight scene described by the bartender as well as the later flight scene where the mariachi and Carolina must negotiate their escape while chained together, the audience witnesses the pair acting as an intermental unit. They are not only similarly deadly but are able to successfully act as a team in order to outfight or outrun their adversaries. (Where Carolina is somewhat awkward in the flight scene in *Desperado*, comically wearing two different shoes, in *Once Upon a Time in Mexico* she is every bit the mariachi's equal.)[8] However, all of these scenes are given in either dream or flashback, as Carolina has been killed prior to the events depicted in the movie. On the one hand, this allows the mariachi to again take up the role of vengeance seeker; on the other hand, however, this also allows his character to continue his intermental development.[9]

As with the first two movies, Rodriguez continues his use of shot/reverse-shot filming to suggest when two lead characters are not in an intermental relationship; most importantly, this technique is used when filming the mariachi's initial conversation with Sands, as well as their later conversation in the church confessional. Unlike the previous two movies, these two lead characters will not later develop an intermental relationship.[10] Nor is the mariachi conceived of as a loner; after passing Sands's test in the church, Sands tells him to "assemble [his] team" for their role in Sands's scheme. Reminiscent of his band in *Desperado*, his "team" is a pair of musician-assassins who form a small intermental unit with the mariachi. However, there is no significant intermental development with this band, whose primary importance in the mariachi's development will come near the end of the movie when he defines his band as "sons of Mexico." Here then, the mariachi is announcing the last stage of his intermental development, essentially as one with Mexico, or to adapt Palmer's terminology, as part of "the Mexican mind."

So the most important question at this point is: how does Rodriguez signal this development to his audience? He cannot use eye-line matching and extreme close-ups with the mariachi and, essentially, the Mexican population. Nor can he employ the kind of narrator that George Eliot uses in *Middlemarch*[11] to establish the *Middlemarch* mind, in usages such as "decided according to custom" or "[t]he rural opinion about the new young ladies . . ." (qtd. in Palmer 68–69). Instead, Rodriguez diminishes the role of the mariachi in the plot, making him one of a larger cast who all play important roles in determining which force ultimately knows the mind of Mexico and best serves her interests. This all-star cast—Antonio Banderas, Johnny Depp, Willem Dafoe, Mickey Rourke, and Pedro Armendáriz, Jr.[12]—all work in some way to either exert influence and control the Mexican people or, in the case of the mariachi, free them from such manipulations. There are three specific forces contending for the soul of Mexico: the President (Pedro Armendáriz, Jr.), who seeks to assert political power and protect his country from Barillo; Armando Barillo (Willem Dafoe), a crime lord who manipulates through violence as well as bribery; and the mariachi, who once again takes up the mantle of vengeance seeker in order to liberate the people from the aforementioned competing forces. It is also worth noting at this point that the title for the third installment, *Once Upon a Time in Mexico*, is the only title in the trilogy that does not refer explicitly to the mariachi himself.

Other than taking on a smaller role in the plot, the mariachi is also filmed in such a way as to suggest his connection with the people (as opposed to the way he is shot in his conversations with Sands, addressed above). Much of the time that the mariachi seems to be a solitary figure (given the murder of his wife and child) he is shot not just with others, but specifically as a man among people; the mariachi is an integrated part of the local community in ways he was not in the previous two movies. For instance, the opening credits show him walking through town—through the market, the town square, and ultimately to a rooftop where he may look down upon the entire town—playing a guitar (as opposed to carrying his guitar case full of guns), connecting him back to the popular figure of traditional Mexican culture. He is not filmed in shadow, nor is there any attempt to obscure his face, signaling to the audience that the mariachi has changed drastically from the previous movie in his ability to form relationships and interact with others. That the guitar is unfinished may note that the mariachi himself is unfinished in his development, both as a character and as a symbol for Mexico. Similarly, he is known to and beloved by the guitar makers, who would rather die than give him up to the assassin Cucuy (Danny Trejo).[13] The Mariachi gives himself up to Cucuy, sparing the lives of others in an uncharacteristic act of self-sacrifice suggesting his larger symbolic importance.

However, how does all of this lead to reading the mariachi as part of a larger intermental unit, as opposed to functioning as a symbol for Mexico? In other words, how does Rodriguez demonstrate that he shares their mind, and not just their values? I would like to posit that the mariachi's final act in the movie marks his participation in what we might call "the Mexican mind." The end of the movie demonstrates the mariachi's growth from a man without a community to one who is integrally—and intermentally—connected to his community. In addition to defining him and his band as "sons of Mexico"—the first such identification in the trilogy—the mariachi is the one character in the above-mentioned power struggle who understands what the people want and gives it to them without any strings attached. Unlike the President, Barillo, or Sands, the mariachi is not looking to bribe, cheat, or manipulate the people. Rather, what he gives them in the end he gives freely, much as the guitar maker gave him a guitar—not for any kind of return but rather as a gift. His actions demonstrate that he shares the communal mind because, unlike any of the other power players, he understands their needs and their desires.

After the violence has ended and the players move on, it is important to note that the mariachi's bandmates leave town with their pockets, belts, and guitar cases stuffed with money. The mariachi, however, has left all of his profits with the people. Significantly, he leaves his money in an open guitar case; having replaced his guns with money, the mariachi is now giving to the people what they need. No longer the harbinger of death and destruction, as promised by Buscemi and Belini, the mariachi is now the bringer of economic improvement. On the same rooftop where we saw him in the opening credits, looking down upon the same town, we see money floating through the air; his gift, in other words, was for the community itself. While on the one hand it may seem that the mariachi is still a loner, because he does not seem to be in any relationship with others, I would like to suggest that his relationship is now with the community itself. His intermental growth has brought him from forming individual relationships to developing a connection with the mind of the people more broadly. His final memory of Carolina highlights his intermental connection to the community. Carolina asks him what he wants, and his reply is "to be free." He shares the same desire as the community, which sought freedom from the President (who left), Barillo (who died), and Sands (who has been left blind).[14]

The final shot of the mariachi has him walking out of town, carrying his guitar case. There is no reason to believe that it is filled with money (as were his bandmates' cases), nor do we suspect that he is carrying his guns (as he no longer has any need for them). Rather, it would appear that he is carrying his guitar, leaving the trilogy much as he entered it. Similarly, while in the previous movies it was suggested that he was leaving something behind, this time the mariachi is walking towards something. Donning a sash representing the Mexican flag, the mariachi is returning to Mexico more broadly. The look of hope in his eyes as the camera moves in for an extreme close-up suggests that the mariachi has found the peace he once sought and has finally become what he originally wanted to be: mariachi. Where before he was a loner, the mariachi has now become the very symbol of Mexican community, one representing boundless charity and love of the arts.

In addition to all of the accolades he has earned with respect to the Mexico Trilogy,[15] Rodriguez should also be commended for his development of the figure of the mariachi for American audiences. The mariachi is now reconceived as a vehicle for significant character development, cultural critique, and possibly even reconfigurations for how American audiences understand Mexico. Recall, for instance, the mariachi's first attempt at paid work in *El Mariachi*: upon offering his services to a bartender, he is told the bar already has entertainment, at which point a cartoonish "one man band" quickly performs a muzak version of traditional mariachi music. The mariachi himself is dismayed at his inability to find work, as well as what appears to be an acceptance of inferior entertainment as a result of modern musical technology. In *Desperado*, the mariachi performs with his band and later gives a lesson to a young boy looking to learn the guitar. And in *Once Upon a Time in Mexico*, the mariachi is given a guitar that we are led to believe he carries with him as he leaves town. Thus, Rodriguez makes a compelling case for reinvesting the mariachi with cultural significance, demonstrating that he can be a greater vehicle than Hollywood has previously demonstrated.

The mariachi persists as a symbol for Mexican art and culture. To give but one related example: Mariachi Films, a boutique film company in Mexico City providing services from pre- through postproduction, advertises with the slogan "Tu Ventana a México" ("Your Window to Mexico").[16] The mariachi has long stood as a positive symbol for Mexican culture, and with the Mexico Trilogy, Robert Rodriguez has breathed new life into that symbol for American audiences long used to stock footage and simple characterization.

Notes

1. Among the many such figures that American audiences may recall are Lee Van Cleef's performance in Sergio Leone's *For a Few Dollars More* (1965) or music legend Johnny Cash, whose "Folsom Prison Blues" (1955) includes the lines "I shot a man in Reno/just to watch him die."

2. Including Palmer's *Fictional Minds* (2008), as well as Dorrit Cohn's *Transparent Minds: Narrative Modes for Presenting Consciousness in Fiction* (1978). Another recent work that explores social minds in narrative fiction is Lisa Zunshine's *Why We Read Fiction: Theory of Mind and the Novel* (2006), which discusses how novels explore Theory of Mind and metarepresentational ability. Such an approach could also be usefully adapted to film narratives.

3. Zunshine's opening example, Peter Walsh's trembling in Virginia Woolf's *Mrs. Dalloway*, does not mention the face at all, instead reading "Walsh's body language" (3).

4. I would like to note here that sharing a social mind should not imply anything about the kinds of thought that the characters share. What's important here is not the content of those thoughts, but that two characters can share them so that explicit statement of them is rendered unnecessary. Moco's relationship with his attendant is not to be seen as a caring relationship between two equal partners.

5. In *El Mariachi*, the mariachi was mistaken for Azul; in *Desperado*, a hit man was mistaken for the mariachi. This chiasmus helps establish the inverted parallelism of the two movies, allowing the audience to understand *Desperado* as sequel and remake simultaneously.

6. In the same dream, the mariachi who tends to Dominó's dead body, who

is then shot in the hand, is played by Antonio Banderas. This helps to establish a plot continuity that the introduction of the band might otherwise frustrate.

7. The audience familiar with *El Mariachi* may also connect Carlos Gallardo to his previous role and see his character as both musician and gunslinger.

8. Once again, there are several parallels between *Desperado* and *Once Upon a Time in Mexico*, one of the most important at this point being the similarities between the two flight sequences, specifically the fact that both chase scenes end in explosions. These similarities tie the scenes together and, I argue, help the audience to understand the development of the intermental relationship between the mariachi and Carolina.

9. I'm not suggesting that characters must die in order for others to experience such growth. In this case, Carolina's death forces the mariachi to create new bonds and allows Rodriguez the space to make the character into a national symbol.

10. It should be noted that Sands will become a new manifestation of the man in black, a vengeance-seeking gunslinger in all black, who ends the movie as the loner that the mariachi was introduced as in *El Mariachi*. While I certainly do not develop them all, interested viewers are encouraged to uncover the various parallels and chiasmi Rodriguez employs throughout the trilogy.

11. That is to say, Rodriguez *could* use such a narrator, but not without drastically altering his method of storytelling in the trilogy.

12. American film audiences may recognize Armendáriz, Jr., from his role as Don Pedro in *The Mask of Zorro* (1998) and *The Legend of Zorro* (2005)—opposite Antonio Banderas—but may not know that he has appeared in over 100 movies, more than a dozen televisions series, and nearly two dozen telenovelas.

13. The audience may recognize Trejo from his role as Navajas in *Desperado*.

14. Again, the importance of the eyes cannot be overstated. If the eyes are the means by which individuals can form intermental relationships in film, Sands's blindness may suggest that he never was able to—nor will he now ever—form meaningful intermental relationships with others. This, of course, is in addition to the traditional suggestions of blindness in Western art as a means of suggesting an ironic new kind of knowledge.

15. *El Mariachi* won the audience award at both the Sundance and Deauville American Film Festivals, as well as Best First Feature at the Independent Spirit Awards. *Desperado* was nominated for the Bronze Horse at the Stockholm Film Festival. *Once Upon a Time in Mexico* was nominated for two Satellite Awards. Additionally, Salma Hayek, Antonio Banderas, and Rubén Blades were all nominated for and/or awarded individual awards for their performances.

16. http://www.mariachifilms.com/ESP/index.html.

IT'S A WRAP

CHAPTER 10

Tarantino & Rodriguez: A Paradigm

ILAN STAVANS

I find the forking paths of Quentin Tarantino's and Robert Rodriguez's careers (the former calls the latter "my bro") endlessly thought-provoking. They are both successful American filmmakers with an obsession for B-movies. And they distill a sensibility unequivocally derivative; that is, their style is defined by parody, often poking fun at other movies such as spaghetti westerns. However, their success is built on divergent premises. The result is that Tarantino is a dandy of the intellectual elite whereas Rodriguez is seen as painfully dull to the point of irrelevance, a manufacturer of bad taste and cheap entertainment.

The two traffic in violence. Tarantino makes narratives that are shaped as a critique of history. He doesn't shy away from tackling large ideological issues, such as blackness in America, the sexist legacy of martial arts, slavery, and Hitler's fascism. From *Pulp Fiction* (1994) to *Kill Bill 1* and *2* (2003 and 2004), from *Inglorious Basterds* (2009) to *Django Unchained* (2012), suffering in his films plays out as a joke: his protagonists are vigilantes eager to subvert the past. Rodriguez, in contrast, is oblivious of history. His plots are sloppy and his message lighthearted. With a flair for excess, he goes from the rambunctious to the incoherent. Starting with the low-budget *El Mariachi* (1992) and evolving to the fancy *Once Upon a Time in Mexico* (2003), and declining in the trite *Machete* (2010), Rodriguez's movies are for the most part irredeemably innocuous.

And yet, they ought to be seen as pathfinders—especially since they owe a similar debt to Sam Peckinpah's cinematic explorations of human aggression—although the path they each find makes for a study in contrast. I don't need to expand on Tarantino's legacy since he has a legion of admirers (among which I count myself, obviously). Rodriguez, instead, is in urgent need of context. What makes him stand out is his readiness to swim against the current. At a time when U.S.-born Latino directors hardly register in the Hollywood landscape (unless they come from Mexico with pedigree, like Alfonso Cuarón, Guillermo del Toro, and Alejandro González Iñárritu), he is an island unto himself, an all-purpose producer whose films pay attention to an unattended segment of the population. Indeed, Rodriguez has made it his mission to hire Hispanic actors (Jessica Alba, Antonio Banderas, Salma Hayek, Michelle Rodriguez, Danny Trejo . . .), alone and en troupe, handing them roles where their ethnicity isn't a token. And his movies strive to commercialize Chicanismo: to put Mexican Americans on-screen, not in anodyne situations but with a vengeance. In his plots, Anglos are commonly evil whereas *Mexicanos* are heroes. Where else in the United States does such equation exist? In other words, *revanchismo* is his modus operandi.

Not surprisingly, Tarantino and Rodriguez have collaborated in myriad projects, which signals a porous friendship. For instance, each of them was in charge of an episode of the anthological movie *Four Rooms* (1995): Tarantino in charge of "The Man from Hollywood," Rodriguez of "The Misbehavers." They were together again in the double feature *Grindhouse* (2007), Tarantino behind the segment *Death Proof*, Rodriguez behind *Planet Terror*. (*Machete* was based on a fake trailer in Rodriguez's portion of *Grindhouse*.) They have also worked for one another: Tarantino occasionally directs a scene in a Rodriguez movie, and, more ambitiously, *From Dusk till Dawn* (1996) was directed by Rodriguez from a Tarantino screenplay. In other words, there is an easy come, easy go quality to their liaison. Has something unique emerged from this collaboration? If not unique, at least suggestive: Tarantino and Rodriguez do work with the same raw material, even if their end results are altogether different.

Again, why is Rodriguez disdained and Tarantino championed? It is because Rodriguez doesn't appear to demand much of his talent. He gives the public cheesy, forgettable fun. Don't get me wrong: I'm a lover of camp. In Spanish, the word for kitsch is *cursi*, the realm where telenovelas thrive, a universe defined by rough, overdrawn emotions. Rodriguez firmly makes *lo cursi* his realm. His movies are melodramatic to a fault. He isn't as much a master of *sensiblería* (like Pedro Almodóvar) as he is a slave to it: he presents Hispanic themes uncritically, afraid of taunting their limitations, which is what an artist should do. Tarantino, ever a demanding artiste, only touches the edges of camp, never for a second indulging in it. Every scene in his films is meticulously built. While the response is therefore calibrated, I'm never sure how much in Rodriguez's movies is intentional. I have sat in almost-empty theaters across the country, from

Massachusetts to California, laughing, mostly alone, at what unfolds on-screen. Is the director in charge of what I like? Am I laughing with him or at him? Attending a Tarantino screening is the polar opposite: the theater is packed to saturation, and people's attention always feels syncopated.

Therein is the paradigm: both Tarantino and Rodriguez indulge in violence, one to meditate on how we have become immune to it, the other to use it as thrill and, in doing so, give Latinos a break. Our appreciation of them is a study in empathy.

CHAPTER 11

Five Amigos Crisscross Borders
on a Road Trip with Rodriguez

FREDERICK LUIS ALDAMA, SAMUEL SALDÍVAR,
CHRISTOPHER GONZÁLEZ, SUE J. KIM,
AND CAMILLA FOJAS

Frederick Luis Aldama: To wrap up this volume of essays, I'd like to ask the four of you scholars on Robert Rodriguez and Latino popular culture generally why it is that Robert Rodriguez is the most prolific Latino director working today, yet he has yet to be embraced by the Latino scholarly community?

Christopher González: Hearing that question makes me balk, quite frankly. I would wager that the average person walking down the street, if asked to name a Latino director, would name Rodriguez pretty readily above most others. And yet the lack of scholarly engagement with his films reveals a curious disconnect. One reason for this lack might have to do with Rodriguez's choice of aesthetic decisions, which are more in the genre-bending (or genre-busting) realm of cinema than in what we might call highbrow cinema. Now, I don't say that as a pejorative; in fact, I personally think it is one of Rodriguez's most important characteristics—his conscious decision to remain autonomous and free to choose the types of films he makes. But unlike directors such as Luis Valdez, Ramón Menéndez, and Edward James Olmos, Rodriguez isn't interested in easily defined Latino cinema. *Stand and Deliver* (1988) and *La Bamba* (1987), two straightforward biopics, engage issues of Latinidad head-on because that is what motivates those films at the level of audience. They seek to enlighten and entertain, in other words. Rodriguez, on the other hand, is pure entertainment.

I know this sounds like Graham Greene's famous distinction regarding his "serious" novels and his "entertainments," but I think Rodriguez sees serious art and pure entertainment as completely compatible. *El Mariachi* is damned entertaining while also being an example of top-notch craft. That film alone should've spawned many more critical essays and books than it has. Because of his approach, his films require a Latino scholarly community that recognizes the sublime in the outrageous. Perhaps it is that the Latino scholarly community, having staked its ground for so long on issues of identity, gender, and representation, has only recently begun to see Rodriguez's work as worthy of examination—though a few Latino scholars such as Charles Ramírez Berg recognized this as long ago as "Bedhead" and *El Mariachi*—the latter having been inducted by the Library of Congress into the National Film Registry in 2011. If Latino scholars haven't been paying attention to Rodriguez, I can't imagine that lacuna lasting very much longer.

Samuel Saldívar: Chris, you bring up some very good points concerning Rodriguez's aesthetic decisions as they relate (or don't relate) to a Latino scholarly community. I have to admit that what has always interested me about Rodriguez's films is their general invisibility among Latino academics. And while your idea of recognizing the sublime in the outrageous may be one of the struggles Latino scholars face when interacting with a Rodriguez film, I would also like to add that what fascinates me about a Rodriguez flick are his constant moves to complicate perceived ideas of Latinidad—a Latino-ness traditionally identified as the embracing of a Latino cultural identity à la *Stand and Deliver* and *La Bamba*. If we were to place a Rodriguez film like *Spy Kids* with its center-staging of racially ambiguous protagonists (as Sue mentions in her essay in this volume) into the scholarly mix, we necessarily need to revise and complicate our preconceptions of a *filmic Latinidad*. This particular move, among many others, is what makes Rodriguez films so fun to watch. As a director, Rodriguez makes conscious decisions to include Latinos in prominent roles, but their racial/ethnic makeup is rarely a central focus or driving force of his films. Instead what Rodriguez creates are films that invite audiences to focus on cinematic narratives that are fun to watch, rather than works that focus first on identity or racial struggle of one particular character and *then* the film itself.

Sue J. Kim: I'd agree with both Chris and Samuel—which I suspect I will be for most of this conversation. I'll add that I think part of the lacuna comes from two trends in scholarly cultural studies in the past few decades. On one hand, you have an emphasis on texts that deal thematically and explicitly with issues of ethnicity and identity; films like *Stand and Deliver* explicitly invite such analysis. On the other hand, film criticism in the late twentieth/early twenty-first century (and even earlier) privileged experimental cinema, what Chris mentioned above as "highbrow" cinema. These critical reading practices, descended in large part from that whole *Cahiers du Cinema* tradition, have shaped the tastes and approaches of film critics and students for several decades. Not that this is true across the board—Charles Ramírez Berg being an excellent example—but as in literary studies, I think that has turned our attention generally to more avant-garde works. Rodriguez's work doesn't fit either of these critical lenses in any obvious way. As Sam notes, many of his films don't centralize race and ethnicity thematically, and many of his films are "lowbrow." You see this divide even in what scholarship does exist on his films; more has been written about *El Mariachi*, an "art house" movie, and *Sin City* than the *Spy Kids* series, which some people may see as just fluff for kids. But many people are actually *watching* Rodriguez's "fluffier" fare, and I think they are infinitely more fascinating.

Camilla Fojas: I agree with much of what has been said, particularly how Rodriguez plays with genre and audience expectations in a way that makes his work difficult to summarize and perhaps capture by scholars with particular projects or theoretical or archival attachments. However, I would argue that Rodriguez has clear roots in Latino cinema and that his early work did benefit from the cultural and industrial transformations that took place during the rise of what has been dubbed "Hispanic Hollywood," a designation that includes the films cited by Chris—*La Bamba* and *Stand and Deliver*. In fact *La Bamba* was one of the films used to test the vitality of the Latino market in Hollywood; it was released simultaneously to a Spanish-language and English-language market to great success, proving that there was a great market share for Latino and Spanish-language fare. *El Mariachi*, a Spanish-language border film, succeeded both as an independent production to an indie market, also on the rise in the 1990s, and as a Spanish-language film to Spanish speaking and/or Latino audiences. The same process of dual marketing is at work with the *Machete* franchise that appeals to a mass market and to a more targeted, though also very large, Latino market. In this way, I think Rodriguez is able to cross generic boundaries and extend his filmic observations beyond localized cultural conflict and identity formation to explore issues linked to national identity and political debates. I've noticed that *Machete* has drawn considerable scholarly attention within Latino Cultural Studies for its reflection on immigration, drug trafficking, and the politics of the border region. As an artist, Rodriguez brings his aesthetic innovations to a number of genres and audiences, and while all of his films should be studied as parts of a whole, his work includes important Latino cultural productions that impact the cultural mood around the status of immigration and the immigrant and Latino populations in the U.S.

FLA: In many ways the essays gathered in this volume present the first collective move to enrich our understanding of how Rodriguez makes films that complicate our sense of Latinidad as well as how he can create genre films that entertain and offer social critiques . . .

CG: I think that's really the sort of critical direction to begin engaging with Rodriguez's films. We can't use the same sorts of critical lenses that are used in examining, say, Quentin Tarantino's films. That's not to say Tarantino doesn't take up issues of race and ethnicity in his films; he does. But in Rodriguez we have a director who self-identifies as a Latino, is infused with a Latino worldview at a personal level, and isn't afraid to have that worldview manifest in his films. (Ilan points to this in his discussion herein of Rodriguez in relation to *lo cursi*.) Indeed, his films complicate our understanding of Latinidad because his films are deceptively complex. Something like *Planet Terror*, which looks like a cheap B-flick (today we might say a direct-to-video film), is actually quite technically sophisticated and, as I argued in my essay in this collection, subtly critiques issues that are very important to Latinos and Americans in general—immigration, as well as this nation's penchant for "Othering." In her essay, Sue identifies the importance of the sociopolitical vis-à-vis Latinos in Rodriguez's films, and specifically, within his "kids" films, which is often anathema in films made for children. That Rodriguez can weave these important matters of identity into films that are humorous and delighting in child's play ought to be seen for what it is: a real technical achievement.

In *From Dusk till Dawn* and *Sin City* Rodriguez does something that may be one of the most impressive things of all, which is his ability to successfully collaborate with a coeval. That he can manage to create such significant films, not with a full-time partner such as the Coen brothers have, but with another independent creative mind such as Tarantino or Frank Miller, is a rare gift. Emily R. Anderson's essay really shows just how invested in each other Rodriguez and Miller were when adapting *Sin City*, and I think it pays off in the film in a big way. These collaborations yield such interesting chimeras that it pushes an audience to consider the film in a new way, which leads to seeing longstanding sociopolitical and identity issues in new ways as well.

SS: I agree with you, Chris, in saying that Rodriguez's constant moves to complicate Latinidad is a fantastic area for further exploration. To continue a bit with my opening comments about Rodriguez's move to complicate Latinidad, I think here of Frederick's formulation in *The Cinema of Robert Rodriguez* of his *will to style* as a way of using the devices of film to craftfully shape stories that bridge the individual director's vision with the sociocultural collective. In all of Rodriguez's films we see this willful desire to *make new* our perception, thought, and feeling toward Latino characters that radically complicate "traditional" notions of Latinidad. *Machete*'s Agent Sartana Rivera (played by Jessica Alba) is a case in point. The choice to have Rivera not speak with a truncated, broken Spanish highlights a Latinidad that is *not* inherently tied to language. Rodriguez chooses to take from the building blocks of reality—that today for many Latinos Spanish is not their mother tongue—and then embrace and *naturalize* this aspect of our Latinidad. He even makes *new* our perception of language when he chooses to stylize Rogelio Torrez's (played by Steven Seagal) Spanish as heavily English-accented. Through language, Rodriguez presents a much more fluid linguistic Latino community. Such stylizing of language is one element of many that allow Rodriguez to *make new* the audience's understanding of issues of immigration, migration, and corruption.

SJK: I also believe strongly that what we learn from approaching "minority" filmmakers like Rodriguez should inform how we approach white filmmakers. For instance, to pick up on something that Chris said above, I would say that while we wouldn't approach Tarantino's films in quite the same way as we would Rodriguez's, I think scholarship of Rodriguez's films can point to some of the blind spots in, say, studies of Tarantino. As we know, ethnicity isn't limited to ethnic minorities; the dominant term (white) is also a constructed ethnicity. So this might mean, for example, exploring how whiteness is constructed by and in Tarantino's films, and what constructions of whiteness inform his films. And "whiteness" here is obviously not one thing; rather, what constructions of whiteness go into the films' contents and contexts. I know it's been said a lot, but I think that any minority or female filmmaker should have as much freedom of "will to style" as any white male director. By the same token, I think the insights and methodologies we learn from studying the marginal authors and texts *should* inform the way that we also study "mainstream" filmmakers.

CF: I agree that Rodriguez challenges typical notions of Latinidad. To varying degrees, his narrative worlds are inflected with the experience of the borderlands and a cultural proximity to Mexico that enhances the narrative unfolding of identity as a dynamic and dialectical process. Rodriguez destabilizes Latinidad by representing a proliferation of cultural identities, often as an effect of border culture, and through showing a different kind of family and community formation. This is most obvious in *Machete* when, for example, the idea of being "Mexican" is depicted as both a set of signifiers and a state of being. There are other more spectacular and outrageous ways that identity is exploded as ultimately flexible and unstable—for example, in *From Dusk till Dawn* where anyone can become a vampire and turn against their own family. His use of mixed-genre filmmaking, spectacular and cartoonishly blood-drenched scenes, overt eroticism, recognizable stars, and action-inducing editing makes each film highly entertaining for a general audience. Yet within this mainstreaming are, as others have mentioned, some very complex ideas about race and ethnicity and tacit critiques of major social and political issues.

FLA: We all know well that films like *El Mariachi*, *Desperado*, *Spy Kids*, and *Sin City* have been critical and commercial successes. Yet, others like *From Dusk till Dawn* have been less so. For the most part, the critics panned *From Dusk till Dawn*. And, while it had big stars like Harvey Keitel (as Jacob Fuller) and Juliette Lewis (his daughter Kate Fuller) as well as George Clooney (as Seth Gecko) in his first crossover role from TV to film, *From Dusk* didn't do so well at the box office . . .

CG: I think the commercial failure of *From Dusk* is a prime example of the disconnect that often occurs between certain expectations of an audience and the expectations a film has for its audience. Tarantino was riding high after the runaway success of *Pulp Fiction*; Rodriguez had just released his first film with a major studio in *Desperado*, a film that made Salma Hayek and Antonio Banderas household names in America. Both Tarantino and Rodriguez had already established a specific kind of following in terms of audience. Neither director had even suggested an interest in genre films at that time, though both would collaborate again in an even more over-the-top genre of the exploitation film with *Grindhouse*. To have audiences who were expecting another *Pulp Fiction* or *Desperado* carry those expectations with them into *From Dusk till Dawn* yielded a disastrous result at the box office, albeit a courageous move on the part of both directors. (Careers have been ruined for less egregious risks.)

Moreover, the first half of the film comports with an expectation of a Tarantino film—the gun violence, the snappy dialogue, the sense of claustrophobia that always seems to accompany Tarantino's most riveting scenes from his oeuvre, and so on. Then suddenly there's Chet Pussy (Cheech Marin) as Master of Ceremonies advertising all types of "pussy," and an audience is forced to readjust their expectations or else just throw their hands up and say, forget it. I think in its initial box office run, the latter was the case, which led to moviegoers' avoiding the film altogether. But time has a way of resurrecting things in interesting ways, and so how perfect is it that *From Dusk till Dawn* managed to become a cult classic. When taken on its own terms, I think the film succeeds quite brilliantly.

SS: I agree with Chris about Rodriguez gambling a bit on *From Dusk till Dawn* with an audience that may have been expecting another type of film—one more akin to *Desperado*. I wonder, however, if perhaps the film's marketing had more readily embraced the vampire trend of the day whether this might have changed its initial reception. Recall that *From Dusk* was released in 1996, following in the wake of TV shows like *Buffy the Vampire Slayer* (1992) as well as films such as *Interview with the Vampire* (1994) and *Vampire in Brooklyn* (1995). Perhaps if audiences had been more primed for the vampire genre that crystallizes after the first third of the movie, it might have had more of a commercial success in its day. Audiences might have expected less a Tarantino road flick and might have been more prepared for when the hyperbolic monstrous bloodbath ensues.

SJK: I have to admit, the first time I saw this movie I really agreed with one movie reviewer who said that, cinematically, Rodriguez and Tarantino should run fast and far away from each other and never collaborate again. Chris's discussion of the film, however, showed me the depth of intertextual sources Rodriguez was playing with. Its failure certainly had to do with audience expectations that were likely put off by the stylistic, thematic, and generic Tarantino/Rodriguez pastiche.

CF: I think that *From Dusk till Dawn* makes sense in relation to all the other films of his oeuvre even if it did not stand alone as a commercial success. From it you can trace his use of the same or similar themes; for example, the action happens when someone is in the bathroom or emerges from it, the boundaries of identity are shown to be unstable, and the border is a key point of reference. It transitions from the border provenance of his earlier films by crossing into Mexico and having the latter part of the story line take place there. But it might seem that the action that takes place south of the border is unrelated to that which happened previously. As others have mentioned, this confused audiences and upset expectations.

FLA: At a certain point, Rodriguez decided he didn't want to be a hired hand to Hollywood producers, breaking entirely from the studio system. One of the films that led him to solidify this decision was *The Faculty* . . .

CG: Looking back at all of his films so far, it's easy to see why Rodriguez wanted out of the studio system, especially if *From Dusk till Dawn* and *The Faculty* are any indication. He seems to have an eclectic nature of storytelling and a very specific way of bringing his stories to film. Rodriguez is notorious for working at a near-frantic shooting pace, one that often takes actors by surprise. He consistently pushes for a more efficient way of creating his films, as his "Ten Minute Film School" shorts constantly emphasize. Wanting to work in that manner must be counterintuitive to the studio system, and breaking free from that system, though initially a huge risk, seemed to fit Rodriguez's work ethic and vision quite well.

Frederick, you note that *The Faculty* seemed to be the one that forced Rodriguez's hand in terms of moving away from the studio system. That film is intriguing, and isn't necessarily a bad film. But we can view *The Faculty* against the rest of his films and see that what makes a Rodriguez film a *Rodriguez film* is clearly lacking. There is little of the self-reflexive in it, and the film is clearly a progeny of Kevin Williamson, the writer of *Scream* and *Scream 2*. It was a Dimension Films product, buoyed by the *Scream* franchise, and was yet another opportunity to have teens in harm's way, only this time what they feared is literally otherworldly. So Rodriguez is brought in to direct when Williamson cannot, and he is subject to the very constraints he dislikes when shooting a film. However, because the story and script are not his, Rodriguez has little control and less leverage with the studio. In the end I think he needed to direct *The Faculty* if only so that it could motivate him to get out of the studio system once and for all and lead him to films he wanted to create.

SS: Chris mentions many of the issues that certainly straightjacketed Rodriguez's creativity. Indeed, Rodriguez's move away from the studio system afforded him the opportunities to explore and reevaluate his filmmaking process in ways that pushed him beyond a shortsighted directional lens. Aside from his notorious pace and inventiveness as director, Rodriguez has his hand in almost every aspect of his films. His involvement includes script writing, directing, scoring, and editing. This total involvement is certainly frowned upon in the Hollywood studio system. With massive restrictions on his involvement it's no wonder he felt like a hired hand in the making of *The Faculty*.

SJK: I agree; *The Faculty* wasn't necessarily a bad film on its own terms, but it certainly wasn't a Rodriguez film. As a young filmmaker, he probably had to experience that to realize just how unworkable the Hollywood system is and convince him to take off on his own.

CF: I have to say that the break from the studios seems entirely inevitable given Rodriguez's independent beginnings. I agree with all of the comments above in that it is a sign of his artistic integrity and unique vision that he chose to find his own way outside of the studio system.

FLA: Given that the essays in *Critical Approaches to the Films of Robert Rodriguez* only touch briefly on *From Dusk*, I'd like to focus the rest of our conversation ("road trip") on this film. While Sam brings up the incipient presence of vampire TV shows and films in the early to mid-1990s, the genre really seemed to take off after *From Dusk*. Perhaps with all the vampire-themed TV shows and films made since 1996, *From Dusk* might not appear to be as innovative as it was . . .

CG: It may not appear innovative to viewers now, but we have to consider *From Dusk* within the context of the lead-up to its release. Sam mentioned a few movies that preceded *From Dusk*, and it's worthwhile to note them again. 1992 is a significant year in terms of vampire films, thanks to two movies in particular: Francis Ford Coppola's *Bram Stoker's Dracula*, starring Gary Oldman and Winona Ryder, and the film version of *Buffy the Vampire Slayer*, starring Kristy Swanson. These two films resuscitated this genre, if you'll pardon the pun, which in the 1970s had gone from bad Christopher Lee/Peter Cushing movies to worse, with George Hamilton starring in *Love at First Bite*. In 1994 *Interview with the Vampire* was released, which starred Brad Pitt, Tom Cruise, and Antonio Banderas. The disastrous *Vampire in Brooklyn*, starring Eddie Murphy, quickly curtailed any enthusiasm about the resurgence of the vampire film in 1995. So, unlike the postmillennial explosion of the vampire (and zombie) film, Rodriguez takes a huge gamble with *From Dusk*.

What's innovative, however, about *From Dusk* is that the film is this interesting chimera. It's part Tarantino crime shoot-'em-up, complete with Tarantino trademarks such as cheeseburgers from the fictitious Big Kahuna Burgers joint that appears in *Reservoir Dogs*, *Four Rooms*, *Pulp Fiction*, and *Death Proof* (Rodriguez includes a reference in *Sharkboy and Lavagirl*), to the Gecko brothers crime duo that mirrors Vincent Vega (played by John Travolta) and Jules Winnfield (played by Samuel L. Jackson) in *Pulp Fiction*, to similar scenes of the crime duos shot from the perspective of someone inside a car trunk, and so on. And yet, there is an unambiguous turn to Rodriguez's style once the cast of characters arrives at the Titty Twister in Mexico. None of the vampire films I just listed have such a bifurcated structure. The only thing that comes close to such a similar one-two punch is the Tarantino/Rodriguez *Grindhouse* collaboration, but even that was billed as a double feature. *From Dusk till Dawn* is almost like a double feature within the same film, if you take my meaning.

SS: Chris describes *From Dusk* as a chimera that broke from the reinvigorated predecessors, a point I would like to keep running with. This identification of the film ties to my earlier mention of the problematics of its reception. In many ways, the film functions as a double feature—a double feature that is deliberately divided by the Texas–Mexico border.

Yet, both sides of the double feature are tied together. This raises the question of what techniques (motifs, for instance) might have been used to prepare the audience for this suturing of the two parts. The elements that begin to suture one to the other don't seem to appear until we are already south of the border and in the Titty Twister bar. I think of Rodriguez's careful inclusion of shots of a knife with slime green blood. The image begins to suture the first half with the second half, but does so just before the attack and feeding begin. This suturing moment might have come too late for audiences.

SJK: *From Dusk* may also have been part of a shift to a new generation or new way of treating of vampire stories. Chris's comments remind me that *Buffy the Vampire Slayer*, the *television* show, started in 1997, one year after *From Dusk* was released. As is well known, Joss Whedon was very unhappy with the Hollywood film (echoes of Rodriguez again) and decided to remake the show according to his original vision on television. Both *From Dusk* and *Buffy* are self-conscious, irreverent, and experimental, and both put historically marginalized peoples at the center of the tale: Latinos and women. It's interesting because I'm not as familiar with *True Blood* or *Twilight* (which I know are *very* different), but I don't think the current vampire texts have the same kind of irreverent wit that we began to see with *From Dusk* and that gained momentum in the late 1990s.

CF: I think the film is split by a divergent aesthetic that is actually a binational split that coincides with the crossing of the border between the U.S. and Mexico. Everything north of the border happens in a kind of realistic, though cartoonishly Tarantino-like blood-soaked, manner, and the trip across the border moves the film in another more fabulous and allegorical space as if we were entering another dimension. In some ways Rodriguez is exploiting U.S. audiences' expectations of the magic and otherworldliness of everything south of the border. But the film also critically exposes these colonial ideas. It is no accident that the domain of the vampire is the bar that is open from dusk till dawn. As in the classic border film *Touch of Evil*, Mexico is identified with night and darkness, also the domain of things related to the chaos and instability of the unconscious. A figure of the undead, the vampire combines human and monster and subverts and distorts family relations—which for Marx is one of the effects of capitalism. The vampire, like capitalism, is a dehumanized and dehumanizing agent that extracts the life force of humans and turns them into soulless beings who then become caught up in this endless cycle. A possible reading of the film would follow the flow of globalization across the border and its vampirizing of the Mexican labor force in the maquiladoras. Rather than, as with some of the teenage vampire television narratives, being about the fantasy of power and transcending socially imposed boundaries, the vampire story in Mexico is a potentially powerful allegory for examining binational relations on the heels of NAFTA.

FLA: With a relatively small budget of twenty million dollars (compared to Hollywood action/horror films, that is), the only way Rodriguez could make the film in Hollywood was with a nonunion crew . . .

CG: Rodriguez understandably took heat from his decision to go with a nonunion crew, as he details in the documentary of the making of *From Dusk* titled *Full Tilt Boogie*. Indeed, here we have a director who cut his teeth on making the most with what he had in terms of limited budget, extreme time constraints, and so on. It's a part of his innate (or instilled) work ethic to produce his films in as efficient and cost-effective a manner as possible. In essence he solves logistical problems with little consideration of the studio system in mind. Frederick, in your book *The Cinema of Robert Rodriguez* you detail how he butted heads with the studio simply because he knew Frank Miller was doing significant enough work on the film version of *Sin City* that Miller deserved codirector credit. This of course goes against the policy of the Directors Guild of America. Rather than compromise his principles, Rodriguez decided to renounce his DGA membership. In the case of *From Dusk*, his choices were to compromise his project because of a lack of funds or to circumvent the budget issue with innovative thinking that happened to go against the union. His decision angered many folks, but Rodriguez is hardly a stranger to that when his craft is at stake.

SS: This question does not surprise me at all given his history with the DGA and working with limited budgets. Chris's comments highlight just how far Rodriguez is willing to go to guarantee his creative freedom. Rodriguez dared to reject a career as a hired hand to the studios because he was most invested in preserving that space to be able to realize his vision in the making of films that run the gamut of genres. I think it might be worth our scholarly time to consider Rodriguez under the light of other directors who have chosen to step outside the Hollywood system.

SJK: Undoubtedly, working with a nonunion crew is a thorny issue. On the one hand, I really think it's important on principle to support unions, particularly in a time in this country where labor is really being attacked and most people don't have the benefit of a union. People in service and temporary jobs are almost never unionized, and unfortunately this particularly affects women and people of color. That being said, Hollywood is a really different ballgame, with all the money involved, and limits on attribution make less and less sense in a world of, say, increasing inter-medium collaboration or crowdsourcing. In the case of *Sin City*, union rules needed to catch up with the contemporary reality. In other words, unions can become part of the problem, although in most other spheres, I think we need *more* unions, not less.

CF: The labor backstory of the production runs against my earlier intervention about the vampire as a critique of capitalism, making the film a symptom of the contradictions of capitalism. But I think Chris makes a good point in that the film would not have been made but for the use of the nonunion crew which is itself a sign of how Rodriguez is able to make the most within the strictest of limitations. And as Sam emphasizes, this decision is part of a series of strategic moves to preserve his artistic freedom. But I would like to heed Sue's reminder that those excluded from the protection of the unions are often the most marginalized social groups.

FLA: By the time he made *From Dusk* Rodriguez had already made *El Mariachi*, the Showtime *Roadracers*, and *Desperado*. We see the building up of what we might call a Rodriguez Star System: Clooney, Cheech Marin, Salma Hayek, Quentin Tarantino, Michael Parks, John Hawkes, Danny Trejo, Tom Savini appear in other of his movies . . .

CG: This is an interesting aspect of Rodriguez's filmmaking in that he continually reuses certain actors time and again. Here again we see why he and Tarantino get along so well. Tarantino has a similar penchant for reusing actors; Uma Thurman, Harvey Keitel, and Samuel L. Jackson leap quickly to mind. He also has the tendency, again as does Tarantino, of hiring actors that may be seen as has-beens or washed up. There is little doubt that Tarantino reinvigorated John Travolta's film career, and Rodriguez has no problem including the likes of Steven Seagal and Charlie Sheen (rebooted as Carlos Estévez for *Machete Kills*). I think the result is an intriguing contradiction. On the one hand audiences see an actor they may have typecast in another role in something completely different (Seagal as a Spanish-speaking Mexican gangster) while also seeing Rodriguez cast once again actors like Danny Trejo and Tom Savini. Trejo in particular serves as a kind of connective tissue in Rodriguez's films, and even certain props appear from one film to the next. Here I'm thinking of the codpiece gun Savini, as Sex Machine, uses in *From Dusk*. The same codpiece gun appeared earlier in the guitar-case arsenal in *Desperado*, when Carolina (Salma Hayek) quips, "I don't even want to know what that's for." The result of this intermingling of Rodriguez's storyworlds enriches a devoted audience that has watched Rodriguez's films carefully.

SS: Rodriguez's star system does work as a connective tissue between his films that can and does lead to our crating of total Rodriguez filmic world. In our minds, the character Machete (Danny Trejo) lives beyond the film *Machete*. His roles in *From Dusk*, *Desperado*, and *Spy Kids*, for instance, transform him in our minds into an omnipresent figure. The same could be said about Cheech Marin who also appears in all of these films—and more. In *From Dusk* Marin becomes omnipresent within the film itself. He plays variously a border patrol agent, Master of Ceremony Chet Pussy at the Titty Twister, and the gangbanger Carlos. This is to say, Rodriguez's star system works in the mind of the viewer to create a network of connective tissues between the films (and within a given film). This allows for the making of omnipresent figures as well as the kind of "intertextploitation" Chris formulates in his essay in this collection.

SJK: To me, this is one of the most interesting and important contributions of Rodriguez. Rodriguez and Elizabeth Avellán, the cofounder of Troublemaker Studios (and his former spouse), have created an entire infrastructure for making films outside of Hollywood. This process included not only hiring Latino/a actors, but also involving industry folks out in Texas. They've helped to build Austin into a creative center for all kinds of arts. I'm really interested in the larger economic and social processes in which filmmaking is embedded, and I find it really admirable that they were able to create a different model that involves so many people and supports many other artists.

CF: I agree with the idea that the use of a stable of actors creates a kind of coherence to the Rodriguez corpus of films that transcends story lines and generic differences. It is also the mark of an auteur and, as Sue remarks, an industrial formation that is very much linked to a local economy. Also, like other prolific directors of Latino cinema who use the same actors again and again, for example, Edward James Olmos or Gregory Nava, this practice serves to support the Latino artistic community.

FLA: What are we to make of the critical and commercial flops of the direct-to-video sequels to *From Dusk*: *From Dusk till Dawn 2: Texas Blood Money* and the prequel *From Dusk till Dawn 3: The Hangman's Daughter*?

CG: Failure or fun? For me that's a key question in thinking of the sequel and prequel to *From Dusk*. My guess is that these films have a very specific aesthetic they aspire to, and it's not to be nominated for an Academy Award. If the aim is to make money, these films have generated a profit because they cost roughly around $5,000,000 each to make. Compare that with the $20,000,000 budget of the original. It's also important to remember that Rodriguez is producing these films and not directing them. But there is a clear low-budget aesthetic that both Tarantino and Rodriguez hold in high regard that can even be seen in their films that aspire to a highbrow aesthetic. Tarantino has mined spaghetti westerns and Zatoichi films for all they are worth. Rodriguez continually hearkens to the slapstick cartoon sensibility even in a film such as *Desperado*, as Frederick notes in *The Cinema of Robert Rodriguez*. But perhaps the most telling thing of all is that *From Dusk* has achieved a cult status, and the subsequent films are aimed at those die-hard fans that so enjoyed the first. These specific audiences, one might call them the films' ideal audiences, understand that the low-budget feel of these flicks is part of their charm, irrespective of their status among film critics.

SS: Considering that these films had a smaller budget and were both released the same year (1999), I second Chris's observation that the sequel and prequel were intended for an ideal audience that was no doubt outside of a mainstream viewership. Rather than attempt comparisons to other made-for-DVD films, or even to the original *From Dusk*, I see them working as entertaining films for an ideal audience that is interested in expanding the storyworld introduced in the vampiric second half of *From Dusk*.

SJK: Ha! I didn't even realize that there were sequels and prequels for *From Dusk*. Well, Rodriguez said that he initially intended *El Mariachi* to go straight to video, so you can say that he was sticking to his roots.

CF: I think this follows what Charles Ramírez Berg noted as the economic logic of border film production where a series of films of a similar kind are made quickly and furiously for maximum profit. I agree with what Chris said about these films' being aimed at fans more concerned with the cult status of the films than their aesthetic valuation.

FLA: Music scoring is often overlooked in Rodriguez's films. Yet we see in all his films how he carefully choreographs the music score to intensify our emotional response. In *From Dusk*, we hear the rhythms and pauses of the Latino rock band Tito & Tarantula (one song's titled "Angry Cockroaches") carefully synched with the peaks and troughs of action . . .

CG: Graeme Revell scored *From Dusk*, which I find interesting because soon thereafter Rodriguez would come to score his own films. Interestingly, I find Revell's score to be less potent and evocative than the soundtrack, which relies heavily on country music and electric guitar rock. The film's music is decidedly country during the first half that is set in Texas during the day. When the main group of characters cross into Mexico and darkness falls, the signature sounds of Tito & Tarantula dominate, as well as Stevie Ray Vaughan and even Jimi Hendrix's Woodstock rendition of the "Star-Spangled Banner" that plays ever so quietly when Frost (Fred Williamson) recounts his Vietnam experience. Of course, music plays a crucial role in the dance of seduction, which Frederick identifies in *The Cinema of Robert Rodriguez* as a key moment in *From Dusk*. That scene is absent of dialogue, and it lasts the entirety of the song, accompanied with Hayek's sensual body gyrations. In essence, the audience is being mesmerized by the dance and the song, just as Richie Gecko is. Fortunately for us, we survive the encounter, mostly unscathed.

SS: Rodriguez carefully uses music to laser-focus our attention to shifts in theme and action; the music sutures audiences to shifts in the camera-eye's visual registers. For instance, the country music in *From Dusk* aurally takes audiences into the geocultural region of Texas just as the sound space created by Tito & Tarantula takes audiences into the geocultural region of Mexico. With Satánico Pandemónium's dance of seduction, Rodriguez uses the audio channel to create a sound space (ballad of seduction that includes lines like "watching her strolling in the night") that mirrors Hayek's choreographed body movements. At the same time, the lyrics anticipate the horror to come: We will "feel the fever of [our] doom." And, Rodriguez is careful in his use of silent pauses. One such pause takes place as the audience (and the story's barflies) moves from its aural/visual trance-like state into the hyperfrenetic state of fear and agitation when the vampires attack and feed.

SJK: Yes, Rodriguez is skilled at both combining elements very traditionally yet at the same time playing with our expectations. I'm thinking not only of the Pandemónium dance in *From Dusk*, but also of the neo–film noir scenes at the beginning of *Spy Kids 3*, which are very funny. I agree that part of Rodriguez's signature style is his own music. I don't think any of the children's films would really work without that signature music.

CF: I do think that the soundtrack is a key player in *From Dusk till Dawn* for melodramatic effect, to mark the shift to Mexico, and to target a younger MTV'd audience. Rodriguez's use of music and his musical style is a key part of his own filmic journey which, we might recall, has origins in the figure of the mariachi.

FLA: *From Dusk* is based on a screenplay that Tarantino wrote and sold for $1,500 dollars. Certainly, the presence of Tarantino is felt throughout the film, especially in the extended dialogues between characters. As I discuss in *The Cinema of Robert Rodriguez*, however, it is only after an hour into the film that the story becomes wholly Rodriguez. This happens at the end of the above-mentioned dance seduction scene when Hayek as Satánico Pandemónium morphs into a hybrid human/serpent monster and when Tarantino as Richie Gecko turns into a vampire and is killed . . .

CG: The moment you're alluding to, Frederick, is like the suture of the film in my estimation. In fact, I think we can begin to see the transition of the two parts of the film once the RV crosses into Mexico. It's evident in Seth Gecko's demeanor, which goes from businesslike criminality guided by a sort of moral relativism (he robs banks; he doesn't rape and murder women like his brother), to an undisciplined purveyor of violence. When Jacob Fuller (Keitel) asks Seth, "Are you so much of a fucking loser that you don't know when you've won?," it's nearly an unfair question. Seth has essentially gone from being in a Tarantino film to being in a Rodriguez film. His character necessarily changes to fit the appropriate ethos of the storyworld. The moment he wakes up Richie in the RV, the transition from Tarantino to Rodriguez in the film has begun. Rarely does Tarantino have more than ten actors in many of his scenes because the tension of the dialogue is what grabs the audience.

But the carnivalesque Titty Twister bar is pure Rodriguez. It's a demented Tarasco bar from *Desperado*. And the slapstick humor that lies just beneath the surface of Rodriguez's films now becomes manifest. The codpiece gun, the campy lines from Savini, Danny Trejo as the bartender, the heavy dose of visual effects, a dead body fashioned into a guitar (!), the splatter and exploding bodies that are a notable homage to Sam Raimi and John Carpenter, they are as much markers of Rodriguez's "will to style" as the gunplay and rapid-fire dialogue are for Tarantino. It's fitting that it seemingly becomes a Rodriguez flick when Tarantino's character is killed off, as Frederick notes. That cannot be an accident. Also, I don't think the two parts of the film are slapped together haphazardly. But as I've said, this moment in the film that Frederick points to is the "take it or leave it" moment for an audience. Nothing in the film has set up the audience to accept the possibility of a vampire shoot-out before Hayek's transformation. The audience is asked to go from a hyperrealistic world of Tarantino violence to scenes from a Carpenter film. Looking back at our earlier discussion, I can now confidently say that this is why *From Dusk* failed at the box office.

SS: This suture that takes place once we cross the Rio Bravo marks a massive shift in style, tone—and worldview—in the film. There is a discernable change in character: Seth appears liberated as an "officially" self-proclaimed "Mexican," and Jacob Fuller and his otherwise passive family become active agents in their fight to survive, for instance. And, there's a marked shift in filmic style: the lens and lighting play up the neon-baroque look of the exterior and interior of the Titty Twister, for instance. This shift from the Tarantino road flick that feels somewhat constrained to the Rodriguez horror-baroque that feels suddenly liberated occurs in and through the passage across the U.S.–Mexico border; that is, the suture happens within the borderlands, or the limitlessly imaginable and possible space *la frontera*.

SJK: These descriptions of the transitions between Tarantino and Rodriguez's styles in *From Dusk* make sense to me. I think the first time I saw the film, I was less put out by the seeming incoherence of the film than the underutilization of Salma Hayek, who is one of my favorite actresses. But it's interesting that she serves as kind of the catalyst of this transition in this film.

CF: I agree with what Frederick, Chris, and Sam remark about the moment of the shift in directorial tone. I would add that while the characters cross the border and move into Mexico, they are still contained in the RV and have the same rapport and dynamic they had before leaving the U.S. Even as they enter the Mexican bar, the sense of the first part of the film remains. It is only when there is direct contact with the "magical" elements on the Mexican side of the border, with the actual transformations of the characters into vampires, that the film fully unleashes a new style and sensibility.

FLA: *From Dusk* is full of pop culture allusions: from the *Wild Bunch* to *Spartacus* to Tex Avery cartoons to disco to drive-ins to comic books (the x-ray vision special effects used to show the kidnapped bank teller in the trunk of the Gecko brothers' Mercury Cougar XR-7) . . .

CG: Again I think Tarantino and Rodriguez show why they're cut of a similar cloth. Both of these filmmakers dip into other aspects of the cinematic world and pop culture. These intertextual moments are a quick way of establishing nuance to the film's world while also rewarding an audience in the know. Near the 31-minute mark Seth Gecko says, "Okay, Ramblers. Let's get ramblin'," which is a near verbatim rendition of what the character Joe Cabot (Lawrence Tierney) says to his cadre of hit men (Mr. Orange, Mr. Pink, etc.) in the opening scene of *Reservoir Dogs*. Like Big Kahuna Burgers, the audience knows it's in a Tarantino world when they hear this line. Or consider Sex Machine's line when they discover how easy it is to make a cross to fight the vampires: "Peter Cushing does that all the time!"—an allusion to Cushing's frequent portrayal of Van Helsing opposite Christopher Lee's Dracula, as Sam noted earlier. In fact, that scene is a gleeful reminder that the characters are doing exactly what an ideal audience is doing when the characters argue over the best ways of killing vampires. "Has anybody here read a real book about vampires, or are we just remembering what some movie said? I mean, a *real* book," Jacob asks. Sex Machine replies, "You mean . . . you mean like a Time-Life book?" "I take it the answer's no," Jacob admits sarcastically. I think it's a great scene that puts Rodriguez's gallows humor in concert with audience expectation. We know the audience members are going through the same repertoire of how to kill vampires in their own minds—a repertoire that is based completely on film and pop culture. Holy water, garlic, wooden stakes, and even the effectiveness of silver are debated. Rodriguez is at the top of his game here. And in both parts of the film, all of these tiny allusions accrete into a rich viewing experience because, arguably, the audience is participating in the film by bringing their knowledge of these allusions to bear on the film. It's a sort of interactive experience, or at least an active (rather than passive) viewing experience.

SS: I was struck by these as well as more geographically particular cultural allusions and references that Rodriguez inserts into *From Dusk*. The film doesn't have to tell us we're in Texas. All the references and accents simply locate us there: The cowboy-hat-wearing Texas Ranger with his six-pack of Lone Star beer and Texan drawl, for instance. And, when we cross the Rio Bravo into Mexico, again the film doesn't have to tell us we're in Mexico, we simply are. The Titty Twister has Tequila ads and Mesoamerican women painted all over its interior walls. The dancing women sport Mesoamerican sartorial wear. Tito & Tarantula are dressed in traditional mariachi outfits. This is to say that Rodriguez's careful use of allusion and reference show more than tell of the film's geocultural locations.

SJK: I think this is part of what really distinguishes many turn-of-the-millennium and twenty-first-century texts from what came before. Postmodern art is said to break down the boundaries between high and low art, but I think it's really these kinds of films and television shows, embedded in pop culture, that really do away with that distinction. A novel like Thomas Pynchon's *Gravity's Rainbow* may reference all kinds of high and low culture, but in doing so it's still self-consciously trying to make capital-A *Art*. Whereas I think the motivation for Rodriguez and others is still to make art, but popular culture is just like the air they breathe, not a repository of materials to dip into sometimes.

CF: The film captures the mood and tone of the western emphasized by references to films like *The Wild Bunch*. Also the bar with the women dancing on tables looks very much like the bar in the border town in *Duel in the Sun*. Yet, as others mentioned, the use of certain actors creates a pop cultural intertext that moves it beyond the genres and styles it references.

FLA: We see the influence in *From Dusk* of Hong Kong action films (when Fred Williamson as Frost pulls the heart out of a vamp there's even a direct reference to Bruce Lee's *Enter the Dragon*) as well as 1970s drive-in classics like John Carpenter's *Assault on Precinct 13* and George Romero's *Dawn of the Dead* . . . as well as Italian horror flicks like those of Dario Argento and Mexican horror films of the 1960s and 1970s—even Brazilian gore auteur José Mojica Marins . . .

CG: Let's not forget what happens to the heart Frost holds in his hand. Sex Machine stabs it with a wooden pencil, which kills the vamp! That's the type of scene that is reminiscent of these other films you mention, Frederick. The kind of dark humor we've come to expect from Sam Raimi's *The Evil Dead* films starring Bruce Campbell, who incidentally was cast in *From Dusk till Dawn 2: Texas Blood Money*, so there's yet another connection. Again, I think the ties *From Dusk* has to 1970s horror and exploitation films cannot be understated in trying to understand an audience's engagement with the film. If an audience isn't aware that the film resonates with Carpenter, Romero, Argento, and Raimi, it's missing out on an important ingredient of the film. For example, just consider what happens to the vampire bodies when they are dispatched in the film. They tend to melt, explode, or burst into flames. The high volume of splatter and gore is meant to hearken audiences to Carpenter and Raimi in particular. Just as in *Planet Terror*, the gore is not meant to be realistic, it's meant to be stylized and over-the-top. I think Tarantino and Rodriguez do a tremendous service to American audiences by reaching back to these niche films. *Django Unchained* isn't possible without Sergio Corbucci's *Django* starring Franco Nero. *From Dusk* isn't possible without Sam Raimi's *The Evil Dead*. The unsteady, off-kilter zoom that is way too fast is a Raimi signature, and we see it when Jacob makes his way to the storage room with his makeshift shotgun/baseball bat cross. An audience can't fully appreciate *From Dusk* without any knowledge of these important precursor films.

SS: Certainly, Scott Fuller's *Precinct 13* T-shirt acts as a visual shout-out to John Carpenter's *Assault on Precinct 13*. It acts as a constant reminder to the audience that this is a film in the mode of Carpenter's over-the-top gore. (In looking back at my earlier response to motifs, perhaps Scott's T-shirt does work to stitch the film's two parts together.) Rodriguez's allusions provide a big payoff to those in the audience who have a huge repertoire of films in their memory bank. There's added pleasure for those who do make the Carpenter connection. The casting choices also add layers of meaning. With Tom Savini as Sex Machine, audiences in the know will register all variety of 1970s horror films; indeed, Rodriguez alludes directly to this when he has Savini morph into a kind of rat–werewolf and not a vampire.

SJK: This relates to the previous conversation about popular culture; whereas Romero and Carpenter may have been trying to shock, Rodriguez's generation takes these texts as a tradition. That is, Romero and Raimi also drew on horror and genre traditions, but those traditions were more obscure, whereas Romero and Raimi themselves helped make these genres widespread and commonplace. Although obviously there are different audiences for these films, the filmmaker and the core audiences, I think, really just take this cinematic context as a given. The breadth of this tradition also speaks to globalization as well as advances in technology. In order to see an obscure film, by the 1990s, you could just get a videotape instead of sending away for some reel of film, and then by the early 2000s, digitization (which Rodriguez has also helped pioneer) has made spreading texts even easier. It's all very exciting and, hopefully, will encourage even more cross-pollination.

CF: Though the film is a combination of action, crime story, western, and horror, the dominant strands in the latter part of the film are horror and action. The fight sequence pacing is reminiscent of a Hong Kong action film yet with the added spectacle of gore through bloodied, shape-shifting, and exploding bodies. The Rodriguez–Tarantino audience expects a cross-genre spree that is self-reflexive but that also indulges the pleasures of the original genre.

FLA: In *From Dusk* we begin to see Rodriguez's visual trademark styles: fast cuts and unusual angles . . .

CG: I agree, and I think that part of this has to do with the type of film we're talking about here. It's easy to call *From Dusk* an experimental film. Two big-name directors. Two distinct feels to the film. Two blended styles. And yet, because it seems to dispense with traditional ways of filmic storytelling (here I'm talking about genre or style blending), I think Rodriguez, perhaps encouraged by Tarantino, was able to experiment with how to shoot the film in terms of the visual trademarks you note. The unusual angles fit with the kinetic energy of the fight scenes, for example. But I also think the extremely fast cuts are used to great effect, especially in the scene where Seth discovers Richie has raped and murdered the hostage in the hotel room. The cuts are so quick that I literally cannot blink or I will miss the image. And even then I'm only left with a sense of what Seth is seeing. Here the blistering cuts back and forth allow Rodriguez to draw out the moment where Seth processes the bloody mess he's seeing.

Rodriguez increases the audience's anticipation and delays final realization of what has happened to the hostage, which evokes a sense of dread and horror. This is a different kind of horror than we will find at the Titty Twister, but it is horrific nonetheless. Now, compare how this scene of violence encourages a reaction of horror as opposed to the now-famous scene from *Pulp Fiction* when Vega shoots Marvin in the face, splattering the inside of Winnfield's car. That's not treated as horror but rather dark comedy, if not slapstick.

SS: The juxtaposition of cinematic styles (Tarantino then Rodriguez) in *From Dusk* undoubtedly challenges Hollywood approaches to filmmaking where the aim is to create a uniform style so as not to break the cinematic illusion. In Rodriguez's more recent films like *Planet Terror* and *Machete* we see him continue to play with the juxtaposition of styles in ways that create an added layer of meaning for audiences. In many ways, Rodriguez performs a kind of *montage* but not in the splicing together of disparate scenes but in the putting together in one film of disparately global styles. In this way, he makes new our perception, thought, and feeling of the whole.

SJK: That makes sense, since it's on the eve of his departure from Hollywood and really coming into his own not just stylistically but in terms of his production process.

CF: With *From Dusk* Rodriguez deepens and complicates his use of the fast cut, oblique camera angles, and editing to create action and set the mood. He not only consolidates his filmic style with this film, he also applies this style to a different genre *and* he changes the sense of that genre, the horror film, with these techniques. He makes horror, as Chris notes, into slapstick.

FLA: There are other allusions in the film such as the Fullers' Pace Arrow RV and the end shot with the camera panning out to show that the Titty Twister bar is actually the top of a partially buried Mayan temple. They seem to allude to a subtext of indigenous myth . . .

CG: Rodriguez uses the Mesoamerican pyramid in a really interesting way, just as he later does in *Planet Terror*, as I argued in my essay for this collection. It seems that in both instances, the final image of the pyramid forces the audience to reconsider everything they've seen to that point. It's the sort of moment made famous by Charlton Heston when he sees the ruined Statue of Liberty at the end of *Planet of the Apes*. Suddenly you realize Heston was on Earth the entire time. Likewise, you realize that the Titty Twister is the top of a Mesoamerican pyramid, and it's like, have these vampires been around since before the Conquistadors? I feel it's a creative use of indigeneity, one that moves us away from victimization and passivity. Of course, Rodriguez can't undo the atrocities committed upon native peoples, but on the other hand he's not creating the kind of film that is bound to the obligation of historical facts. In *From Dusk* he imagines a genre film (horror/vampire) where Latinos, descended from indigenous peoples, are the aggressors. On the other hand, we could view this decision to connect predatory vampires with the indigenous as a commentary on the rationalization of the extermination of brown people. It's actually a tough spot for Rodriguez to be in. It's good to see Latinos creating genre films and literature, but it is problematic to make Latinos the ones who need exterminating. Perhaps it would be different if, say, Antonio Banderas played the role of Seth. I guess this speaks to the delicate nature of filmmaking vis-à-vis race, ethnicity, and the sociopolitical.

SS: Rodriguez builds in this subtext of indigenous myth in other subtle ways, like the inclusion of Seth Gecko's "tribal"-inspired tattoos that run from his wrist to his neck (also called a sleeve). Of course, there's the albino snake wrapped around Satánico Pandemónim with her skull pendants that conjures images of Luis Valdez's *Pensamiento Serpentino* and the Mesoamerican Goddess Coatlicue—both of which have greatly influenced Chicano/a, Latino/a, and Indigenous Studies. Coatlicue is known as a devourer who is usually depicted as adorned by a necklace of skulls, hearts, and hands.

SJK: I have to admit, I missed the indigenous subtext in *From Dusk* the first time I saw it. Thank goodness for scholarship such as this!

CF: I found the pyramid to be a reminder of the geopolitical context of the events. In a sense the caravan of characters that traverse the border remind us of the colonial encounter of the U.S. with Mexico. It offers a send-up of how Hollywood depicts Mexico as a land of sunny escape from the troubles left behind in the U.S., since for these characters there is no escape and the real trouble begins in Mexico. The pyramid is a potent symbol of the complex history of this ancient civilization that is not only beyond the comprehension of the U.S.-based characters, it is also out of their range of vision. Thus the pyramid registers as ominous and signals the persistence of the mystical forces encountered in the bar.

FLA: In *The Cinema of Robert Rodriguez* I talk about how in *From Dusk* Rodriguez creates an aesthetic relation in which beauty is found in the transgression of norms and in the rehabituation of our perception of the object. I especially focus on the Salma Hayek as Satánico Pandemónium's transformation into a monster that combines the beautiful with the ugly . . .

CG: I mentioned this above as "recognizing the sublime in the outrageous." Rodriguez often brings together two seemingly incongruous things that an audience would rarely, if ever, see in the same space. Hayek's transformation is a perfect example of this. Yet the sensuous areas of her body, her breasts, her hips, remain human. It's her face that becomes monstrous. I think that's very telling, and it speaks to issues of the desirability of brown bodies. But there are also these heartfelt moments between family members. Seth mourns for his brother even though Richie has done some really horrible things. Jacob makes his kids swear to God that they will kill him when he becomes a vampire. Those moments are squarely in the realm of the absurd, and yet, there's something beautiful in them because of the tenderness of emotion. So it's not only physical beauty, but also a metaphysical beauty that underpins many of these incongruous moments in the film. That's where I think Rodriguez is doing something different than just revisiting Carpenter, Romero, and Raimi. He's making a very conscious creative decision to have these really beautiful moments comingled with the outrageous. I think here of Cherry Darling (Rose McGowan) in *Planet Terror*, who loses her leg and has it replaced with a wooden table leg, and later, an automatic rifle (and rocket launcher?). Her go-go dancer's body is suddenly part machine, and she's the one who ends up becoming the savior of the survivors at the end of the film. One last example comes to mind: the handsome Johnny Depp sans eyes near the end of *Once Upon a Time in Mexico*. It's a grotesque disparity for a man noted for being so handsome to have his eyes gouged out and walk around with these gaping, bloody holes in his face. In each of these instances, Rodriguez sees an aesthetic in conflating the beautiful with the ugly, as Frederick states.

SS: Recognizing the sublime in the outrageous or finding the beauty in the transgression of norms distills *From Dusk* to its essence. It is not only to be found physically, but also at the level of character interaction. For instance, just before Scott becomes a live human buffet to the vampires, Scott whispers a plea to his sister to kill him before he is dismembered or turned into a vamp. Rodriguez combines moments of tenderness with those of violence to create new emotions in the audience.

SJK: That's a really good way to put it, "the sublime in the outrageous." Because Rodriguez really does have a "heart" to his films, in the sense of not just trying to provide thrills and gore (e.g., *Saw* films), but in trying to say something about desire, fear, difference. I think that's what draws me to the children's films; they're so cinematically outrageous and yet really very positive and affirmative.

CF: I think that beauty and a sense of aesthetic freedom are part of the transgression of borders and norms in Rodriguez's films, particularly in *From Dusk*. There is something beautiful in the monstrous and something liberating in embracing the anxiety about difference in the other by becoming that other. This is an idea that Rodriguez seems to return to repeatedly in his films, the idea of transformation into the other. For example, in *El Mariachi* it is the confusion of the Mariachi with the drug trafficker, in *Machete* of the white Senator becoming Mexican, and in *From Dusk* it is the human becoming vampire.

FLA: *From Dusk* depicts a world where women (and children) seem to be the victims of an incredibly dysfunctional patriarchal system—one that breeds psychopaths like the Gecko brothers. What are we to make of the gender politics in the film?

CG: With the exception of Jacob Fuller and his son, there is certainly a lack of good men in the film. On the other hand, I'm not sure that the vampire community is as patriarchal as the "real" world Seth and Jacob know. They almost have to slap themselves in order to understand that, despite their disbelief in vampires, the first wave of vampires they fought off was very real. I also consider Satánico Pandemónium's threat to Seth, about essentially making him her dog. It's also revealing to examine the women that appear in Texas and those that appear in Mexico. All of the Texas women are victimized with the exception of Kelly Preston as a vacuous reporter. On the other hand, the women in Mexico are straight-up killers when night falls. Satánico Pandemónium's murder of Richie (after a dance of seduction) seems like just desserts for a murdering rapist. It's only fitting (1) that he is seduced by a woman (this time an actual, not imagined seduction) and (2) that a powerful woman is the instrument of Richie's demise. Seth, for his part, actually seems to want to keep Kate Fuller (Juliette Lewis) safe from his own brother. This doesn't make him a champion of women by any stretch of the imagination, but it does show the difference between the two Gecko brothers. I mentioned Jacob Fuller a moment ago, and he is the clear symbol of failed patriarchy. He's the proverbial man of faith who's lost his faith, and the impetus for his loss of faith is the loss of his wife. That he doesn't make it to the light of day is indicative of failed patriarchy. His only success, if we're trying to find one, is that he seems to have somehow gotten through to Seth, even if it's just enough to influence him to do the right thing with Kate at the film's end.

SS: When considering the gender politics of this film it's difficult to find a male character that does not fall into some sort of patriarchal oppressive role. This may be the film's strongest point of contestation. Women just don't fare well in *From Dusk*.

SJK: I'd agree that the film shows a world of patriarchal domination, and that women of color don't make out so well in the film. And as I said above, I was irked that Salma Hayek's role was so limited, even though her character is pivotal to the structure of the film. Overall, I'd say it's not his best in terms of gender politics, but I've also been convinced that it's not as bad as I first thought it was.

CF: I think in this sense, Rodriguez inherits the gendered norms of the genre or genres of which the film partakes. The question is whether or not the audience finds these norms challenged or disrupted. One could say that Salma Hayek is a typically phallic woman who is punished and ultimately eliminated as a threat. The women seem to be adjuncts of or subordinate to the men rather than agents or subjects. This seems to change somewhat over the course of Rodriguez's career, culminating in gendered revisions of generic norms in *Machete*.

FLA: What are we to make of the race politics in *From Dusk*?

CG: Texas does not have the best record when it comes to political correctness and issues of race politics. Texas Ranger Earl McGraw goes on and on about the "mongoloid boy" in the opening scene of *From Dusk*, and yet, Jacob Fuller has a son of Chinese descent whom he loves and defends unconditionally. Two Texas men with differing levels of compassion for someone who might be considered as "Other." Again, a lot of the good in the film rests squarely on Jacob, and he seems to have the greatest capacity for empathy in the entire cast. The Titty Twister bar is truly a diverse environment, and it's no accident that it's where we see the greatest concentration of people in the entire film. I believe Chet Pussy when he describes the variety of "pussy" available at the Titty Twister. There the diversity is welcomed, but it is welcomed for a nefarious reason. It's a film where, like *Planet Terror*, a group is forced to cross *into* Mexico in order to escape something in Texas. Rodriguez is a native Texan, and he must be very keen as to the politics of race and immigration in his state. Indeed, he has taken this to the next level in his *Machete* films.

SS: *From Dusk* is made by a Latino director yet race is never really complicated; it certainly doesn't exist as central ingredient as it does in *Machete*. However, there are interesting complications such as the casting of a U.S. Border Patrol agent as Latino (Cheech Marin) and the total rejection of a long tradition of representing Latinos as marginal, passive figures. How much more active can they be than as marauding vampires?

SJK: The border issues are present in *From Dusk*, although muted in relation to some of his other films. The fact that Tarantino wrote the script certainly informs that mutedness.

CF: I think the racial politics are embedded much more in the vampire narrative than in the explicit politics of representation. Through the symbolic figure of the vampire we might read race as inherently mutable and subject to transformation, that is, all humans might become the other represented by the vampire.

FLA: I wonder, too, if the politics of representation shift when we move more from the fugitive story where we feel Tarantino's heavy hand (the first hour of the film) to the vampire comic book story where we have the clear presence of Rodriguez (the south-of-the-border latter part of the film) . . .

CG: I agree, and I think that's where I may have been going in my response to the last question. It's not that Tarantino doesn't deal with issues of race or politics (e.g., *Jackie Brown*, *Pulp Fiction*, *Django Unchained*), it's just that he doesn't deal with it in *From Dusk*. The politics of representation can really only come into play in terms of Scott Fuller, Jacob's Chinese son. Seth calls Scott a Jap, only to be corrected by Jacob. Beyond this brief moment, there is little to do with representation in the film until night falls on the Mexican side of the border. The fact that we ultimately learn the Titty Twister is the apex of a Mesoamerican pyramid with bloodstains from its portals screams of identity and representation issues. While it's not an overt issue in the vampiric second half of the film, the presence of race and representation is far more palpable here than in the first half of the film. If the night section in Mexico is only mildly concerned with representation, the day section in Texas is even less so.

SS: The idea of the film as suturing borders in the making of a borderlands might open up ways of exploring how the film turns upside down some elements of stereotypical representations, especially in the more fully owned Rodriguez part of the film.

SJK: Absolutely. The latter part of the film has layers upon layers of complexity (Satánico Pandemónium, the vampires themselves as monstrous others, the bar on top of the temple) whereas, at least in terms of racial politics, the first part is much less interesting.

CF: The politics of representation necessarily shift once the border is crossed. The story becomes less about the two brothers and more about the interactions of all the characters with the occupants of the bar. It is as if the latent racial politics along the border erupt in Mexico where we find a mix of people from the U.S. and Mexico in a collective carnivalesque space.

FLA: If *From Dusk* brings an irreverent worldview—the carnivalesque?—to all of matters of its content, can we single out issues of representation (gender or race) for our criticism?

CG: I think that's what I'm finding so difficult in terms of this aspect of *From Dusk*. The carnivalesque inverts roles and the dynamics of power. That's why I noted Satánico Pandemónium's position of power in what Frederick identifies as the moment the film goes from Tarantino to Rodriguez. If you only consider the dialogue, and please correct me if I'm wrong here, but race is never mentioned by any of the characters once they arrive at the Titty Twister. That's not to say it's not present, but the characters never make it an issue, outside of Scott's race early on in the film. Frost is an African American, former Vietnam vet, but his race is not an explicit issue. The Mexican characters don't speak Spanish, so even language isn't an issue to single out for examination. All of this leads me to think that the overriding issue has to do with patriarchy and gender roles, with the Mesoamerican pyramid that serves almost as an epilogue.

SS: I would level my criticism at the violence toward women and the absence of Spanish in the film. So while *From Dusk* innovates in its geographic juxtapositions (U.S.–Mexico) and cinematic crossings (Tarantino/Rodriguez styles), there could have been more of a will to style when it came to the characterization of women and bilingual or code-switching English/Spanish play.

SJK: I'm not sure it's ever entirely possible to single out an issue for criticism. One always has to consider something like gender and race in relation to context and other considerations. For instance, my reading of *From Dusk* would be different (worse) if I wasn't aware of Rodriguez's other films as well as his impact in the world of filmmaking.

CF: I think that gender, ethnicity, and race work together as expressions of U.S. hegemony. We can't forget that these characters are almost typical Westerners who originate from the U.S. and "make a run for the border" to escape the law. They include the family man, his adopted racialized son—reminiscent of the adopted Native American adjuncts of the western hero, and the virtuous young white woman who must be protected from the villainous outlaw. Their expectations about what they will find in Mexico are upset by the intervention of another genre, the horror/vampire film, which shifts the coordinates of the hegemonic Western narrative to another more allegorical scene.

FLA: Might *From Dusk* be the *first* borderland film in form and content made by a Latino film director?

CG: *El Mariachi* and *Desperado* are borderland films set entirely in Mexico. However, if we are talking about a borderland film wherein there is a crossing from the U.S. into Mexico in the content of the story, and one in which there is a crossing of *styles* within the very structure of the film, then I don't think there is any dispute that *From Dusk* is a first. As I mentioned earlier, there aren't many films like *From Dusk*, and anytime there is a first in some category there are going to be missteps and imperfections inherent. *From Dusk* may have flaws, but it also carves out new ground in storytelling and technical achievement. It takes a lot of risks, and I think time has been kind to it and not the reverse. After a decade and a half, the film still holds up well. In fact, I enjoy it now more than I did the first time *because* I can now situate it in bas-relief with Rodriguez's body of work (before and since), as well as Tarantino's. Incidentally, though Tarantino is far from a great actor, his best acting role is without question Richie Gecko—and not just because he appears in over half the movie. He actually plays a convincing, complex character and not just some version of Tarantino himself, which is a testament to the film as well. Ultimately, *From Dusk till Dawn* is a film that managed to do some very significant things with the tiniest of budgets. And for me, that's what makes it worthy of study at the level of form and content.

SS: I mentioned already how I think this film in form and content is of *la frontera*. We might even consider it as extending a Latino borderland film tradition that includes Cheech Marin's (this guy is everywhere, ¿qué no?) *Born in East L.A.* (1987) and runs all the way up to Rodriguez's *Machete*.

SJK: I don't know enough about the genre of borderland films to weigh in on this, but I would definitely say it's the first for Rodriguez, and indicative of many good things to come in his career.

CF: I think it definitely fits into the border genre and is one of the first of its kind to mix it with the horror genre. The film makes very explicit linkages between the western and the border genre while expanding and exploring connections to other filmic traditions and types—for example, those mentioned earlier like Hong Kong action films. Also, the connection of the racialized other and the vampire and how these arbitrary divisions might be traversed is a unique approach to the symbolic boundaries explored in border narratives.

Postproduction in Robert Rodriguez's "Post-Post-Latinidad"

ALVARO RODRIGUEZ

It is a paradox that Robert Rodriguez's entrance, much less his success, was both supposed to—and never could possibly—happen. Our fathers' brotherhood made us first cousins, Robert some two-plus years older than myself, as enigmatic as he was alluring to my child eyes as we sat in the back of a pickup truck in Rio Grande City in the early 1980s, waxing large about a new R-rated film neither of us could see but both seemed to know something about: John Carpenter's *Escape from New York*. Robert definitely knew more than I did, by that time already a fully-fleshed fanboy doing close readings of *Fangoria Magazine* for facts and figures that other kids our age surely would have found esoteric had they the word in their pubescent vocabularies. As our bodies stank in the sweltering South Texas heat, our minds occupied a fire-lit world after the fall of New York, Manhattan Island walled off into a maximum security prison whose inductees could elect self-annihilation and save themselves from the circles of Hell that awaited them inside. Robert also had another view, cataloging for my eager ears a run-through of how Carpenter shot this sequence and that, already informing what would become his own style. (Later, upon the release of Albert Pyun's *Dangerously Close*, Robert cheerfully remarked upon a critic's statement that the film contained "more style than substance," "How cool is that? That's the kind of movie I want to make!")

From the day in the truck bed to my arrival as a freshman and resident at St. Anthony's High School Seminary, an all-boys boarding school that Robert attended as a day student (his house located conveniently across the street), I didn't see him much, he growing up in San Antonio, I attempting to do the same, four hours straight south on Highway 281 in Edinburg, Texas, a college town that seemed never to have learned how to behave like one. But as I attempted to navigate the skull-and-bones cryptoworld of the Oblate-run gulag, I soon saw "Video Bob" (as he preferred to be known) as my lifeline, unwittingly signing an invisible contract for access to his library of film scores, VHS bootlegs, and trips to the Eisenhower Road flea market to buy Rambo-esque hunting knives for use as film props. Returning to the paradox, it was evident to me then Robert had the potential to be the Next Steven Spielberg—maybe. How many more thousands of Robert Rodriguezes were there spread across the continent, sequestered in their bedrooms between two mammoth VHS tape decks, splicing their juvenilia and augmenting them with borrowed bits of Jerry Goldsmith and *The Lost Boys* soundtrack? I didn't know. I wasn't sure. I would not have hazarded a guess. But this Robert Rodriguez was mine, and if I wasn't going to seize the opportunity to attach myself to him like Chang and Eng, I would at least attempt to both emulate and monitor his progress while I read my movie novelizations in paperback and thumbed through *Siddhartha*, the Beats, James M. Cain, and Charles Bukowski.

Like a lemming, I followed him to the University of Texas at Austin (a pre-freshman year visit to the town resulted in a three-movies-in-three-theaters-in-one-day blowout along with his roommate Christian McLaughlin with whom he would film the outré short "Reform School Sluts" and who would become a novelist and television sitcom writer) and kept tabs on his maturation as an artist. His comic strip *Los Hooligans* was a primer in storyboarding and building his visual sensibilities even as it insidiously attacked his back with at times crippling, chronic pain. I watched as he made his video shorts; he openly lamented his grades were not quite good enough to get him into the film production classes. But as his dual-deck mini-movies began to garner attention, it became obvious he would not be deterred from his desire to put his third brain on display in some form of cinema.

Three semesters of creative writing in poetry and a stint as an assistant entertainment editor at the *Daily Texan* (where *Los Hooligans* shared space with my film, music, and book reviews) began to form my own alternative film school as Robert toiled on his first real movie, *El Mariachi*, a quickie whose purpose was to showcase his talents as a director, writer, editor, and cinematographer ("They might hate my direction but like my editing, and I'll get a job as an editor," he quipped) and to facilitate a quick turnover to the Mexican video market with enough profit to shoot a "better, bigger" movie. I lent my questionable talents as a budding songwriter to his soundtrack and graduated with my B.A. in English, wishing him the best of luck with his little $7,000 experiment that sure had some nifty moments with a bus and some squibs.

It wasn't long before he became something of a self-propagating myth ("Why do I want to be a man when I'm already a legend?" Machete asks toward the end of his first full-length adventure), the "rebel without a crew" who single-handedly made a quirky, entertaining first feature in Spanish on a shoestring and walked away with an IFP award, a nod from the Sundance audience, and a deal with Columbia Pictures.

This was the new wave, suddenly crashing through the glass doors of Hollywood and flooding the offices of agents, producers, and executives with the endless possibilities and promises of streets paved with gold. Our collaboration began in earnest with a new spec script, a "supernatural action comedy" uncleverly titled *Till Death Do Us Part*, written with an unknown actress in mind in whom Robert saw endless potential. Her name was Salma Hayek.

Despite the fact that the script did not go into production (Robert later mined its rough pages for sequences he would use in *Spy Kids* and *Once Upon a Time in Mexico*), what I'd secretly, unconsciously hoped for was finally happening. I was writing screenplays, and Robert was opening doors. In the old Dewey fashion, I was learning by doing, as I would continue to hold onto the "student mind" for nearly two decades, always looking for teachers and acknowledging Robert as one of the most gifted and important.

Working with him has always had its share of difficulties and triumphs, of missed opportunities and modest successes. As many of the preceding chapters have posited, Robert became an expert smuggler, fine-tuning the electric undercurrents of his popular narratives with themes of identity, family, and a "post-post-Latinidad." It didn't matter if it took the form of a kids' film, a *Breakfast Club*–meets–*Invasion of the Body Snatchers* teen sci-fi, or a grindhouse Mexploitation picture. There was always something *there*, bubbling up from under. It took me a while to develop a vocabulary to quantify it, but it was present from the beginning. It was a sense of a shared boyhood, informed by the magic of celluloid and the sanctity of the cinema, even if only shared on badly cropped VHS (plus a few bucks' "pain in the ass fee"). All these years later, after many interactions credited and uncredited, this is the word made digital (née filmic) flesh that comprises the still-evolving canon of an unlikely auteur. It has been a privilege to play a small part in the process, to have recognized what others are now seeing in the films of Robert Rodriguez, and to face the challenges of continuing to create with him and realize our shared truck-bed dreams.

Works Cited

Alba, Richard. "Mexican Americans and the American Dream." *Perspectives on Politics* 4 (June 2006): 289–296.

Aldama, Arturo J. "Fear and Action: A Cognitive Approach to Teaching *Children of Men*." *Analyzing World Fiction: New Horizons in Narrative Theory*. Ed. Frederick Luis Aldama. Austin: U of Texas P, 2011. 151–161.

Aldama, Frederick Luis. "*The Adventures of Sharkboy and Lavagirl*: A Journey of Perceptual Chunking in Audiovisual, Visuotextual, and Textual Media Forms." Visual Perception and Narrative. Annual Meeting of the International Society for the Study of Narrative. Harrahs, Las Vegas, NV. 16 Mar. 2012.

———. "Characters in Comic Books." *Characters in Fictional Worlds: Understanding Imaginary Beings in Literature, Film, and Other Media*. Ed. Jans Eder, Fotis Jannidis, and Ralf Schneider. Berlin: Walter de Gruyter, 2010. 318–328.

———. *The Cinema of Robert Rodriguez*. Austin: U of Texas P, 2014.

———. "Putting a Finger on That Hollow Emptiness in Roth's Indignation." *Philip Roth Studies* 7.2 (Fall 2011): 131–142.

———, ed. *Toward a Cognitive Theory of Narrative Acts*. Austin: U of Texas P, 2010.

Alleva, Richard. "Blood Sport: Sin City and Walk on Water." *Commonweal* 132.9 (2005): 21–22.

Alonso Gallo, Laura P. "Latino Culture in the U.S.: Using, Reviewing, and Reconstructing *Latinidad* in Contemporary Latino/a Fiction." *KulturPoetik* 2.2 (2002): 236–248.

Anderson, Kristin J., and Christina Accomando. "'Real' Boys?: Manufacturing Masculinity and Erasing Privilege in Popular Books on Raising Boys." *Feminism and Psychology* 12.4 (2002): 491–516.

Anonymous. "52% Support Arizona-Like Immigration Law in Their State." Rasmussen Reports. ⟨http://www.rasmussenreports.com/public_content/politics /current_events/immigration/52_support_arizona_like_immigration_law_in _their_state⟩. Retrieved May 1, 2012.

Anzaldúa, Gloria. "Chapter 7: *La conciencia de la mestiza*: Towards a New Consciousness." *Borderlands/La Frontera: The New Mestiza*. *The Norton Anthology of Theory and Criticism*. Ed. Vincent B. Leitch. New York: Norton, 2001. 2211–2222.

Applebaum, Stephen. "Robert Rodriguez, Film Director." *Robert Rodriguez: Interviews*. Ed. Zachary Ingle. Jackson: UP of Mississippi, 2012. 160–162.

Arnott, Luke. "*Blam!* The Literal Architecture of *Sin City*." *International Journal of Comic Art* 10.2 (2008): 380–401.

Ashcraft, Brian. "The Man Who Shot Sin City." *Wired Magazine* 13.4 (Apr. 2005). ⟨http://www.wired.com/wired/archive/13.04/sincity.html⟩.

Baker, Timothy C. "The (Neuro)-Aesthetics of Caricature: Representations of Reality in Bret Easton Ellis's *Lunar Park*." *Poetics Today* 30.3 (2009): 471–515.

Banita, Georgiana. "Chris Ware and the Pursuit of Slowness." *The Comics of Chris Ware: Drawing Is a Way of Thinking*. Ed. David M. Ball and Martha B. Kuhlman. Jackson: UP of Mississippi, 2010. 177–190.

Belton, John. "Painting by the Numbers: The Digital Intermediate." *Film Quarterly* 61.3 (2008): 58–65.

Beltrán, Mary C. *Latina/o Stars in U.S. Eyes: The Making and Meanings of Film and TV Stardom*. Chicago: U of Illinois P, 2009.

Biddulph, Steve. *Raising Boys: Why Boys Are Different—and How to Help Them Become Happy and Well-Balanced Men*. Berkeley: Celestial Arts, 1998.

Borde, Raymond, and Étienne Chaumeton. "Towards a Definition of *Film Noir*." *Film Noir Reader*. Ed. Alain Silver and James Ursini. New York: Limelight Editions, 2003. 17–25.

Bordwell, David. *Narration in the Fiction Film*. Madison: U of Wisconsin P, 1985.

Bordwell, David, and Noël Carroll, eds. *Post-Theory: Reconstructing Film Studies*. Madison: U Wisconsin Press, 1996.

Botting, Fred. "A-ffect-less: Zombie-Horror-Shock." *English Language Notes* 48.1 (2010): 177–190.

Bould, Mark. *Film Noir: From Berlin to Sin City*. New York: Wallflower, 2005.

Bourdieu, Pierre. *Distinction: A Social Critique of the Judgment of Taste*. Trans. Richard Nice. Cambridge, MA: Harvard UP, 1984.

Buchanan, Pat. *The Death of the West: How Dying Populations and Immigrant Invasions Imperil Our Country and Civilization*. New York: Thomas Dunne Books, 2002.

Buñuel, Luis. *Viridiana*. Screenplay by Julio Alejandro de Castro and Luis Buñuel. Unión Industrial Cinematográfica, 1961.

Caldwell, Thomas. "River of Life and Death: Women, Religion, Power and Purity in *Water*." *Screen Education* 64 (2012): 115–120.

Cameron, Douglas M. "Representation of the Border in Contemporary Cinema: The Imbrication of Cultures in *El Mariachi*." *MACLAS Latin American Essays* 9 (1995): 3–17.

Canavan, Gerry. "'We *Are* the Walking Dead': Race, Time, and Survival in Zombie Narrative." *Extrapolation* 51.3 (2010): 431–453.

Carroll, Noël. "Horror and Humor." *Journal of Aesthetics and Art Criticism* 57.2 (1999): 145–160.

———. *The Philosophy of Motion Pictures*. Malden: Blackwell, 2008.

———. "The Specificity of Media." *Journal of Aesthetic Education* 19.4 (1985): 5–20.

Chatman, Seymour. *Story and Discourse: Narrative Structure in Fiction and Film.* Ithaca: Cornell UP, 1978.

Chavez, Leo R. *The Latino Threat: Constructing Immigrants, Citizens, and the Nation.* Stanford: Stanford UP, 2008.

Cohn, Dorrit. *Transparent Minds: Narrative Modes for Presenting Consciousness in Fiction.* Princeton: Princeton UP, 1978.

Cohn, Neil. "The Limits of Time and Transitions: Challenges to Theories of Sequential Image Comprehension." *Studies in Comics* 1.1 (2010): 127–147.

Cornejo Polar, Antonio. "*Mestizaje* and Hybridity: The Risks of Metaphors." *The Latin American Cultural Studies Reader.* Ed. Ana del Sarto, Alicia Ríos, and Abril Trigo. Durham: Duke UP, 2004. 760–764.

Cornelius, Wayne A. "Ambivalent Reception: Mass Public Responses to the 'New' Latino Immigration to the United States." *Latinos: Remaking America.* Ed. M. Suárez-Orozco and M. Paez. Berkeley: U of California P, 2002. 165–184.

Dagleish, Tim, and Mick Power, eds. *The Handbook of Cognition and Emotion.* West Sussex: John Wiley & Sons, 2000.

Dalle Vacche, Angela. "Painting Thoughts, Listening to Images: Eric Rohmer's *The Marquise of O . . .*" *Film Quarterly* 46.4 (1993): 2–15.

Damasio, Antonio. *Descartes' Error: Emotion, Reason, and the Human Brain.* New York: Putnam, 1994.

Damico, James. "*Film Noir*: A Modest Proposal." *Film Noir Reader.* Ed. Alain Silver and James Ursini. New York: Limelight Editions, 2003. 95–105.

Dickens, Charles. *Little Dorritt.* New York: Penguin Classics, 2004.

Durgnat, Raymond. "Paint it Black: The Family Tree of the *Film Noir.*" *Film Noir Reader.* Ed. Alain Silver and James Ursini. New York: Limelight Editions, 2003. 37–51.

Ebert, Roger. *Once Upon a Time in Mexico.* Review. RobertEbert.com. 12 Sept. 2003. Web.

———. *Sin City.* Review. *Chicago Sun-Times.* 31 Mar. 2005. Web.

Eisner, Will. *Comics and Sequential Art.* Paramus: Poorhouse, 1985.

———. *Graphic Storytelling and Visual Narrative: Principles and Practices from the Legendary Cartoonist.* New York; London: W. W. Norton, 2008.

Eliot, George. *Middlemarch.* New York: Penguin Classics, 2003.

Evans, Dylan, and Pierre Cruse, eds. *Emotions, Evolution, and Rationality.* Oxford: Oxford UP, 2004.

Fehrle, Johannes. "Unnatural Worlds and Unnatural Narration in Comics? A Critical Examination." *Unnatural Narratives: Unnatural Narratology.* Ed. Jan Alber and Rüdiger Heinze. Berlin: de Gruyter, 2011. 210–245.

"15-minute film school with Robert Rodriguez." *Sin City: Recut, Extended, Unrated.* Dimension Studio, 2005.

Flagg, Gordon. "Frank Miller's *Sin City*: The Making of the Movie (Book)." *Booklist* 101.17 (2005): 1558.

Flanagan, Martin. "Process of Assimilation: Rodriguez and Banderas, from *El Mariachi* to *Desperado.*" *Ixquic: Revista Hispánica Internacional de Análisis y Creación* 3 (2001): 41–59.

Foucault, Michel. *The History of Sexuality: An Introduction, Vol. 1.* [1976] Trans. Robert Hurley. New York: Vintage, 1990.

Fragola, Anthony. "Art as a Source of Imagistic Generator for Narrative." *Journal of Film and Video* 42.3 (1990): 41–50.

Fregoso, Rosa Linda. *The Bronze Screen: Chicana and Chicano Film Culture*. Minneapolis: U of Minnesota P, 1993.

Frijda, Nico H. *The Emotions*. Cambridge: Cambridge UP, 1986.

Fuller, Graham. "Colour Me Noir." *Sight and Sound* 15.6 (2005): 12–16.

Gallese, Vittorio, et al. "Action Recognition in the Premotor Cortex." *Brain* 199.2 (1996): 593–609.

———. "The Roots of Empathy: The Shared Manifold Hypothesis and the Neural Basis of Intersubjectivity." *Psychopathology* 36.4 (2003): 171–180.

———. "The 'Shared Manifold' Hypothesis: From Mirror Neurons to Empathy." *Journal of Consciousness Studies* 8.5–7 (2001): 33–50.

Gardner, Jared. *Projections: Comics and the History of Twenty-First-Century Storytelling*. Stanford: Stanford UP, 2012.

———. "Storylines." *SubStance: A Review of Theory and Literary Criticism* 40.1 (2011): 53–69.

Gaut, Berys. "Identification and Emotion in Narrative Film." *Passionate Views: Film, Cognition, and Emotion*. Ed. Carl Plantinga and Greg M. Smith. Baltimore: Johns Hopkins UP, 1999. 200–216.

Genette, Gerard. *Narrative Discourse: An Essay in Method*. Ithaca: Cornell UP, 1983.

Gobineau, Arthur de. *The Inequality of Human Races*. Trans. Adrian Collins. London: William Heinemann, 1915. pdf file.

Goldberg, Ilan I., Michael Harel, and Rafael Malach. "When the Brain Loses Its Self: Prefrontal Inactivation during Sensorimotor Processing." *Neuron* 50.2 (2006): 329–339.

Goldberg, Stephanie. "TV Can Boost Self-Esteem of White Boys, Study Says." *CNN.com*. 1 June 2012. Web.

González, Christopher, ed. *The Films of Robert Rodriguez*. Special Issue of *POST SCRIPT: Essays in Film and the Humanities*, forthcoming.

Griswold, Jerry. *Feeling Like a Kid: Childhood and Children's Literature*. Baltimore: Johns Hopkins UP, 2006.

Gutierrez-Albilla, Julian Daniel. "Picturing the Beggars in Luis Buñuel's *Viridiana*: A Perverse Appropriation of Leonardo da Vinci's *Last Supper*." *Journal of Romance Studies* 5.2 (2005): 59–73.

Halberstam, Judith. *Female Masculinity*. Durham: Duke UP, 1998.

Hartlaub, Peter. "Blood and Guts and Guffaws in 'Mexico.'" Rev. of *Once Upon a Time in Mexico*. *San Francisco Chronicle*. Sfgate.com. 12 Sept. 2003. Web.

Hasson, Uri, et al. "Intersubject Synchronization of Cortical Activity during Natural Vision." *Science* 303.5664 (2004): 1634–1640.

Herman, David. "Re-Minding Modernism (1880–1945)." *The Emergence of Mind: Representations of Consciousness in Narrative Discourse in English*. Ed. David Herman. Lincoln: U of Nebraska P, 2011. 243–272.

———. "Stories as a Tool for Thinking." *Narrative Theory and the Cognitive Sciences*. Ed. David Herman. Stanford: Center for the Study of Language and Information, 2003. 163–192.

————. *Story Logic: Problems and Possibilities of Narrative*. Lincoln: U of Nebraska P, 2002.

————. "Storytelling and the Sciences of the Mind: Cognitive Narratology, Discursive Psychology, and Narratives in Face-to-Face Interaction." *Narrative* 15.3 (Oct. 2007): 306–334.

————. "Toward a Transmedial Narratology." *Narrative across Media: The Languages of Storytelling*. Ed. Marie-Laure Ryan. Lincoln, NE: U of Nebraska P, 2004. 47–75.

Hervey, Benjamin A. *Night of the Living Dead*. London: British Film Institute, 2008.

Hesse, Hermann. *Siddhartha*. Trans. Hilda Rosner. New York: New Directions, 1951.

Hill, Aaron. "Robert Rodriguez's CGI-Overload, *Shorts*." *The Village Voice*. VillageVoice.com. 18 Aug. 2009. Web.

Hogan, Patrick Colm. *Affective Narratology: The Emotional Structure of Stories*. Lincoln, NE: U of Nebraska P, 2011.

————. *Cognitive Science, Literature, and the Arts: A Guide for Humanists*. New York: Routledge, 2003.

————. *The Mind and Its Stories: Narrative Universals and Human Emotion*. Cambridge: Cambridge UP, 2003.

————. *Understanding Nationalism: On Narrative, Cognitive Science, and Identity*. Columbus: Ohio State UP, 2009.

Holden, Stephen. "Growl, and Let the Severed Heads Fall Where They May." Review of *Machete*. *New York Times* 2 Sept. 2010. ⟨http://www.nytimes.com/2010/09/03/movies/03machete.html?pagewanted=all&_r=0⟩.

Hopgood, Fincina. "The Politics of Melodrama in Deepa Mehta's *Water*." *Metro Magazine* 149 (2006): 142–147.

Huang, Priscilla. "Anchor Babies, Over-Breeders, and the Population Bomb: The Reemergence of Nativism and Population Control in Anti-Immigration Policies." *Harvard Law & Policy Review* 2.2 (2008): 385–406.

Huntington, Samuel P. "The Hispanic Challenge." *Foreign Policy* (Mar./Apr. 2004): 30–45.

Husain, M. F., dir. *Meenaxi: Tale of 3 Cities*. Written by M. F. Husain and Owais Husain. Yash Raj Films, 2004.

Ingle, Zachary, ed. *Robert Rodriguez: Interviews*. Jackson: UP of Mississippi, 2012.

Inskeep, Steve. "Interview: Frank Miller and Robert Rodriguez Discuss Their Comic Book Movie 'Sin City.'" *Morning Edition (NPR)*. 1 Apr. 2005.

James, C. T. "The Role of Semantic Information in Lexical Decisions." *Journal of Experimental Psychology: Human Perception and Performance* 1.2 (1975): 130–136.

Johnson, Alaya Dawn. "The Bechdel Test and Race in Popular Fiction." *Angry Black Woman: Race, Politics, Gender, Sexuality, Anger*. 2 Sept. 2009. Web.

Kant, Immanuel. *Critique of Judgement*. Trans. J. H. Bernard. London: Hafner Press, 1951.

Kauffman, Linda S. *Bad Girls and Sick Boys: Fantasies in Contemporary Art and Culture*. Berkeley: U of California P, 1998.

Kay, Glenn. *Zombie Movies: The Ultimate Guide*. Chicago: Chicago Review Press, 2008.

Keen, Suzanne. *Empathy and the Novel*. Oxford: Oxford UP, 2007.

Kidd, Kenneth B. *Making American Boys: Boyology and the Feral Tale*. Minneapolis: U of Minnesota P, 2004.

Kindlon, Dan, and Michael Thompson. *Raising Cain: Protecting the Emotional Life of Boys*. New York: Ballantine, 1999.

Kounios, John, and Phillip J. Holcomb. "Concreteness Effects in Semantic Processing: ERP Evidence Supporting Dual-Coding Theory." *Journal of Experimental Psychology: Learning, Memory and Cognition* 20.4 (1994): 804–823.

Kousta, Stavroula-Thaleia, et al. "The Representation of Abstract Words: Why Emotion Matters." *Journal of Experimental Psychology: General* 140.1 (2011): 14–34.

Koven, Mikel J. *Blaxploitation Films*. Herts, UK: Kamera, 2010.

Kraniauskas, John. "Hybridity in a Transnational Frame: Latin Americanist and Postcolonialist Perspectives on Cultural Studies." *The Latin American Cultural Studies Reader*. Ed. Ana del Sarto, Alicia Ríos, and Abril Trigo. Durham: Duke UP, 2004. 736–759.

Kristeva, Julia. *Powers of Horror: An Essay on Abjection*. New York: Columbia UP. 1982.

Lacan, Jacques. *Écrits: A Selection*. New York: W. W. Norton, 1977.

Lane, Richard D., and Lynn Nadel, eds. *Cognitive Neuroscience of Emotion*. New York: Oxford UP, 1999.

LeDoux, Joseph. *The Emotional Brain: The Mysterious Underpinnings of Emotional Life*. New York: Touchstone, 1996.

Leen, Catherine. "Three Border Films: *El Mariachi*, *El Jardín del Edén* and *Lone Star*." *Cultural Popular: Studies in Spanish and Latin American Popular Culture*. Ed. Shelley Godsland and Anne M. White. Bern: Peter Lang, 2002. 97–112.

Lefèvre, Pascal. "Some Medium-Specific Qualities of Graphic Sequences." *Sub-Stance: A Review of Theory and Literary Criticism* 40.1 (2011): 14–33.

Levy-Drori, Shelly, and Avishai Henik. "Concreteness and Context Availability in Lexical Decision Tasks." *American Journal of Psychology* 119.1 (2006): 45–65.

Lwin, May O., Maureen Morrin, and Aradhna Krishna. "Exploring the Super-additive Effects of Scent and Pictures on Verbal Recall: An Extension of Dual Coding Theory." *Journal of Consumer Psychology* 20.3 (2010): 317–326.

Macor, Alison. *Chainsaws, Slackers, and Spy Kids*. Austin: U of Texas P, 2010.

Mallan, Kerry. "Challenging the Phallic Fantasy in Young Adult Fiction." *Ways of Being Male: Representing Masculinities in Children's Literature and Film*. Ed. John Stephens. New York: Routledge, 2002. 150–163.

Mar, Raymond A., and Keith Oatley. "The Function of Fiction Is the Abstraction and Simulation of Social Experience." *Perspectives on Psychological Science* 3.3 (2008): 173–192.

Martindale, Colin. "Creativity and Connectionism." *The Creative Cognition Approach*. Ed. Steven Smith, Thomas Ward, and Ronald Finke. Cambridge, MA: MIT P, 1995. 249–268.

Martins, Nicole, and Kristen Harrison. "Racial and Gender Differences in the Relationship Between Children's Television Use and Self-Esteem: A Longitudinal Panel Study." *Communication Research* 39 (June 2012): 338–357.

Marvis, Mary J. *Robert Rodriguez*. Childs, MD: Mitchell Lane, 1998.

Massumi, Brian. *Parables for the Virtual: Movement, Affect, Sensation*. Durham: Duke UP, 2002.

Matheson, Richard. *I Am Legend*. Garden City, NY: Doubleday, 1954.

May, Jeff. "Zombie Geographies and the Undead City." *Social & Cultural Geography* 11.3 (2010): 285–298.

Mayer, Richard E., and Roxana Moreno. "A Split-Attention Effect in Multimedia Learning: Evidence for Dual Processing Systems in Working Memory." *Journal of Educational Psychology* 90.2 (1998): 312–320.

McCarthy, Cormac. *No Country for Old Men*. New York: Knopf, 2005.

McCloud, Scott. *Understanding Comics: The Invisible Art*. New York: Harper Perennial, 1994; Northampton, MA: Kitchen Sink Press, 1993.

McHale, Brian. *Postmodernist Fiction*. New York and London: Methune, 1987.

Mercer, John, and Martin Shingler. *Melodrama: Genre, Style, Sensibility*. London: Wallflower, 2004.

Migneco, Fabio. *Il cinema di Robert Rodriguez*. Piombino (Livorno), Italy: Il foglio, 2009.

Mikkonen, Kai. "Presenting Minds in Graphic Narratives." *Practical Answers* 6.2 (2008): 301–321.

Miller, Frank. *Frank Miller's* Sin City: *The Hard Goodbye*. Milwaukie, OR: Dark Horse Books, 2005. 199.

———. *That Yellow Bastard: A Tale from Sin City*. Milwaukie, OR: Dark Horse Comics, 1997.

———. *The Big Fat Kill: A Tale from Sin City*. Milwaukie, OR: Dark Horse Comics, 1996.

Miller, George A. "The Cognitive Revolution: A Historical Perspective." *Trends in Cognitive Sciences* 7.3 (Mar. 2003): 141–144.

Mitchell, Elvis. "Interview with Frank Miller." *The Treatment*. KCRW. 30 Mar. 2005. Radio.

Modleski, Tania. *Feminism without Women: Culture and Criticism in a "Postfeminist" Age*. New York: Routledge, 1991.

Molina-Guzmán, Isabel. *Dangerous Curves: Latina Bodies in the Media*. New York: New York UP, 2010.

Naremore, James. *More than Night: Film Noir in Its Contexts*. Berkeley: U of California P, 1998.

Noriega, Chon A. *Shot in America: Television, the State and the Rise of Chicano Cinema*. Minneapolis: U of Minnesota P, 2000.

Noriega, Chon A., and Ana M. López. *The Ethnic Eye: Latino Media Arts*. Minneapolis, MN: U of Minnesota P, 1996.

Oatley, Keith. *Such Stuff as Dreams: The Psychology of Fiction*. Hoboken: John Wiley & Sons, 2011.

O'Halloran, Kay L. "Visual Semiosis in Film." *Multimodal Discourse Analysis: Systemic Functional Perspectives*. Ed. Kay L. O'Halloran. London, England: Continuum, 2004. 109–130.

Ortony, Andrew, Gerald L. Clore, and Allan Collins, eds. *The Cognitive Structure of Emotions*. Cambridge: Cambridge UP, 1988.

Paivio, Allan. "Dual Coding Theory and the Mental Lexicon." *Mental Lexicon* 5.2 (2010): 205–230.

———. *Imagery and Verbal Processes*. New York: Holt, Rinehart, and Winston, 1971.

———. *Mental Representations: A Dual Coding Approach*. Oxford: Oxford UP, 1990.

Palmer, Alan. *Fictional Minds*. Lincoln: U of Nebraska P, 2008.

———. *Social Minds in the Novel*. Columbus, OH: The Ohio State UP, 2010.

Pérez-Torres, Rafael. *Mestizaje: Critical Uses of Race in Chicano Culture*. Minneapolis: U of Minnesota P, 2006.

Phelan, James. *Worlds from Words: A Theory of Language in Fiction*. Chicago: U of Chicago P, 1981.

Pizzino, Christopher. "Art that Goes BOOM: Genre and Aesthetics in Frank Miller's *Sin City*." *English Language Notes* 46.2 (2008): 115–128.

Place, Janey, and Lowell Peterson. "Some Visual Motifs of *Film Noir*." *Film Noir Reader*. Ed. Alain Silver and James Ursini. New York: Limelight Editions, 2003. 565–575.

Plantinga, Carl. *Moving Viewers: American Film and the Spectator's Experience*. Berkeley: U of California P, 2009.

———. "The Scene of Empathy and the Human Face on Film." *Passionate Views: Film, Cognition, and Emotion*. Ed. Carl Plantinga and Greg M. Smith. Baltimore: Johns Hopkins UP, 1999. 239–255.

Pollack, William. *Real Boys: Rescuing Our Sons from the Myths of Boyhood*. New York: Random House, 1998.

Pratt, Henry John. "Medium Specificity and the Ethics of Narrative in Comics." *Storyworlds* 1 (2009): 97–113.

Puig, Claudia. "Depp Fans Flames in Quirky 'Mexico.'" Rev. of *Once Upon a Time in Mexico*. *USA Today* 11 Sept. 2003. Web.

Pynchon, Thomas. *Gravity's Rainbow*. New York: Viking Press, 1973.

Ramírez Berg, Charles. *Latino Images in Film: Stereotypes, Subversion, and Resistance*. Austin: U of Texas P, 2002.

———. "Stereotyping in Films in General and of the Hispanic in Particular." *Latin Looks: Images of Latinas and Latinos in the U.S. Media*. Ed. Clara E. Rodríguez. Boulder: Westview Press, 1997. 105–120.

———. "A Teaser before the Show." Foreword. *The Cinema of Robert Rodriguez*. Frederick Luis Aldama. Austin: U of Texas P, 2014. ix–xii.

Richardson, Alan, and Ellen Spolsky, eds. *The Work of Fiction: Cognition, Culture, and Complexity*. Aldershot: Ashgate, 2004.

Robertson, Barbara. "VFX Heads Reveal How Frank Miller and Robert Rodriguez Shared Directing Duties on *Sin City*." *Animation* 19.7 (2005): 46–47.

Rodriguez, Richard T. *Next of Kin: The Family in Chicano/a Cultural Politics*. Durham: Duke UP, 2009.

Rodriguez, Robert. Audio Commentary. *El Mariachi*. Dir. Robert Rodriguez. Columbia, 2005. DVD.

———. "Behind the Scenes." Interview. *Frank Miller's* Sin City. Dir. Robert Rodriguez and Frank Miller. Buena Vista Home Entertainment, 2005.

Rohmer, Eric. *Die Marquise von O . . .* Written by Eric Rohmer, from the story by Heinrich von Kleist. Janus Films, 1976.

Rose, James. "28 Days Later." *Beyond Hammer: British Horror Cinema Since 1970.* Leighton Buzzard: Auteur, 2009.

Rubin, David C. "51 Properties of 125 Words: A Unit Analysis of Verbal Behavior." *Journal of Verbal Learning and Verbal Behavior* 19.6 (1980): 736–755.

Sadoski, Mark. "Embodied Cognition, Discourse, and Dual Coding Theory: New Directions." *Discourse, of Course: An Overview of Research in Discourse Studies.* Ed. Jan Renkema. Amsterdam: John Benjamins, 2009. 187–196.

Sadoski, Mark, and Allan Paivio. *Imagery and Text: A Dual Coding Theory of Reading and Writing.* Mahwah: Lawrence Erlbaum, 2001.

Sarkeesian, Anita. "The Oscars and the Bechdel Test." *Feminist Frequency: Conversations with Pop Culture.* 15 Feb. 2012. Web.

Schrader, Paul. "Notes on Film Noir." Ed. Alain Silver and James Ursini. *Film Noir Reader.* New York: Limelight Editions, 2003. 53–63.

Scott, A. O. "Guitar in His Hand, Revenge in His Heart." Rev. of *Once Upon a Time in Mexico. The New York Times* 12 Sept. 2003. Web.

Shakespeare, William. *The Tragedy of Othello, the Moor of Venice.* Ed. Alvin Kernan. New York: Signet, 1986.

Shen, Dan. "What Narratology and Stylistics Can Do for Each Other." *A Companion to Narrative Theory.* Ed. James Phelan and Peter J. Rabinowitz. Malden, MA: Blackwell, 2005. 136–149.

Shklovsky, Viktor. *Theory of Prose.* Trans. Benjamin Sher. Intro. Gerald L. Bruns. Elmwood Park, IL: Dalkey Archive Press, 1991.

Siegel, Robert. "Injecting Noir into a Comic-Book Classic." *All Things Considered (NPR).* 26 Dec. 2008. Web.

Silverman, Kaja. *Male Subjectivity at the Margins.* New York: Routledge, 1992.

Smith, Greg. *Film Structure and the Emotion System.* Cambridge: Cambridge UP, 2003.

Smith, James P. "Assimilation across the Latino Generations." *American Economic Review* 93.2 (2003): 315–319.

Smith, Robert Courtney. *Mexican New York: Transnational Lives of New Immigrants.* Berkeley: U of California P, 2006.

Solso, Robert. *Cognition and the Visual Arts.* Cambridge, MA: MIT P, 1996.

Spivak, Gayatri. "Can the Subaltern Speak?" *The Norton Anthology of Theory and Criticism.* Ed. Vincent B. Leitch. New York: Norton, 2001. 2197–2207.

Stam, Robert, and Toby Miller, eds. *Film Theory: An Anthology.* Hoboken: Wiley-Blackwell, 2000.

Stratton, Jon. "Zombie Trouble: Zombie Texts, Bare Life and Displaced People." *European Journal of Cultural Studies* 14.3 (2011): 265–281.

Szanto, George. *Theater and Propaganda.* Austin: U of Texas P, 1978.

Tan, Ed S. *Emotion and the Structure of Narrative Film.* Trans. Barbara Fasting. Mahwah: Lawrence Erlbaum, 1996.

Tarantino, Quentin, and Robert Rodriguez. *Grindhouse: The Sleaze-Filled Saga of an Exploitation Double Feature.* New York: Weinstein Books, 2007.

Tobar, Héctor. *The Barbarian Nurseries*. New York: Farrar, Straus and Giroux, 2011.

Torres, Hector A. "Chicano Doppelgänger: Robert Rodriguez's First Remake and Secondary Revision." *Aztlán* 26.1 (2001): 159–170.

Travers, Peter. "El Mariachi and the Sundance Kid." *Rolling Stone* 18 Mar. 1993, 652.

———. Rev. of *Once Upon a Time in Mexico*. *Rolling Stone* 8 Sept. 2003. Web.

Valdivia, Angharad N. *Latina/os and the Media*. Malden, MA: Polity, 2010.

Varela, Francisco J., Evan Thompson, and Eleanor Rosch. *The Embodied Mind: Cognitive Science and Human Experience*. Cambridge, MA: MIT P, 1991.

Vasconcelos, José. *The Cosmic Race: A Bilingual Edition*. Trans. Didier T. Jaén. Baltimore: Johns Hopkins UP, 1997.

Verstraten, Peter. *Film Narratology*. Toronto: U of Toronto P, 2009.

Wannamaker, Annette. *Boys in Children's Literature and Popular Culture: Masculinity, Abjection, and the Fictional Child*. New York: Routledge, 2008.

Weiner, Robert G., and John Cline, eds. *Cinema Inferno: Celluloid Explosions from the Cultural Margins*. Lanham, MD: Scarecrow, 2010.

Welcome, Suzanne, et al. "An Electrophysiological Study of Task Demands on Concreteness Effects: Evidence for Dual Coding Theory." *Experimental Brain Research* 212.3 (2011): 347–358.

West, W. Caroline, and Phillip J. Holcomb. "Imaginal, Semantic, and Surface-Level Processing of Concrete and Abstract Words: An Electrophysiological Investigation." *Journal of Cognitive Neuroscience* 12.6 (2000): 1024–1037.

Whaley, C. P. "Word-Nonword Classification Times." *Journal of Verbal Learning and Verbal Behavior* 17.2 (1978): 143–154.

Winter, Jessica. "Rodriguez's Desperado Hours Drag, but Johnny Be Good." Rev. of *Once Upon a Time in Mexico*. *Village Voice*. Villagevoice.com. 9 Sept. 2003.

Wolk, Douglas. *Reading Comics: How Graphic Novels Work and What They Mean*. Cambridge: De Capo P, 2007.

Woolf, Virginia. *Mrs. Dalloway*. Eastford, CT: Martino Fine Books, 2012.

Zaitchik, Alexander. "Does Rodriguez's 'Machete' Advocate 'Race War'? *The Huffington Post*. ⟨http://www.huffingtonpost.com/alexander-zaitchik/does-robert-rodriguezs-ma_b_712003.html⟩. Retrieved May 1, 2012.

Žižek, Slavoj. *The Fright of Real Tears*. London: British Film Institute, 1999.

Zunshine, Lisa, ed. *Introduction to Cognitive Cultural Studies*. Baltimore: Johns Hopkins UP, 2010.

———. "Theory of Mind and Fictions of Embodied Transparency." *Narrative* 16.1 (2008): 65–92.

———. *Why We Read Fiction: Theory of Mind and the Novel*. Columbus, OH: The Ohio State UP, 2006.

Notes on Contributors

FREDERICK LUIS ALDAMA is Arts and Humanities Distinguished Professor of English and University Distinguished Scholar at the Ohio State University, where he is also founder and director of LASER: Latino & Latin American Studies Space for Enrichment and Research. He teaches Latino/a and Latin American postcolonial literature, film, and comics, as well as narrative theory and cognitive science approaches to culture. He is the author and editor of over twenty books. He coedits the series Cognitive Approaches to Literature and Culture (University of Texas Press) as well as World Comics and Graphic Nonfiction (University of Texas Press). He also edits several additional book series, including Latino Pop Culture (Palgrave) and Contemporary Latino Authors and Directors (Ohio State University Press). He sits on the executive council of the International Society for the Study of Narrative and on the editorial boards for journals such as *Narrative* and the *Journal of Narrative Theory*, and is a member of the standing board for the Oxford Bibliographies in Latino Studies.

EMILY R. ANDERSON is an Associate Professor of English and the Chair of Film Studies at Knox College. Her previous articles on cinematic narration and unreliability and on epistemological crises in gothic fiction have appeared in *Journal of Narrative Theory* and *Eighteenth-Century Fiction*. She is currently writing on the ways cognitive and rhetorical approaches to narrative complement each other and together might explain narration across media.

JAMES J. DONAHUE is Associate Professor of Literature at SUNY Potsdam. His research interests include ethnic American literary studies, narrative theory, and twentieth-century American literary culture. He has published work on Jack Kerouac and James Welch and is currently working on several projects at the intersection of ethnic studies and narrative theory. He is coeditor of the forthcoming volume *Narrative, Race, and Ethnicity in the Americas.*

ERIN E. EIGHAN is a PhD student at the University of Connecticut, Storrs, where she is working on a dissertation that uses the tools of cognitive science to analyze a range of narrative fiction formats such as film, comics, television, and novels.

CAMILLA FOJAS is Vincent de Paul Professor and Director of Latin American and Latino Studies at DePaul University, where she teaches classes and does research on the construction and representation of race and national borders in film and popular culture. Her books include *Cosmopolitanism in the Americas* (2005), *Border Bandits: Hollywood on the Southern Frontier* (2008), and *Islands of Empire: Pop Culture & U.S. Power* (2014). She is coeditor of *Mixed Race Hollywood* (2008) and *Transnational Crossroads: Remapping the Americas and the Pacific* (2012).

ENRIQUE GARCÍA is Assistant Professor of Hispanic Visual Culture at Middlebury College. His research focuses on Latino/a American film and comic books. He has published a number of articles on Mexican and Caribbean comic books. He is currently finishing a book on Cuban Cinema as well as writing a monograph on the works of U.S. Latino comic book writers/artists Jaime and Gilbert Hernandez for Frederick Luis Aldama's "Contemporary Latino Authors and Directors" series. His future projects include a book on the representation of race in the works of Mexican comic book author Yolanda Vargas Dulché, as well as a monograph on Latino musicals.

CHRISTOPHER GONZÁLEZ is Assistant Professor of English at Texas A&M University–Commerce, where he teaches twentieth- and twenty-first-century literatures of the United States. He has published articles on authors such as Edward P. Jones and Philip Roth, the comic-book artist Jaime Hernandez, and filmmakers Alex Rivera and Robert Rodriguez. He is managing editor of *Philip Roth Studies.* He is special issue editor of *POST SCRIPT: Essays in Film and the Humanities,* which focuses on the films of Robert Rodriguez, is coauthor with Frederick Luis

Aldama of *Latinos in the End Zone: The Brown Color Line in the NFL* (2013), and has forthcoming an in-depth examination of the works of Junot Díaz.

PATRICK COLM HOGAN is a professor in the Department of English and the Program in Cognitive Science at the University of Connecticut. He is the author and editor of twenty books, including *Cognitive Science, Literature, and the Arts: A Guide for Humanists* (2003), *Understanding Indian Movies: Culture, Cognition, and Cinematic Imagination* (2008), *What Literature Teaches Us about Emotions* (2011), *How Authors' Minds Make Stories* (2013), *Narrative Discourse: Authors and Narrators in Literature, Film, and Art* (2013), and the coauthored book with Frederick Luis Aldama, *Conversations on Cognitive Cultural Studies: Literature, Language, and Aesthetics* (2014).

ZACHARY INGLE is a PhD student in Film and Media Studies at the University of Kansas. He is currently writing his dissertation, exploring Rodriguez and contemporary scholarship on the auteur theory. He is editor of *Robert Rodriguez: Interviews* (2012) and coeditor of *Identity and Myth in Sports Documentaries: Critical Essays* (2013).

SUE J. KIM is Professor of English at the University of Massachusetts, Lowell. She is the author of *Critiquing Postmodernism in Contemporary Discourses of Race* (2009) and essays on race, aesthetics, and ideology in journals such as *Narrative*, *Modern Fiction Studies*, the *Journal of Asian American Studies*, and *College Literature*. She is the guest editor of a special issue of *JNT: Journal of Narrative Theory* on "Decolonizing Narrative Theory." Her book *On Anger: Race, Cognition, Narrative* (2013) examines race, emotion, cognition, and narrative form.

ALVARO RODRIGUEZ is a screenwriter who has coauthored the films *Shorts* and *Machete*, both directed by Robert Rodriguez, as well as *The Hangman's Daughter*, a prequel to *From Dusk Till Dawn*. A frequent panelist and presenter at the Austin Film Festival, he has also curated an "Epoca de Oro" Mexican film series at the Museum of South Texas History and has presented on the smuggled subtext(s) in *Machete* at South Texas College. His border-influenced short fiction has appeared in multiple publications, both physical and digital, including *Along the River* (edited by David Bowles, 2011) and *After Death* (edited by Eric J.

Guignard, 2013). He is one of the writers for Robert Rodriguez's *El Rey* television network while juggling fatherhood and family in and along the South Texas border.

SAMUEL SALDÍVAR is a PhD candidate in the Chicano/Latino Studies and English Departments at Michigan State University. He is the author of "Unwanted Extraterrestrials . . . or Dirty, Stinking, Aliens: Latinos in Today's Sci-Fi Televisual Blueprints," in *Latinos and Narrative Media: Participation and Portrayal* (2013), edited by Frederick Luis Aldama. Saldívar teaches and publishes on all matters concerning Latino popular culture.

PHILLIP SERRATO is Associate Professor of English and Comparative Literature at San Diego State University, where he is on the faculty of his department's children's literature program. He has published widely on matters of identity, sexuality, and gender (especially masculinity) in Chicano/a literature, film, and performance. Presently, Serrato is at work on two books: an examination of masculinity in Chicano/a literature, film, and performance from the nineteenth century to the present day, as well as a critical survey of the emergence, history, and development of Chicano/a children's literature.

ILAN STAVANS is Lewis-Sebring Professor in Latin American and Latino Culture at Amherst College. He has published dozens of books, including *All the Odes* (2012), by Pablo Neruda, which he edited; *¡Muy Pop! Conversations on Latino Popular Culture* (2013), which he coauthored with Frederick Luis Aldama; and *A Most Imperfect Union: A Contrarian History of the United States* with cartoonist Lalo Alcaraz (2014).

Index